Advocate for the North

Judge John Parker
His Life and Times in the Northwest Territories
1944 - 1958

by
Frank Wade

Note for Librarians: a cataloguing record for this book that includes Dewey Decimal
Classification and US Library of Congress numbers is available from the Library and Archives
of Canada. The complete cataloguing record can be obtained from their online database at:
www.collectionscanada.ca/amicus/index-e.html
ISBN 1-4120-4243-7
Printed in Victoria, BC, Canada

TRAFFORD

Offices in Canada, USA, Ireland, UK and Spain
This book was published on-demand in cooperation with Trafford Publishing. On-demand
publishing is a unique process and service of making a book available for retail sale to the
public taking advantage of on-demand manufacturing and Internet marketing. On-demand
publishing includes promotions, retail sales, manufacturing, order fulfilment, accounting and
collecting royalties on behalf of the author.
Book sales for North America and international:
Trafford Publishing, 6E–2333 Government St.,
Victoria, BC v8t 4p4 CANADA
phone 250 383 6864 (toll-free 1 888 232 4444)
fax 250 383 6804; email to orders@trafford.com
Book sales in Europe:
Trafford Publishing (uk) Ltd., Enterprise House, Wistaston Road Business Centre,
Wistaston Road, Crewe, Cheshire cw2 7rp UNITED KINGDOM
phone 01270 251 396 (local rate 0845 230 9601)
facsimile 01270 254 983; orders.uk@trafford.com
Order online at:
www.trafford.com/robots/04-2050.html

10 9 8 7 6 5 4 3 2

Acknowledgements

Many kind people helped me complete this biography. Thanks go to my friend Brenda Clark, without her I could have not have finished this book. She advised on format, scanned all the photographs, drawing and maps, produced numerous editions for editing including the final layout, as well she encouraged me. Also, to my dear friend, the late Evelyn Robbins, BC government cartographer who drew the map outlines. She also helped me with my first book. Many thanks to my editor, the expert Peter Colanbrander, who edited and reshaped the book. Frank McCall, with his encyclopaedic knowledge of the north was supportive and extremely helpful. The late Dr. Kelsall, Canadian wildlife expert, was also most helpful.

The famous Gordon Robertson and the late Louis Audette, who were both members of the NWT Council, Robertson being the chairman, both graciously allowed me to talk to them. The late Roy Minter, Order of Canada, Yukon expert, encouraged me greatly. Others in this list were Barbara Hunt, Ruth Stanton, Barbara Parker, Erik Watt, famed northern jounalist, Ray Mahaffy, Leonard Ingraham and the late Bent Sivertz, former NWT Commissioner.

Also, Doug Whyte, Canadian national Archives, Ottawa, Vancouver and West Vancouver reference librarians, Len McCann of the Vancouver Maritime Museum, Edward Atkinson and Francoise Chartrand of the National Archives, Anna O'Neill and Shirley Borden of the NWT Archives, Yellowknife, Susan Baer of the NWT Court Library, Yellowknife, Paul Banfield of the Queens University library, Kingston, Tim Campbell of the Canadian Photography Museum, Ottawa, Linda Johnson of the Yukon Archives, Whitehorse, Eaon McEwen, northern biologist. Friend Lucy Street did a thorough edit of the manuscript. Also the famous Canadian Yukon Territories artist Ted Harrison permitted me to use his picture on the cover

Friend and Mediterranean naval war veteran Ken Gibson, who has worked with me on other projects, did the excellent art work. Friend and lawyer, Wally Beck and Bill Dunn, mining engineer, looked over the manuscript of the book. I must also thank my wife Ruth for her assistance and Claire Parker for her support.

List of Drawings

List of Maps

Chapter 1
Early Days

John Parker had the unusual experience for a young boy of being given the chance to choose his country of adoption. This came about because his father, an Englishman, was transferred to the United States and gave his son the responsibility of making this decision. Parker was born on 26 November 1911 in Brentwood, Essex, in England. In 1920, when he was nine, his father was moved to New York to represent the Westminster Bank. Parker attended a local school for two years and then his father asked him to consider his further education. He was given three options; he could go to an American private preparatory school, or a boarding school in England or Canada. Parker thought about these choices for a while and decided that he wanted to keep his British connections. Canada was closer to home and was part of the British Empire so he chose to further his schooling there. His father visited Canada and decided on St. Andrews School, a good Presbyterian Academy in Toronto.[1] As a result, Parker became a Canadian.

Eight years later, he enrolled in an arts course at Queen's University in Kingston, Ontario, with the idea of becoming a lawyer. His plan was to study law at Osgoode Hall in Toronto after graduation. Kingston was an attractive old university town, and possessed both the university and the Royal Military College. There were residences for female students in those days but none for males, so Parker had to look for cheap lodgings or band together with other students to rent a house. He ended up in a garret in an old Victorian boarding house for students run by the Misses Daly. They were both over seventy and had rather fixed ideas about student behaviour. When they found a case of beer in young John's room they threatened to inform his mother. However, for their age and the time, they were quite long-suffering, no doubt as a result of many years of experience, and John had a pleasant stay there.

Like most Queen's students then, he was taught by some of Canada's best brains. His teachers included Norman Rogers who was later Minister of National Defence, Dr. McIntosh who was chief economic adviser to the federal government during the Second World War and later principal of the university, and Dr. Gregory Blastos, an outstanding philosophy professor. He admitted, in retrospect, that his aim then had been to secure a degree with the minimum of effort and the maximum of enjoyment. Luckily he had such good teachers that he couldn't help but be influenced for the better by them.

He conceded that any success that he had in later life was largely due to them.

There was not too much pressure on students in the arts programme in those days. The emphasis was on reading as many books as possible more than on attending classes. He cut quite a few for other more pleasurable pursuits. A university student in those days could manage on $90 for annual fees, $20 for books, and $50 a month for board, lodging, and extras. On the other hand, it was very difficult to get work because of the Depression, so he spent the summer at his parent's cottage or studying for courses that he failed. On looking back at his university days, he considered that he had been highly irresponsible.

In his final year, he shared a house with four other students and found it a very rewarding experience. He felt that he learned as much from his numerous discussions with them as he did from the lectures. One of these friends was killed overseas in the war that was just over the horizon. Eric Gilmore, another, became head of the consular service in the Department of External Affairs. A third, Jack Weir, ended up as a leading Canadian counsel and president of the Canadian Bar Association.

In April 1934, John Parker graduated and became apprenticed — as they called it then — to an established law firm in Toronto and attended Osgoode Hall law school for two hours a day. This continued for the next three years and happy and good years they proved to be. He was the only student in the firm and he was treated royally. This firm took its training responsibilities seriously and did not use students as office boys or just for searching titles or other routine jobs. Some of his class-mates were much less fortunate.

Sir Alan Aylesworth, who had been minister of justice in the Laurier cabinet, was the nominal head of the firm and would attend at the office one or two days a week when he was not in Ottawa performing his duties as a senator. He had been one of Canada's finest counsel in his day, but by the time that Parker was in the firm he was an old man, stone deaf, and an eccentric figure. On one occasion, Parker was talked into taking money to Aylesworth's house. This had to be done every Saturday morning so that the old man had some change for the church collection on Sunday, and to save on the interest that would otherwise accrue. But he insisted that this was not his job and only did it once.

Parker worked with all members of the firm at one time or another and experienced a broad range of legal work alongside outstanding practitioners. This laid the basis for his later career as a generalist lawyer. He worked with A. Murray Garden QC, who specialised in estate work, Hamilton Stuart who handled corporate litigation, and C.A. Thompson and Wilfred Judson who did the court work. Judson ended up on the Supreme Court. John remembered all of them with pleasure for being extremely helpful and kind to him.

John Parker owned a Buick touring car and made himself useful by driving Judson around Ontario when he had to appear in circuit court. He enjoyed this not only because he could get out of the office and see the countryside but also because he could learn from Judson, a fine mind as well as a charming and sociable companion. Judson enjoyed stopping to have a pint of beer at one of the many small breweries that dotted Ontario in those days. The details of each case would be fully explained to him and the weaknesses and strengths of the firm's position gone over. Then he would watch how his mentor conducted himself in the cut and thrust of examination and cross-examination in court. Later, after John had moved north, he would consult Judson by mail if he had a particularly difficult case. Soon a detailed reply would be received at a very nominal fee — the Yellowknifers never realised what top legal advice they were getting.

He also worked with three younger members, H.C. Stanbury, E.W. Burke, and Norman O. Seagram. Seagram was memorable because of his attractive personality and sense of humour. When the old Woodbine Race Track had its spring or fall meet he would take Parker along to examine property in the east end of Toronto and they would move on to the track for the last few races. On one occasion, they put bets on the nose for the last four races and won them all, for Seagram knew the form of many of the horses. They then repaired to his huge house where they celebrated with forty-five-year-old rye whiskey.

John was called to the bar in the spring of 1937 and now faced the worrying task of getting a job. Times were still hard and it was difficult for a young lawyer to gain entry into a Toronto law firm. Even if one was hired, the pay wasn't that good, $60 a month. There were no signs that his training firm wanted him and he didn't like to ask. Luckily, he came across a class-mate, Charles Hill, who was also looking for work. Hill had had the bright idea of visiting Charles McCrea, who had been minister of mines in Ontario and now practised law in Sudbury. McCrea had told him to get a partner and to open a practice in one of the small mining communities in northern Ontario. These communities were fairly prosperous and he would have a far better chance of making a half-decent living there than in the big city.

After much soul-searching, Parker and Hill formed a partnership and considered where they should set up their shingle. They visited Timmins, Larder Lake, and Kirkland Lake, because these were supposedly the most prosperous mining towns. Larder Lake had good possibilities because the nearby Curtis Mine had just gone into production and there were other promising properties in the area. However, it was quite a small community and already had two lawyers. Timmins was a much bigger centre and they would probably have trouble getting established there.

Then they ran into a friend in Kirkland Lake, who was taking over his father's mining supply company. He said the place was booming and urged them to set up there. The town had a population of 23,000 and had several very successful gold-producing mines nearby it. Even though it already had eighteen lawyers, there was felt to be enough business for another small law partnership. So they decided on Kirkland Lake and quickly established an office there.

One of their biggest concerns was that someone would come in with a thorny legal problem that they couldn't handle, and this, indeed, was soon the case. Parker thought back to a talk he had heard at Osgoode Hall by R.S. Robinson QC, a leading counsel who later became Chief Justice of Ontario. He had told the students that they needn't worry about difficult questions if they went into practice on their own, since most of their work would be routine. Moreover, if they were in any doubt about the law, they could always write to one of their instructors for advice. This they did on this occasion and it worked well. In fact Wilfred Judson once spent a whole day with Parker in the court of appeal for a charge of a mere five dollars. However, Parker and Hill never did have too many difficult cases and they prospered on largely routine legal work, at least until the outbreak of war two years later. When it began in the fall of 1939, like most able-bodied men, they packed up the practice and joined the services. Parker went into the RCAF and Hill the army.

Hill was killed on the third day of the Normandy invasion while serving with a Canadian division, but Parker fared much better and ended up in the supply branch of the RCAF. He was eventually posted to Washington DC, because of his legal experience, to work in the British Air Mission. He was given the rank of Flight Lieutenant and was later promoted to Squadron Leader. He served as a liaison officer with the American government, arranging for contracts and the delivery of spare parts for the American aircraft being used in the Commonwealth Air Training Programme in Canada. In the circumstances, this was a very comfortable posting and he remained in the job for the duration of his war service. The work was interesting and Washington and the Maryland and Virginia areas couldn't have been better places to work and live in.

By October 1944 the war was going well in Europe and the allies were pressing on the German border. The training programme for airforce personnel in Canada was just about over. It had been estimated that possibly 2,000 aircrews would be lost each day during the first three days of the D Day invasion of Normandy. Actually not even five crews were lost, so a major surplus of trained aircrew resulted. Knowing of this inside information, Parker thought that the time was ripe to get out.

Around this period, he had noticed several pages in the Toronto Globe and Mail on the gold mining boom in Yellowknife in the Northwest Territories. Several gold mines were starting there, two with particularly huge reserves.[2] The Toronto Stock Exchange was experiencing a small revival as a result, even though the war was not over. With his Kirkland Lake experience and his knowledge of the mining industry, John saw the possibility of setting up a law practice there. He insisted that it wasn't the call of the wild that prompted this rather rash decision but merely mercenary considerations. He still recalled his days in Toronto when it was so difficult for a lawyer to get a job and how he and his partner had done well in Kirkland Lake.

However, there must surely have been something of a romantic streak in him, and the thought of some adventure in the back of his mind. In those days there was much more interest in the Canadian north than there is today, prompted in part by the likes of Albert Johnson, the mad trapper of Rat River,[3] Nelson Eddy (the Mountie) and Jeanette Macdonald in Hollywood's Rosemarie, and the impostor "Grey Owl." Pierre Berton has written of the great number of movies that Hollywood made about the Canadian north in the twenties and thirties. Canadian Pacific Steamship advertisements showing Indian chiefs standing on the terrace of the Banff Springs Hotel with the Bow River and mountains in the background were posted all over Europe and North America before the war. As things turned out, Parker would probably have made a lot more money in the south, but he would not have led such an adventurous life, known so many colourful characters, and played so important a role in a fascinating chapter of Canadian history.

Parker put in his request for demobilization and, much to his surprise, it was approved. He left Washington on 22 October 1944 for Ottawa for further instructions. Here he contacted people in the government who were responsible for the north. They gave him every encouragement, speaking of prospects in the territories in glowing terms. He arranged to transfer to Calgary, the nearest manning depot to Yellowknife, to complete his discharge procedure. After having a full medical and dental examination, he received about $800 in back pay and was told that other veterans' allowance monies would be coming to him. These amounted to more than $1000 and could be used towards an education or to buy a house or household effects in order to ease the return to civilian life. He was allowed a railway warrant for any destination in Canada, but encountered trouble when he asked for a flight to Yellowknife. However, the transportation officer broke the rules and made out a ticket for Canadian Pacific Airlines and there was no further difficulty. His law books to be brought by airforce plane as soon as space was available.

So, in the second week of December 1944 he boarded a Lockheed Lodestar, the latest twin-engined fourteen-passenger aircraft, bound for Fort Smith where he would spend the night before flying on in a smaller plane to Yellowknife. At Fort Smith, the weather deteriorated with freezing cold, snow, and high winds so the flight to Yellowknife was delayed until conditions improved. In fact, he was there for four days. The weather had cleared by the third day but there were still no calls for the passengers to board the plane. Parker began to realise that he had entered a completely different world. The delay had nothing to do with the weather at all; the pilot of the smaller plane had established a more than friendly relationship with an attractive female passenger. As the walls of the hotel rooms were paper-thin and the woman in question was located next door, John couldn't help being aware of the progress of the affair.

While he was waiting, he had a chance to explore the little town and examine the surrounding countryside. Fort Smith was then the most attractive and mature settlement in the Territories. It was also the oldest, because it was a natural staging post on the Slave River; located downstream from sixteen miles of treacherous rapids, it became the place where travellers could rest after the trials and exertions of such a long portage. The town, John discovered, was well laid out and unexpectedly neat and clean with smartly painted clap-board houses as well as the usual shacks and Native tents on the outskirts. The surrounding country was flat and full of muskeg (soggy moss-like ground cover) and dotted with marshes. In the distance there were low-lying hills covered with spindly spruce and willow trees.

The town lay on a flat ledge on the river's edge, with the river islands and dangerous "Rapids of the Drowned" in the background. These rapids were so named because five white traders, bound for Great Slave Lake (100 miles north) for furs, were lost in their turbulent waters in 1786. There was a Roman Catholic church and school (the headquarters of the northern Roman Catholic diocese), an RCMP post, a Hudson Bay Company (HBC) store and hotel, and also government offices. The town was laid out as a grid but the roads were not yet paved. Apart from the airstrip which Parker's plane had used, small floatplanes were parked near the shore of the frozen river. There were also several stern-wheel river ships and some barges lying frozen in the ice alongside some wharfs, for the place was a busy river terminus in the summer.

Fort Smith was full of history. Many of the early British explorers had visited it, and the HBC had built a fort here in 1874 to trade with the Slave Indians. In 1876, a Roman Catholic mission school and church had followed. The federal government established its first administrative offices here for all the Territories in 1921 and it was from here that the US army had its main staging post for the wartime CANOL project. This misguided scheme saw the construction of an oil pipeline from Norman Wells on the Mackenzie River to Alaska.

The portages for the "Rapids of the Drowned" began at Fort Fitzgerald to the south, just below the 60th parallel in Alberta. They were eventually made into a rough road after larger boats began coming upriver and heavier loads had to be transported overland. As time went by, the river became an increasingly busy waterway extending from Edmonton for over 1,600 miles to the Arctic Sea. At the time of John Parker's first visit, one could go overland on a colourful railroad from Edmonton to Waterways, close to Fort McMurray on the Athabasca River. Here one transferred to paddle steamers. These would then bring you downstream through Lake Athabasca to the Slave River, continuing to Fort Fitzgerald. Once there, a taxi would take you over the portage track to Fort Smith where you would get aboard another steamboat for onward passage to the north.

The area abounded with furbearing animals that provided a fairly good living for the local Natives and a few white trappers. The Slave Indians led a hard life hunting and fishing. The mysterious caribou herds were their lifeblood, providing them with food, clothing, and tents, and they even made thread from sinew and implements from the bones and horns.

The local economy was augmented by the government administrative offices, and there was also a Canadian army radio station in town. These units were located throughout the territories to provide commercial and government communications. A wire could be sent through their offices to the Canadian National or Canadian Pacific telegraphic offices in Edmonton. The units also provided weather information for the Meteorological Forecast Centre in Toronto. This information was also broadcast to northern air terminals and direct to aircraft.[4]

The few days that John spent in Fort Smith gave him a clear foretaste of things to come. Apart from anything else, the town was enveloped in bitter winter cold and almost continuous night. At that time of year, there are about three hours of daylight per day, not the most congenial working environment. As the river was frozen solid, no freight moved north except by the odd Cat train. These were caterpillar tractors that pulled large sleds, like a train, that were loaded with goods and equipment. They travelled over frozen rivers, lakes, and tundra. They even made their way up the Mackenzie River to Great Bear Lake on the Arctic Circle. John began to realise just how isolated this part of Canada was. It was soon explained to him that there were even times of the year when air transportation ceased. This was when, in the spring and fall, the ice was either melting or starting to freeze, thus making it dangerous for floatplanes to take off or land. Generally, this cessation was for three weeks at the end of May and for another three at the end of October. During those weeks, the only communication with the south was by army radio station; physical movement of people stopped, and even emergency dogsled transportation ceased.

After four days, John Parker finally left Fort Smith in the small plane for Yellowknife. The plane was a single-engined monoplane Fairchild 247D which could carry six passengers. It was a sturdy little craft with a large wing above the passenger cabin, and was one of several types of plane that had revolutionised northern transportation by expediting the movement of people and light freight to isolated areas, supplanting the canoe and the dogsled in the process. These small planes, equipped with either floats or skis, could land on practically any level stretch of land or water. The two-hour 200 mile flight was uneventful but informative. The plane was extremely cold because of the draught coming through the ill-fitting door. They flew over flat wooded terrain and then over the frozen, bleak Great Slave Lake, turning northwest to Yellowknife, the temperature on arrival was forty degrees below zero.

Yellowknife Bay lies on the north side of Great Slave Lake, midway between the east and west sides. It is angled due north and is about twelve miles long and averages about a mile in width. Yellowknife town is on a promontory of a tiny north/south bay on the west side of the main bay at its narrowest point. In those days practically the whole town was restricted to a rock-like hill on this promontory, although two small inhabited islands lay close to the north and east of it. The plane landed on a small airstrip south of the townsite. A taxi collected him and drove him through the cold to the Yellowknife Hotel. It was located on the rock with a view looking west over a small sheltered bay.

The terrain was completely different from the hilly country around Fort Smith. This was Canadian Shield country with jagged rock outcroppings occurring everywhere on an uneven harsh-looking landscape. The area was covered with hundreds of lakes, sometimes connected by small rivers, and open bare areas interspersed with small clusters of spindly trees and bushes.

Because of the prevailing gold fever the place was jam-packed. Parker had only been able to get a hotel room because an acquaintance in Edmonton was a personal friend of the colourful owner and Northwest Territories legend, Vic Ingraham. Even so, he was only able to keep it for two nights, and had to look for new accommodations almost immediately. All fourteen hotel rooms were occupied and camp beds were set up in the beverage room at night to cater to the overflow. The hotel was warm, clean, and quite comfortable despite the basic furnishings. Surprisingly, no drunks kept one awake during the night, for Vic Ingraham, who got around on two artificial legs without a cane, ran a tight ship.

Parker soon began to explore his new home town. All over and up the face of the rock several snow-covered streets were strewn with nondescript flat-roofed wooden houses, buildings, and shacks. There was a Hudson Bay store and outbuildings, an RCMP post and barracks, several cafes, two small churches, a bank, and a drug store among several other places of business. Three ski-equipped small planes were tied down on the ice near the shore. Although a little ramshackle, the town had a jaunty, rather confident air about it and Parker, despite his misgivings, felt that the place had possibilities. There was no doubt that gold mining was booming. Two mines were operating within commuting distance to the south (Con and Negus), and another large one not far to the north (Giant) was gearing up. One of the biggest gold deposits in the world lay all around the town. Parker had made his choice and he could only hope that things would turn out for the best.

The Northwest Territories that John Parker now called home comprised about 1.5 million square miles, an enormous area, larger than Europe. Its huge girth embraced all four northern geological regions — Innuitas, Precambrian Shield, Interior Plains, and Cordilleran West.[5] It stretched from the inhospitable northern islands of the high Arctic to the rock-hewn, lake-filled regions further south, and to the lofty mountains of the west. Throughout the Territories the weather is harsh and only July and August are frost-free. Summer temperatures average 50°F but are sub-zero in winter, although they are not quite so extreme in the southern reaches of the Territories. Daylight lasts a few hours in winter but is almost continuous in summer, this range being most accentuated in the higher latitudes.

Few people inhabited the area when Parker arrived and such settlements as existed were widely dispersed. Even now , this situation is little changed. Nonetheless, traces of human habitation going back 5,000 years have been unearthed at Fort Franklin on Great Bear Lake and current thinking is that prehistoric peoples crossed the Bering Sea from Asia some 10,000 or more years ago and gradually moved southward down the North American continent. Over many centuries, two distinct peoples have emerged in the Territories, the Inuit (Eskimo) who live north of the treeline, and the Athapaskan-speaking Dene, most of whom live to the south of that line.

In 1957, near the end of John Parker's sojourn in the Northwest Territories, the Inuit numbered 3,829, and they were spread in more or less equal proportions over Baffin Island, the barren lands, and elsewhere in the region.[6] Many still lived in isolated settlements, relying on sealing and bear-hunting in winter and sea mammals and fish in summer. The barren land bands, however, located on the western littoral of Hudson Bay, were heavily reliant on caribou hunting. Loosely organised socially, the Inuit were (and are) a tough, resourceful, and artistic people.

The Native Indian population was much more heterogeneous in that it had historically comprised eight distinct peoples, each speaking a different dialect.[7] One of these groups, the Yellowknives, had perished in an influenza epidemic in 1928,[8] and the remainder — the Slaveys, Chipewyans, Dogribs (the largest group), Loucheux, Hare, Kutchin, and Kaska — numbered 4,689 in 1957.[9] At that stage the main population concentrations were at Fort Rae, Fort Resolution, and Aklavik, and many Native Indians continued to depend heavily on the caribou herds, and also on fishing and trapping for their living.

White people had first penetrated the barren lands west of Hudson Bay in 1715 when William Stewart, an HBC employee, arrived in the area. The trading fort that he established was later moved northward to the mouth of the Churchill River [10] and it was from this place, Fort Churchill, that Samuel Hearne, guided by the legendary Chipewyan giant, Matonabbee, struck out westwards in 1770 to find copper.[11] During his epic expedition he became the first white man to set eyes on Great Slave Lake and the Arctic Sea. Peter Pond was the first European to visit Yellowknife Bay and by 1785 Great Slave Lake had been surveyed by Alexander Mackenzie.[12]

The most famous Englishman of them all was Sir John Franklin; a sailor, later an admiral and Trafalgar veteran. He led three land expeditions from Fort Churchill from 1816 to 1826. The Yellowknife chief Akaitcho showed his party the way to Coppermine River and later assisted him when many of his men died of starvation. He wintered at Fort Franklin in 1826.[13] He later lost his life and two ships and their ship's companies after being trapped in the Central Artic.[14] Parker visited most of the spots where Franklin went.

For much of the nineteenth century, trading companies, especially the HBC, remained the dominant economic and administrative force in the north. Even after the revocation of its exclusive trading charter in 1870, the HBC continued to be a significant factor in the Northwest Territories where, by 1933, it had forty-one trading posts.[15] The HBC's relationship with the Natives was almost feudal. Its main interest was helping them to trap furs, but it did try to assist in times of distress. It caused problems for the natives because they concentrated on fur-trapping to the detriment of their traditional hunting way of life.

Catholic Belgium Oblate missionaries had begun to appear in 1830 when they established a mission at Fort Resolution. With time, other mission stations were built, some of them as far north as the sub-Arctic, and the Anglicans also began missionary work. There was competition between the two denominations. They tried to provide help to the Natives but only had limited resources. Many priests were devoted and hardworking but some services provided, although well-meaning, were sometimes misdirected, as Parker was to find. They saw themselves as intermediaries between the Natives and the white man.[16]   Today there are seventeen Catholic and ten Anglican churches in the Territories and both denominations have at various times built hospitals and schools, including residential schools, for their Native converts.

Traders and missionaries in the north were joined by the Royal Canadian Mounted Police in 1898 when a detachment was sent to deal with the Klondike Gold Rush.[17] At much the same time, police patrols by land and sea began to occur in what later became the modern Northwest Territories and a growing number of posts were gradually established in the region. Primarily responsible for law enforcement, the RCMP also acted as the sole permanent representative of the federal government in this vast area of wilderness and, as such, discharged various administrative functions.

The old Northwestern Territories had been administered by a governor and his council of appointees. With time, portions of the historic territories were hived off to form a new territory and new provinces, or were ceded to an older province.[18] Nonetheless, the tradition of autocratic government still operated when John Parker came northwards in 1944. Indeed, his arrival almost coincided with the retirement of Charles Camsell, a legendary son of the north who had made his name as an explorer, geologist, and administrator.[19] He had been appointed to the Northwest Territories Council in 1921, and was its chair as well as the commissioner of the Territories and deputy minister of mines and resources between 1935 and 1946. He it was who boasted in 1936 that "six men in Ottawa, of whom I am one, govern the Northwest Territories. We are kindly autocrats who don't have to bother with re-election every four years."[20] In Parker's view, that was the problem with Camsell; friendly, helpful, and charming he may have been, but he'd been in the job for too long.

It was a mining boom that had lured Parker to the north and this, like the tradition of autocracy, had its origins far back in the history of the Territories. As early as the late-eighteenth century, Alexander Mackenzie had observed oil seeping from the Mackenzie River's banks. However, oil exploration had only started in earnest in 1914 and by 1931 oil production was under way at Norman Wells.[21]   This breakthrough had demonstrated that men and machines could operate in the climatic extremes of the north; it also ensured a local supply of fuel for further exploratory expeditions. Mineral prospecting gathered pace, and was made easier by the advent of Cat trains and air travel.[22]. Indeed, the first airline serving the Territories had been formed in 1928 and, after several mergers, was bought out by Canadian Pacific Airlines (CPA) in 1941.

Great Bear Lake was one focus of prospecting activity in the 1930s (and had the dubious distinction of producing the radium-bearing ore that was used for the Hiroshima atomic bomb of August 1945).[23] The future site of Yellowknife was another, which is hardly surprising since it lay above one of the biggest gold veins in the history of Canadian mining. Prospecting began in the area in the early 1930s and in the summer of 1934 "Yellowknife Johnny" Baker and H. Muir staked out what became Burwash Mine across the bay from modern Yellowknife. This gave rise to much publicity and intensified prospecting. At much the same time the Geological Survey sent a party to the area and broadcast its findings to the interested prospectors then gathered at Fort Smith [24].

By 1935, several promising properties in the Yellowknife area had been staked and serious investigation of the ores was under way. The US government pegged the price of gold at $35.00 per ounce in 1934, thus making gold a more attractive investment. The Consolidated Mining and Smelting Corporation from Trail, BC, later known as Cominco, immediately flew in a prospecting party after the news of the gold find at Yellowknife was made at Fort Smith and staked a claim near Yellowknife which became the Con mine. It started production in 1938.

The local Indians watched the goings-on of the white man on their hunting lands with a perplexed interest: wondering what the fuss was all about. They cashed in a little bit; clearing bush, cutting trees and planks and selling caribou meat and fish.

By 1936-7, gold fever had seized the Depression-racked Canadian west, and was inflamed by news of further gold strikes near Yellowknife. By 1938, the excitement had reached boom proportions. One of the little-known sagas of Canadian history was the movement of out-of-work men and families from the prairies north by air, canoe and homemade boat, some extremely original. The outbreak of hostilities the following year, however, led to the stoppage of production and a significant efflux of people. But by 1944, activity in the Yellowknife area rebounded largely as a result of developments at the Giant Mine and Discovery Mine sites. It was this particular spurt of activity that decided John Parker on his new home. Indeed, as legal adviser to Giant, he later got to know the capable and colourful managers who started the mine. There was Thayer Lindsley, an American with, according to Parker, an uncanny nose for valuable ores; Glyn Burge, an English-born ex-pilot; and Dr. A.S. Dadson, a brilliant consultant geologist.[25]   Between them they uncovered and began the development of a rich new gold-bearing zone, thereby triggering a renewed boom, although production only began at the Giant Mine several years later, in 1949.[26]

Parker's new home-town, Yellowknife, had sprung up rather haphazardly in the mid-1930s in the wake of the first gold discoveries. Gradually, the motley collection of cabins acquired the trappings of a settlement. In 1937 a police post was established and in the same year Vic Ingraham laid his plans for a hotel. By 1939, Yellowknife boasted a newspaper, several shops, a bank, a school, and a resident doctor. This was Dr. Ollie Stanton who spent a total of twenty-three years in the north. He delivered 1,000 babies and served all the mines in the area. He and his wife Ruth, who was a physio-therapist and helper were great friends of the Parkers.[27]

The previous year, Federal Government Commissioner Camsell had somewhat tardily recommended the establishment of a town committee, the majority of whose members were to be government appointees.[28]   When new mineral discoveries were made late in the war, the territorial government decided to increase the number of its staff in the town, Fort Smith having hitherto been the main administrative centre. Not only that, but it was decided to locate their offices about a mile to the south of the existing townsite, in the expectation, correct as it transpired, that private businesses would follow suit.

The territorial government had not played much of a role in the development of the town, but once the gold mines were started it began to show an interest. On the contrary, between 1930 and 1935 Camsell and his deputy, R.A. Gibson (described by contemporaries as an unimaginative and autocratic bureaucrat),[29] rigorously visited the Bennett ministry's austerity measures upon the Northwest Territories and the Yukon.[30]

Gibson never did entirely free himself of the austerity mind-set. He retired in 1951. The result was that not only was Yellowknife's progress impeded, but the Native population languished in very poor conditions when Parker first set foot in the north.

C.D. Howe himself , who Parker said approved everything whether it was in his department or not, authorized additional power generation for the proposed Giant Mine and the townsite[31], and an experienced administrator, Fred Fraser, was sent to Yellowknife as Government Agent and Stipendiary Magistrate.[32] This was in late 1944, thus coinciding with Parker's decision to move to the north. Subsequently the two men became friends, although not close ones, and their professional paths often crossed. As Stipendiary Magistrate, Fraser handled only criminal cases, but this included capital offences. According to Parker, he discharged his judicial duties capably and fairly, despite his prior lack of courtroom experience. But Fraser had innumerable other duties and he was virtual dictator of Yellowknife,[33] a circumstance that did not always endear him to Jock McKeekan's Yellowknife Blade, the local mimeographed paper.

The Mining Recorders Office was the busiest of Fraser's departments, so many claims were being registered. It cost $5.00 to buy a prospecting licence then. Land being claimed had to be laid out in squares with sides not more than 1,500 yards long and with corner posts. A map showing the claims plus nearby geographic features had to be registered with Mining Recorder's Office. Eighteen claims could be registered a year.

To relieve Fraser of his duties, Frank Cunningham came north as a Stipendiary Magistrate in 1946 [34]. Parker got to know Cunningham in his legal capacity and rated him as an able lawyer. and capable administrator. They later served together in the Northwest Territories Council.

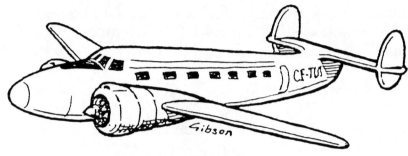

LOCKHEED LODESTAR

Chapter Notes
All unattributed quotations by John Parker and anecdotes originating in tapes and conversations with the author, and also the manuscript that Parker wrote on his life but never published, are not individually cited.

Chapter 1 Notes

1. St. Andrews School was then located in Toronto, but later moved to Aurora, Ontario.
2. After protracted negotiations, Giant Gold mine started diamond drilling. The news got out and a minor gold rush ensured. Giant stock moved from 5 cents to $11.00 in the space of months. Gladys Gould, <u>Jock McMeekan's Blade</u>, (Lambrecht Publications, Duncan, BC, 1990, p 120).
3. Johnson, a trapper, shot and killed a mountie in 1932 and was hunted by plane and dog sled for 48 days in mid winter before being killed.
4. The communication network was never provided for the Yukon Territories because it was not considered necessary. It was much smaller than NWT, less settled and the Yukon river provided good communications between Whitehorse and Dawson city. It was introduced in the 50's as a result of the efforts of Erik Neilson. Erik Neilson, <u>The House is not a Home</u>, (Macmillan of Canada, Toronto, 1989, p 89).
5. J.A. Lower, <u>A Nation Developing</u>, (The Ryerson Press, Toronto, 1970, p 4).
6. Government population from the papers of L. C. Audette, National Archives of Canada. There are considerable differences in the population figures for Canadian

Inuit for this time. The Encyclopedia Britannica gives an estimated figure of 9,733 for all Inuit including the Ungava Peninsular.

7. The American Southwest Indian tribes speak a language very similar to the Canadian Athapaskan.

8. Erik Watt, Yellowknife, How the City Grew, (Outcrop Publishing, Yellowknife, 1989), p22.

9. The Canadian Encylcopedia, (Hurtig, Edmonton, 1988, p 143b). The Indian NWT Brotherhood was formed in 1969. When the Native Indians stated their position on land claims 1975, all the NWT Indians were referred to as "Dene" ("people") in an attempt to encourage the different tribes to coalesce. John Hamilton Arctic Revolution-Social Change in the Northwest Territories 1953-1994, Dundurn Press, Toronto, 1994 p 138, L.C.Audette papers

10 Arthur S. Morton, Hudson's Bay Company (HBC, London, England1934), p 12

11. Matonabbee was the real leader of this expedition because of his wilderness skills and loyalty to Hearne.

12. Arthur S. Morton, Hudson's Bay Company , p 7.

13. Morton, Hudson's Bay Company, p 12.

14. D. Wilkinson, Arctic Fever, (Clarke Irwin, Toronto, 1971), p 57.

15. Hudson's Bay Company brochure on Fort Smith, L.C. Audette's papers.

16. J.A. Lower, A Nation Developing, p 65.

17. The gold rush really lead to the first opening up of the Canadian Northern territories.

18. Manitoba was made a province in 1870, Saskatchewan and Alberta in 1905

19. Charles Camsell, Son of the North Ryerson Press, Toronto, 1954

20. Camsell was born on 8 February 1876, educated at St Johns College, Winnipeg, Universities of Queens, Alberta and Manitoba, and Harvard and M.I.T in the States. In 1900, surveyed the Great Bear Lake with McIntosh Bell of the Canadian Geological Survey, going in by canoe via Fort Norman and coming out south to Fort Rae on the Great Slave Lake, after many adventures. Worked for the Canadian Government and made Deputy Minister of the Dept of Mines and Resources in 1935 and NWT Commissioner from 1935 to 1946. O'Malley, Past and Future Land. p131

21. Today, 3,000 barrels a day flow down a pipeline to Zama. Alberta, 1989 Explorers Guide, Govt. of Northwest Territories

22. Yellowknife Illustrated History, edited by Susan Jackson (Northwest Publishing, Sechelt 1990) p 218

23. Peter C. Newman, Gilbert Labine , the Beaver, spring 1957, p 48

24. Gold indications were found by Blakeney on the mouth of the Yellowknife in the 1890's. Samples were sent to Ottawa and were reported in the Geological Survey but no one followed up on them, Ray Price Yellowknife (Peter Martine Press, Toronto, 1967) p 23. Price writes that Jennyjohn, a student in Dr. Jolliffe's survey party, was the one who found surface free gold near Yellowknife. He gave this information to

two prospectors and Jolliffe was forced to disclose this find to prospectors at Fort Smith. Jolliffe denies this in <u>Yellowknife Illustrated History</u> stating that he did do this but it was not contrary to Survey instructions.

25. Arnold Hoffman, <u>Free Gold, the Story of Canadian Mining</u>, (Rhinehart, Toronto,1947) p 123

26. Price,<u>Yellowknife</u> p 123

27. Edmonton Journal, 31 March 1960

28. Price, Yellowknife, p 27.

29. He tried to interefere in a case concerning a white trapper and an Inuit. He wanted the trapper's game licence revoked and his income tax returns audited and the Inuit stopped from travelling by air by the RCMP. Graham Price, <u>Remote Justice, The Stipendiary Magistrates Court of the Northwest Territories</u> <u>(1905 to 1955)</u> unpublished thesis, p 83.

30. Price, <u>Remote Justice</u> p 86.

31. In 1948, a larger power plant was built by Northwest Territories Power Commission (Northern Canada Power Commision) to augment the Cominco plant. It was further expanded in 1966 and later.

32. <u>Yellowknife Illustrated History</u> p 93.

33. Price, <u>Yellowknife</u>, p 208.

34. Graham Price, <u>Remote Justice</u>, p 118. He ordered a Japanese, found guilty of war crimes to be shot as an example.

Cross section of an Igloo

Fort Smith, 1952, with
the Slave Rive rapids
in the background.

(National Archives of Canada
PA 1018711)

Dr Fred Jolliffe (left).
Outports Islands, NWT

(National Archives of Canada
73926)

CPA Lockheed
Lodestar Aircraft,
Fort Smith, 1944

(Courtesy of Claire Parker)

The Rock, Joliffe
and Latham Islands,
Yellowknife.
From the air, 1952
(Courtesy of E. McEwen)

RC Mission, church,
residence, school
and hospital.
Fort Resolution.
1941
(Courtesy of Claire Parker)

HBC Post, Fort Rae,
1937.
(National Archives of
Canada PA 73923)

Fred Fraser(with paper)
(Yukon Archives/R.Hogan Coll. Print #82/346)

Spring thaw, Great Slave Lake, June 1947
(National Archives of Canada PA 1447791)

Charles Camsell
(National Archives of Canada PA 167041)

Motor Schooner 'St. Roch' in Northern Waters,
1948 (Vancouver Maritime Museum)

'Athabaska River' a paddle steamer at Fort
Fitzgerald, 1946   (Courtesy of Frank McCall)

Chapter 2
Pioneer Life

The night that Parker arrived in Yellowknife, he went down the road from the Yellowknife Hotel to Lil's cafe for supper. No sooner had he sat down, when someone came up to him and, finding out that he was a lawyer, hired him to settle a dispute over a mining claim. He was given ten dollars as a retainer, his first fee in Yellowknife. Work continued to come in immediately after his arrival, and, despite the cold, the poor living conditions, and the primitive town facilities, he liked the place right away. He knew he had made the right decision.

Next morning, he went to visit Fraser to let him know that he was in town and available for any legal work that might be available. He also asked whether there were any rented rooms to be had. Accommodation in town appeared to be very tight and he had to vacate the hotel within three days. Fraser replied that he could stay with him for awhile and that he could move in right away. Parker appreciated this generous offer but wondered about its propriety given that he could be acting as a defence lawyer in front of Fraser in his capacity as presiding magistrate. Fraser told him not to worry, things were different in the north, and there was no other suitable accommodation for him at the moment anyway. He said that when Charles Perkins had been Stipendiary Magistrate in 1941, his wife had been the only other lawyer in town, and they had often acted in different roles in court together.

Fraser's house was on the south end of Jolliffe Island, eastward of the Rock and about 100 yards out in the main bay, it faced the Rock to its west. One could only get to it by boat or by walking across the winter ice. Parker took over the lease of this house later, in 1946, when he got married, and lived in it for several months. It was small but had been quite well built by some early pioneer who had probably put his heart and soul into it to make it sturdy. Unfortunately, it had no insulation, so in winter the temperature in some rooms would drop well below freezing, despite the fact that the oil heater was working away in the living room. One needed plenty of underwear and sweaters and several blankets on the bed at night when the long Yellowknife winters came.

When Parker first arrived, there was no oil for the heater as Fraser had not leased the property in time to put his order in for some. Oil shipments came in once or twice a year during the summer and orders had to be placed well ahead of time. The house was kept warm by an old wood-burning kitchen stove, which went out when the men were away at the office or at night after they had gone to bed. Consequently, it had to be constantly relit in freezing conditions.

There was one bedroom, and another small room just large enough for a bed and a small bureau. The house also had a screened back porch which could serve as a bedroom in summer. Harold "Squeaky" Keys, who worked for the Department of Transport at the airport, was also living there. In winter one of them had to sleep in the living room. Nearby, there was an outhouse open to the main lake. The water in the kitchen sink ran into a bucket which had to be regularly emptied into the lake, failing which there would be a flood on the floor, usually at the most inappropriate of times. Washing and shaving was done in the kitchen sink or beside the lake.

A Heath Robinson shower and a chemical toilet was available in the hotel for those with visiting privileges and one could sometimes get a hot shower at the RCMP post or at Dr. Stanton's house on Con Mine property where a plumbing system had been installed. There was also a shower in a shack attached to a cafe. Customers were restricted to two visits per week, so great was the demand. The cost was fifty cents for advance reservations.   Generally, there wasn't too much bathing done in the winter, only an occasional cold-water body rinse. On special occasions, one could take a bath in a galvanised wash tub in the kitchen filled with boiling water from the stove. After the bath, the hot water would be used to wash clothes and then to clean the floor. The winter water supply was obtained by means of a hole cut into the $4^{1}/_{2}$ inch ice crust on the lake opposite the house. The hole would sometimes ice-over again up to 3 inches thick during the day and at night. This had to be cleared every morning before John Parker went to work so that several buckets of water could be collected.

Parker was able to get a temporary office in a rented room in the two-story Yellowknife Rooms, first built by Vic Ingraham as a hotel but now owned by Oscar Banks. It was centrally located on the west face of the Rock facing the mainland, with all the town stores and businesses located around it. As with many Yellowknife establishments, its oil heater wasn't too effective in the extreme cold, so that Parker had sometimes to work with his coat and gloves on. The outhouse and wash-house were out at the back. Later Banks built some rooms for him in the open foyer on the ground floor of the building. These three small shoe-box rooms housed a secretary, an office, and a bedroom, all separated by curtains. Later still, Parker had his office in a small building nearby.

The law practice grew quickly by word of mouth. Parker tackled a bit of everything: torts (bodily harm, damage, or accident cases); divorces; wills; and real estate work, mainly searching government land-lease records and arranging for land and building transfers. There was also some court work for minor misdemeanours such as petty theft, assault, and drunk and disorderly conduct. Trust funds and financial dealings for persons and companies were also handled. Parker's first major criminal case, the Martha Mafa murder case in Coppermine, did not take place until August 1946. The bulk of the work, however, concerned the mining industry, mostly registering and transferring claims. He also negotiated the sale of his client's claims, as well as his own. At one time he had an interest in 325 claims. Apart from this, he also did most of the legal work for the Giant and Negus mines. The Con Mine had its own legal officers in Trail.

Over the years, thousands of claims were staked in the Yellowknife area. From 1944 to 1947, 200 areas were being investigated. in 1945 alone, over 9,000 were recorded. Millions of shares were bought and sold on the New York, Toronto, Vancouver and other exchanges and money lost and won as the shares went up and down.

There are three stages in starting and developing a mine—the prospecting stage(the riskiest stage), the investigation stage (the critical stage) and finally the financing and building stage (after the mine has found to be viable). The prospecting stage could be carried out relatively cheaply in Parker's time. The investigation stage needed more funds and most claims were dropped or sold off. The final stage required more expertise and large amounts of capital and usually a large mining company with access to financing would take over at this juncture. Sometimes if the claim looked hot a mining company would buy in. The lure of gold has always been part of the human psyche and is still the basis of world economies. Canadian gold stocks have always been attractive to world investors.

In the course of his professional work, he dealt with some famous Canadian mining men. One was John McDonough, a well-known Toronto mining stock entrepreneur, who visited Yellowknife from time to time. In 1945, he called on John complaining that a local prospecting venture that he had financed for two years had come to nothing. At the time, Parker was trying to sell a promising property about 130 miles north of Yellowknife for two local men. One of these, Jack Tibbett, assisted by his wife and another man, had staked out an area that gave evidence of a two-foot wide surface gold vein. Tibbett, a geologist working for the Negus Mine, had, like many Yellowknifers, been prospecting on the side during weekends and holidays. It was on one such outing that he had made this discovery. Parker showed Jack Tibbett's claim to McDonough, who took an instant interest in it. He told Parker not to do anything or tell anyone of their meeting, and that he would return immediately to Toronto to talk to his associates about the matter.

A return airfare to Toronto was wired to Parker within days. Apparently, Canadian Pacific Airlines had been told to give him special treatment. He was met at the Edmonton airport by the CPA manager and escorted to his hotel. Next morning, he got the same treatment in Winnipeg. On arrival in Toronto, he found that a good room had been booked for him at the Royal York Hotel, and the food and entertainment were only of the best.

McDonough wanted to make sure that nothing went awry with the deal. He agreed to pay Tibbett and his partner $30,000 for the property and 700,000 shares in a new company called North Inca Mines. Parker received 10 per cent of this as his fee, which eventually amounted to $35,000, a lot of money for those days. This was a great start to his career and he thought that if this kept up he would be able to retire early as a rich man. The money he made on this deal enabled him to purchase a house on the new townsite.

However, the mine never went into production, although a lot of money was spent on it. What killed it and harmed the Canadian mining industry for a time was the decision of the Liberal government to peg the Canadian dollar at par with the US dollar in 1947. US investment dried up as the Canadian dollar had previously been well below par. This was a great setback to mining activity at Yellowknife and didn't much help Parker's practice either.

Another famous gold mining man that Parker did business with, buying and selling claims for him, was F.M. Connel. His company, Conwest, had a piece of the action in several local operating mines. His wife Joyce had inherited some Giant Mine claims, and he often visited Yellowknife to see the Giant mine officials. He is best remembered for the incident when he gave a Yellowknife prospector $10,000 in cash on a handshake. The man had travelled to Toronto with a gold nugget and some claims to seek a buyer. The mining game had to be conducted without hesitation or someone else would get in on the act.

Apart from his encounters with big names such as these, Parker did labour relations work for the Giant Mine, as adviser to the management committee that handled union negotiations. He recalled that there was never any difficulty in reaching an agreement and there was never a strike in his time. The miners were paid good wages and they usually got a 5 to 15 per cent increase depending upon economic conditions. They worked on a piece-work basis, getting eight dollars per square foot of gold ore extracted. There was no pension in the contract, but the company provided a doctor and a small hospital for its employees and families, and paid for specialist consultations and hospital care and transportation to an outside hospital in cases of serious injury or disease. The men paid a small portion of the health insurance costs to cover outside health charges. This, of course, was in the days before government medical and hospital care benefits. In addition, the company provided proper mining equipment although the miners had to buy their own dynamite for dislodging the ore at the mine face. This was supplied at wholesale costs at the company store. Cheap, good housing, by Yellowknife standards, with central heating and running water, was provided for single men and families, and the company also established a cafeteria which sold excellent cheap meals.

Outside office hours, Parker, like everybody else, tried his hand at prospecting. On one occasion he and his neighbour Kendall Kidder, who was a one-man jack-of-all-trades for the Yellowknife Telephone Company, were partners in a prospecting venture that almost ended in tragedy. Kidder had heard about a very promising area well to the north. Unfortunately this information was acquired in mid-winter. Fearing that someone else would get in before them, they chartered a small two-seater open-cockpit De Havilland Puss Moth aircraft to take them out to the property one weekend. As it was only a two-seater, they had to be flown separately.

The weather was extremely cold when they took off. On arrival, they put up a tent, started a fire, and spent an icy sleepless night worrying about what they would do next day. Intermittent snow flurries began in the morning, sometimes obliterating the distant horizon. However, the country was level and they didn't anticipate too much difficulty in laying out the claims. There were definite quartz outcrops near where they had landed, an encouraging sign, although there were no indications of surface gold. However, such outcrops sometimes meant that there were gold layers in the igneous rock below ground. The area was definitely worth claiming, so they had no hesitation about putting in the square staking plots.

While this was being done, Parker lost sight of Kidder during a sudden snowstorm. After awhile he realised that he had lost his bearings and was unsure about how to get back to the tent. He finished his staking and decided to stay put and call out constantly. This he kept up for about fifteen minutes and was beginning to grow anxious. Then he thought he heard the sound of a distant rifle being fired at intervals. Finally, to his relief, he realised that Kidder was trying to guide him home. Very quickly he made his way back in the direction of the shots and soon found his friend. How lucky it was that they had brought a rifle and plenty of ammunition along with them.

John Parker was sometimes joined by his wife on these prospecting ventures. He met her in 1945 when as Claire Jackson she came to visit her sister and her brother-in-law in Yellowknife. He was a pilot working for Canadian Pacific Airlines. John and Claire were married in Calgary on 27 April 1946.

Before his marriage, Parker had made friends with a kindly neighbour, L.W. "Shorty" Nelson, another Yellowknife character. He was a close friend of the redoubtable McMeekan of the Yellowknife Blade, and, among his many interests, he was active in community affairs, having served for several years on the trustee board in its early days. He was a trained chef and had been a major in the Army Catering Corps during the war. Discarding his career plans, he came north to Yellowknife because of the gold and for a chance of adventure and freedom away from the overcrowded south. It was a good move for him because he took to northern life with relish and, with his lovable nature, was a friend to all. He was apparently making a passably good living by prospecting and doing work for various mining companies. Certainly he was rich enough to feed raw steaks to his sled dogs.

Over the years John and Claire got to know him well. He was very kind to them, showing them the ropes of northern life, and he and Parker entered into several gold deals. Best remembered by John were two that occurred just before he got married. He and Shorty had staked an untouched area near the Giant properties. They laid out eight claims and Shorty then found a Montreal company that wanted to buy them. Around this time, they had also purchased some other interesting claims.

By chance, Parker, who was on his way to get married, met Shorty not long after this in Edmonton. Shorty was full of good news. First, he had sold the purchased claims for $25,000 and a Montreal company had offered $6,000 for the claims near Giant. Parker's share of the $25,000, he said, would be deposited in his, Parker's, bank account and would be waiting for him after his honeymoon. But what to do about the other claim? Should he ask for more money? The claim was near the Giant property (a very substantial mine) and was almost as good as the other claims. Parker told him to do what he thought best.

On their return, John and Claire keenly looked forward to getting their hands on these windfalls. Finances were tight, indeed and they were actually out of money when they landed at Yellowknife. They only got home because the taxi driver, another neighbour, gave them the ride as a wedding present. Next morning, Parker eagerly headed off to savour his new riches. Unfortunately, his account was overdrawn, for Shorty had deposited nothing in it. Both deals had fallen through after Shorty had asked for more money and the Montreal firm had turned him down. Neither claim was ever sold.

Parker's brother Peter, also a lawyer, had joined him earlier in 1946, and was living with John at the Fred Fraser house. When the married couple returned, he moved out and lived in the bedroom off the law office. Even so, Yellowknife was a difficult transition for Claire, especially the extreme cold and the chilly house, but she soon got acclimatised to Yellowknife and came to enjoy the hard work and camaraderie of pioneer life. After all, they were newly married and very much enjoying each others' company. Her first problem, however, was food and household supplies which were difficult to obtain. The two Parker bachelors hadn't stocked the place with much as they had eaten most of their meals at local cafes. At that time of year, the stores were running out of almost everything as the barges didn't arrive until late June, so Claire had to make do with what was left.

As the weather grew warmer, the lake ice became less secure. Two inches of ice will support a person but it is easy to fall through an inch and a half. One has to watch the ice carefully during the June thaw, especially as its depth varies widely over short distances, requiring one to move quickly and carefully, shifting one's weight to safer ice ahead before the surface cracks. At this season, John would take a long pole with him to stretch across to the secure ice on either side in case he fell in. This would keep him afloat until help arrived. Claire would watch him anxiously until he got safely to the other side.

Luckily, he never suffered the embarrassment of falling in. Conditions were safer in the morning after the cold of the night had frozen the ice thicker and more hazardous in the afternoon after the sun had thawed the surface a bit. When the ice reached a really tricky state a canoe had to be dragged along in case of mishap. Claire had a hard time learning to handle an unstable canoe to get over to the mainland after the thaw. Parker made his wife sit astride a chair and practise paddling with an oar. This simulated instruction paid off because she never tipped a canoe and soon grew to love the outdoor life on the lake. Parker himself was an expert canoeist.

These were not the only difficulties Claire had to contend with. The house was twenty feet from the water's edge but in winter it was a cold hard job drawing water every morning from the ice hole; a forty-five gallon drum holds quite a few pails of water. Sometimes a muskrat moved into the hole and started building its nest. When this happened, a brand new four-foot hole had to be dug. There was electricity in the house but it could only power appliances and lights. Only the stove hot plates worked and this made cooking more complicated for a bride not yet well versed in the culinary arts. The use of the open-door outhouse facing the lake, on a pathway used by the other islanders, was most inconvenient, and very cold in winter. Wind direction was always a factor in deciding whether one would venture out or not. Toilet paper was a real problem and impossible to buy. After several months a source of supply was discovered in the ladies room in one of the banks during the course of a party one night. The Parkers weren't customers of this bank but the manager was very kind and told them, after hearing of their predicament, to help themselves. His said that toilet paper was requisitioned as stationery from headquarters, and he had ordered a generous emergency supply.

After the war, the town was still located around the Rock and the two small islands with some expansion into Back Bay. By now it possessed all the basic necessities, but on a limited scale. It had hotels, cafes, air and sea connections, a bank, a dress shop, a shoemaker, a stockbroker, barber shops, bakeries, Burns Meats, and the Pioneer Movie Theatre. It had laundries, grocery stores, oil suppliers, general contractors, the HBC, general and hardware stores, camp outfitters, an insurance agent, a Roman Catholic and an Anglican Church, and, of course, Parker and Parker. All these facilities linked together and to the local gold mines by boat and land taxis.

The postwar mining boom continued unabated. The producing mines, closed during the war, were reopened. Work on over a hundred old or new claims was being done by prospectors, miners, building contractors, geologists, and mining promoters. So, despite the high cost of shipping, most businesses were doing fairly well, although nobody was making a fortune. People had to help one another and use their imagination and skill to survive the hard local conditions. As in any small Canadian community, there was much socializing and partying and many winter sports. Everyone was kept busy at work and in their social activities, and life for most was very satisfying despite the hardships.

The traditional feast days and holidays were honoured with great enthusiasm. Christmas parties for children were held at the churches. Santa landed on the frozen lake off Jolliffe Island and was carried with his bags by dog team to the shore.[35] Christmas Eve visitations were made in the extreme cold with everyone well bundled up and warmed with a hot toddy or two as they moved from house to house across the crisp snow. Usually the sky would be clear and the amazing Northern Lights would present a wonderful backdrop to the proceedings. On one such occasion, Parker said, a trapper, in for the holidays, paid $100 for a bottle of wine and six bottles of beer. this was typical of the crazy behaviour of the trappers and prospectors who had been out on the tundra for months. Shopkeepers felt that it was their responsibility to look after them, and Vic Ingraham usually cancelled a batch of IOUs after the holidays.

The Bank of Commerce manager, Charles Desson, would ensure that customers who had blown all their money on a binge, got back to their traplines or claims. He advanced them enough money to do so and carried the overdraft until they returned six months later. His staff took pity on a particular man who hadn't been out of the Territories for years to see his mother and family. He always spent all his money and had none left over for his travel plans, despite his best intentions. They withheld enough money to get him to Edmonton and personally put him on the plane with some extra cash. Not long after this, they received a letter from him saying he was out of funds and stranded in Edmonton, and had never got to see his family. He had apparently fallen victim to the representatives of certain unscrupulous hotels who await the miners at Edmonton and regale them with stories of the good times that could be arranged for them.[36]

Flying to and from Yellowknife was itself an adventure. Sometimes, the smoke from the frequent forest fires was so bad that aircraft landings at Yellowknife became very difficult.[37] In 1946 and 1947, the original airstrip was replaced by two parallel graded gravel runways. It was only in 1954 that these were paved. The original very rough strip had been cut out of the bush in five days by Ted Cinnamon and his helpers. In 1945, it was Matt Berry who got the contract to build the new runways and also a new airport access road.[38]

At about this time, plans for the new townsite were also being quickly drawn up by government engineers. A grid system was laid out on the new site with Franklin Avenue, which extended south from the Rock and along the small Niven and Frame lakes, going into the core of it. Streets were laid out east and west of Franklin at right angles. The road extended south to Con Mine and north to Giant Mine and west to the airport.

By mid-1946, residents were building houses in the new town at their own cost, all on leased land. Government offices were being constructed or were already up. The biggest building was Vic Ingraham's Yellowknife Hotel on Franklin Avenue. The new hospital, down Camsell Road to the west, overlooking Frame Lake, was beginning to take shape. All the construction had to be done during the four summer months, from June to September, because it was too cold to work outside during the other months. Building was difficult too because everything had to come in by barge during summer. Careful preplanning was thus extremely important if up to a years delay was to be avoided. Orders for supplies had to be placed eighteen months ahead of time.

John Rennie, the surface engineer at Giant a talented amateur artist, supervised the building of some houses at the mine site for Giant employees. Dalton Construction Company of Toronto did the job, bringing their own crews, because skilled carpenters and trades people were unavailable locally. The men worked twelve to fourteen hours in the long summer daylight hours. [39] Claire Parker remembered that these particular houses were not well built and were very cold in winter.

The Parkers had arranged for a new one-story prefab home to be brought in by ship in 1946. It was 800 square feet in size, not too enormous but a great improvement on their quarters on Jolliffe Island. It had a basement with an oil heater that pumped warm air through a centrally located square metal grill to the main floor. The building was expensive for those days, costing $18,000. The Parker's contractor did a good job and he was the best in town. However, he had difficulty finishing the outside before the freeze-up. This was annoying because the Parkers wanted to move in before the really cold weather started. At their urging, to speed up matters, the builder brought in heaters, but they kept shattering the windows because of the extreme difference between the inside and outside temperatures. Once the place was sealed up and the oil heater was operating, the inside finishing was soon completed. John and Claire moved in finally on 22 December 1946. The contractor, probably reflecting attitudes of the times, would only listen to suggestions from the male of the household. Underground water and sewage didn't go in until 1948, so they had to rely on a chemical toilet until then. The contents were dumped into an oil drum in the garden and collected by a man with a truck.

Their friends, Kendall and Jill Kidder, moved in next door. Using imagination, they arranged for a tiny old wooden train caboose to be hauled in by sled and dumped on the property. It was like living in a small mobile home, but very cold in winter with only a wooden stove After a year they moved back to the old town.

The Parker house was in the new town. In the November 1947 elections for the trustee board, 1,358 votes came from the old town, and 1,771 from the new, for a total of 3,079. [40] The new town had finally surpassed the old in population. Yellowknife was now undoubtedly the largest settlement in the north, far outstripping Fort Smith, which was still the government centre. Not everyone was elated at the new town's pre-eminence. McMeekan of the Yellowknife Blade complained about the lack of attention being paid to the old town. He strongly supported a proposal raised by trustee W.E. Cole that if a million was being spent on a sewage system for the new townsite, surely $100,000 could be found for some sort of system for the old townsite. McMeekan added that "the idea of frittering away a million on a system that will probably not work and leaving the waterfront as a gathering place for filth and corruption is stupidity, gross waste, and shows a cynical disregard for the public welfare on the part of the Ottawa administration.[41]   Such was the tone of civic discourse at the time!

By 1947, in response to Yellowknife's new-found prosperity, the federal government and the province of Alberta jointly paid for a rough gravel road to be built from Grimshaw, Alberta, to Hay River. More goods started to come in by truck along this road, and the Yellowknife Transport Company, which operated out of Grimshaw, forwarded it to Yellowknife by Cat train or barge. Nevertheless, the bulk of the shipments north still came from Fort McMurray through to Fort Smith, shipped by the Northern Transportation Company based at Waterways. This company became the sole major operator on the Athabasca River, after the HBC decided to close its transportation division in 1948.

With the construction of the road into Hay River, the businessmen of Yellowknife started to envision a winter road extending through Fort Providence, along the northeast coast of the Great Slave Lake into Fort Rae, and then south to Yellowknife. The Yellowknife Board of Trade, of which Parker was now a member, began to lobby for this option idea. Ted Cinnamon and Vic Ingraham were the prime movers. During the summer of 1948, Ted and a crew did some preliminary work on the proposed 300-mile route. This idea was not to build a year-round road but one that would only be usable during the six month freeze-up from November to April. The land through which it would pass, would be, for the most part, level, which meant that the job wouldn't be too difficult nor the cost too prohibitive.

Private cars would not be able to use the road because they lacked the necessary ground clearance; only buses and trucks would use it. All told, the road would mean that supplies could be brought in more easily at lower cost. Emergency items could be brought during the period in spring and fall when aircraft could not be used. More people could afford to get out to the south, as ground transportation was much cheaper than air travel.

The road was finally built, but only after seven long years. Nothing was done about Cinnamon's proposals by either the government or the locals. However, when the final decision was taken to construct the road, John Parker was directly involved. In January 1955, the matter was discussed by the NWT Council in Ottawa. John Parker had just been elected as a member, and was asked what he thought about the idea. Of course, he strongly supported the project, pointing out that it was long overdue. He called for immediate action by the government authorities, adding that it should only be considered as a stop-gap measure until a properly graded all-season road, with bridges and ferries, could be constructed.

Apparently, a certain Al Hamilton and his brother, of Grimshaw Trucking, had requested permission to build the road under more or less the same conditions as were originally proposed by Ted Cinnamon. Gordon Robertson, then commissioner and council chair, reported that this could not be granted because the land over which the road was to be laid had never been officially surveyed. However, he could see merit in the plan. Bud Drury, the then deputy minister of national defence, and an appointed member of council, said that the proposal had defence implications and he would put his legal officers onto it. The upshot was that an agreement was made with Grimshaw Trucking within the year, and the road finished in 1957.

It proved to be successful. The Cat trains were put out of business, but they had always been costly, dangerous, and not totally reliable. Now Yellowknife could be reached by bus over the winter road, the first Canadian Coachways vehicle arriving in February 1958. The first people to travel the route by car were John Thompson and his wife in their four-wheel-drive Land Rover. This new era of travel coincided with John Parker's departure from the Northwest Territories, but at least he could claim some small credit for bringing it about.

Another new development in Yellowknife concerned the hospital. In 1945, Henry Giegerich, the Con Mine manager, informed Fred Fraser that the tiny company hospital was becoming too small for the community. He suggested that a bigger hospital be built in the new town.

Fraser now spent considerable time in trying to give effect to this suggestion. His task was made no easier by the fact that two options soon emerged, the one involving the Roman Catholic Church and the other the Red Cross. Fearful that a Catholic hospital might inflame sectarian animosity in the community, Fraser prevailed upon the Catholic bishop to allow the Red Cross to take responsibility for the new hospital. In this whole delicate saga, both Fraser and the bishop displayed considerable tact, imagination and magnaminity.[42] At all events, Fraser was able to go to the board trustees and get them to agree to this latest development, and so the Yellowknife Red Cross forty-bed hospital was built. It was the biggest project that the town fathers had ever undertaken. If successful, it would give a big boost to the community's sense of achievement and self-reliance.

The job of raising funds and seeing that the project was successfully completed was given to John Parker. His training and background had been an asset in helping the town deal with complicated governmental and financial matters. He had been very effective as legal counsel to both the town and the school board. People turned to him for advice if legal matters were the least bit complicated. Probably the most important reason that he was chosen was his outgoing, warm personality and his popularity. He also knew everybody of any importance in the Territories. So he was the obvious choice as president of the new hospital board.

He succeeded in raising $215,000, more than enough to construct the building, buy the necessary equipment and furniture, and provide initial supplies. The Red Cross donated $75,000; the federal government, after some serious coaxing, $50,000; Giant Mine $30,000; Con Mine $20,000; HBC $5,000; and Discovery Mine $5,000. There was an anonymous donation of $1,000, the rest being smaller gifts. The contractor was C.N. Buchanan from Edmonton, who had built Vic Ingraham's new hotel, and who, with his experience of working in the north, did a good job on the hospital.

Field Marshal Lord Alexander, the governor general and a handsome figure of a man, paid a visit to the town in July 1947 and officially opened the hospital. He knew and admired Canadians having had them under his command in the Italian campaign and he took to Yellowknife and its inhabitants. They reciprocated in spades. His visit was the biggest social event that had ever happened to the community, and everyone, not just the elite, got a chance to meet or see him close at hand. There was also a stag party for the veterans at night. The women, fed up with all the official dinners for visiting VIPs that were strictly stag affairs, prevailed on the governor general's aide to arrange a very successful luncheon for their special benefit. They dusted off their wedding day "going away" outfits, and hats and gloves were lent, so that everyone, including Claire Parker, could be properly dressed for His Excellency.

However, not all the news out of Yellowknife was this triumphal. One of the major mining stories in the city at the time concerned a mine failure, and this caused quite a sensation in the country. It gave the town something of a bad name and put it back in the national headlines. The mine in question was the Beaulieu Mine, located about forty miles to the east. John Parker maintained that a high percentage of the mining development companies operating in the Yellowknife area then were not well managed. He handled the affairs of many of them and was frequently astonished at how they did things. Beaulieu Mine was a prime example.

The mine had started life when twelve claims were staked in 1939 by S. Hanson and called the Norma vein, probably after his wife or girl friend. It became the Norma Tungsten and Gold Mine and some exploratory work was carried out before the outbreak of the war.[43] In 1945 the property was optioned by Emil Schnee and Toronto partners and the Beaulieu Yellowknife Mine was formed. Schnee was a mining promoter who had a great interest in the Yellowknife area which he visited every summer. He was involved in several properties and Parker handled some of the paper work for him. Parker remembered him for his heavy German accent.

Schnee became the mine manager and drilling was carried out in 1945 and 1946. A prospectus was prepared and shares were sold on the Toronto and New York stock markets. In April 1946, a confusing report was issued stating that a large gold ore body had been found with a potential of 14,000 tons of high-grade gold ore. Further favourable reports followed and the shares started to take off[44]. The national publicity prompted controversy regarding the reliability of the reports, and a group of shareholders hired a reputable mining engineer, Bill McDonald, to investigate the site. He found that the drilling holes were all very close to one another, concentrating upon one small quartz body. His final report was particularly damaging, because he concluded that there was insufficient evidence to sustain the company's claims about the gold ore body.

His report became public, and the Northern Miner printed a stinging editorial about which started "All suckers are not dead." What really annoyed the editorial writer were the fraudulent public relations methods being used. Apparently, the company had purchased some small property from an unsuspecting Spud Arsenault — a resident of Yellowknife — in an effort to bolster its position. In reality, the purchase had nothing to do with the Beaulieu property. Arsenault owned some claims on Gordon Lake and Schnee offered him $100,000 in cash plus shares in Beaulieu. Much to his surprise, Spud was whisked off to Toronto, where, in the glare of maximum publicity, he was paid in one dollar bills. The name of Beaulieu Mines was of course mentioned frequently during the proceedings.[45]

As a result of the Northern Miner's dramatic expose, the shares dropped sharply in price, from $2.50 to $1.00 and lower, and thousands lost their shirts. According to John Parker, very few people in Yellowknife had purchased shares because they had heard the local rumours that the company's reports were far too optimistic.

An investigation by the Securities Commission revealed some pretty tawdry financial dealings by the company. And yet Sam Ciglen, the Toronto partner, continued merrily on as if nothing had happened. Art Ames, who had worked in the Yellowknife government mining record office as a mine inspector, was hired as the new manager of the mine. Parker remembered him as a decent enough fellow who had had some mining experience in Fiji, of all places. He was also known as a bit of a drinker even if he was always the gentleman. Claire Parker recalled that when he had a hangover he would refer to it as "a touch of malaria."

Yellowknifers, many of whom considered themselves fairly expert in mining matters, watched with fascination as money continued to pour in. The share prices started to level off and rise again. Actually the company spent $795,000 before it finally collapsed, and much of it went through Yellowknife. So who were they to complain? Strangely the Yellowknife press — the Blade and the News of the North didn't comment editorially on these events. A year later, Ames reported glowingly that the ore was actually 105,000 tons! A shaft was being sunk and a start was made in constructing a mill. The company DC3 flew ceaselessly in and out of Yellowknife.

The mood of the times is captured in a small notice on page 2 of 23 November 1947 issue of the Blade had a small notice on page 2, which said:

TO POUR BEAULIEU BRICK EARLY DECEMBER.
Results at the Beaulieu property are reported to be highly
favorable and the mill tonnage has been stepped up. Ore is

being taken from development work and from the raise, No. 201.
A ceremonial brick-pouring is to take place in December, when a
large party of guests is expected to come from Outside, as well as
local people. Among the guests will be, it is reported, Gene
Tunney, former heavy-weight champion of the world. Some of the
local sports are planning to have Mr. Tunney referee a bout in
Yellowknife if he can be persuaded to do so.

The date of brick pouring was to be 7 December 1947, and Ames was continually being told by his staff that there simply wasn't enough gold available. Finally a week before the event, the penny dropped and he took off in the company Norseman for Edmonton, and was called to Toronto. On arrival, he was fired, and an announcement made that the ceremony had been called off because of ice conditions. Ciglen, not wanting further scrutiny, hired a consultant to investigate. His findings, published in the new year, stated that the mine had only sufficient ore for two weeks milling, and that was the end of it.

The mine was immediately closed down, only forty-nine ounces of gold, worth $1,715, having been produced. Schnee had the bits smelted in the little furnace in the mine assay office, and they ended up in the Yellowknife Canadian Bank of Commerce in payment of debts. John Parker, who held the fateful lump in his hand, said that it was no more than an inch in diameter.

Not that the rest of the mines in the area were faring too well either. Because of the pegging of the Canadian dollar at par with the US dollar, the Yellowknife gold boom petered out in 1947. Only the two big mines, Con and Giant, could continue and prosper. Ptarmigan closed in 1945 and Akaitcho in 1946. Crestaurum opened in 1946 but closed in 1947. Thompson/Lundmark reopened in 1947 and closed in 1948. Discovery kept going a while longer but closed in 1950.

DH BEAVER

Chapter 2 Notes

35. <u>Yellowknife Illustrated History</u>, p 329

36. <u>Yellowknife Illustrated History</u> p 130

37. Richard Finnie, <u>Canada Move North</u>, (MacMillan of Canada, Toronto, 1948) p 141

38. Price, <u>Yellowknife</u>, p 300.

39. It was difficult building new buildings in Yellowknife in the late 40's because of delays in materiala being delivered on time. Vic Ingraham's new hotel in the new town was delayed a year. Finally finished in June 1947,the estimated cost of $150,000 ended up at $ 200,000. Price, Yellowknife, p197

40. Price, <u>Yellowknife</u>, p 61.

41. Price, <u>Yellowknife</u>, p206

42. Price, <u>Yellowknife</u>, p 228

43. Price, <u>Yellowknife</u>, p 240.

44. Price, <u>Yellowknife</u>, p 240.

45. Price, <u>Yellowknife</u>, p 245.

Yellowknife. 1948 (LtoR) Don Bateman,(Giant Mine),Clare White(Con Mine), John Parker, Merve Hardie, Jock McMeekan,unknown,unknown,unknown, A.Lotzke, Dr. Stanton, Jock McNiven(Nevus Mine). (Courtesy of Claire Parker)

House on Joliffe Island rented by the Parkers 1945-46
(Courtesy of Claire Parker)

Con Mine jetty and mine buildings, Yellowknife, July 1940
(National Archives of Canada PA 101776)

CPA Fairchild 17c aircraft flying from Yellowknife, 1945
(Courtesy of Claire Parker)

Matt Berry's Fairchild aircraft and Dick Finnie's dog sled,
Coppermine, 1931 National Archives of Canada PA 10062

Douglas Dakota aircraft on the frozen lake on the East side of The Rock
(Courtesy of Claire Parker)

Anglican Church, Old Town,
Yellowknife, 1947 (Courtesy of Claire Parker)

Matt Berry

John Parker speaking at a Yellowknife Board of Trade meeting.
(L to R) John Parker, Ted Horton, Don Bateman
(Courtesy of ClaireParker)

Ken Kidder, Claire Parker, John Parker, Jill Kidder on holiday 'outside'. Reno, 1949
(Courtesy of Claire Parker)

Northern Prospector and barge alongside The Rock, Yellowknife, in Latham Narrows. 1941
(National Archives of Canada PA 101785)

Road fromThe Rock, Old Town, Yellowknife to the New Town site, 1947 (Courtesy of Frank McCall)

The Rock, Yellowknife1940
National Archives of Canada PA 15283

The Rock and road leading to New Town
with Latham & Joliffe Island in the background (Courtesy of Frank McCall

The Rock in Midwinter, Back Bay side, 1945
(Courtesy of Claire Parker)

Theatre and Dr. Stanton's Office, New Town,
Yellowknife, 1948 (Courtesy of Frank McCall)

Yellowknife 'Special' House, July 1940
(Canadian National Archives PA 101737)

Yellowknife during thaw out, 1946
(National Archives of Canada 4640)

Left.
Yellowknife Public School in
New Town with
the Con Mine and Great
Slave Lake in the

(Courtesy of Eaon McEwen)

The Famous"Wild Cat" Cafe
(Courtesy of ClaireParker)

Yellowknife, New Town, 1955
(Courtesy of Eaon McEwen)

John Parker and his wife meeting John Diefenbaker
at Whitehorse airport,   July 1961 (Courtesy of ClaireParker)

Chapter 3
Northern Justice

The NWT Stipendiary Magistrate's court was in the tradition of the English medieval court system. When the king's justices got overburdened with work, the king appointed stipendiary magistrates, who received a regular salary, to try cases in the provinces. They dealt with more serious cases than justices of the peace. The NWT magistrates were not always trained lawyers in the early days. Because of the small workload, most of them performed other duties in government service as administrators, policemen, or physicians. Of the twenty-four appointed to the court between its establishment in 1904 and its supersession by Justice J.H. Sissons's court in 1954, sixteen had legal training, two were doctors, three were RCMP, and one was a civil servant.[46]

John Parker recollected that in his time several magistrates were very capable. Fraser and Cunningham have already been mentioned. Luckily, they conducted most of the cases and all the major ones. On balance, he did not have too high a regard for the rest, variously describing them as "hopeless," "nice chap," "knew no law," "very learned," "knew nothing," "charming but not capable".

Most of the work of the magistrates was in the Mackenzie delta and not in the Eastern Arctic. This was because the population in the eastern part of the territory was much sparser, police coverage was not as complete, and the Inuit distrusted the RCMP and often did not report serious crimes. They dealt with them in their own fashion instead.

The Inuit did not understand what was happening at the trials, although, with time, they did come to see that there was some sense in the white man's justice. They had their own ideas on crime and punishment, which, to some extent, made a lot of sense in the conditions of the north. It was very important that the white judiciary understand Native thinking on matters criminal and conduct proceedings with this in mind. This did not always happen, but most of the magistrates tried to take this situation into consideration.

In Native Inuit culture, the husband had total authority over the family. He was the one who made the decisions about where to stop and set up camp, whether to hunt or not, how to deal with problems and crises. A wife's opinion might only be solicited on an important matter.

There was no recourse to a formal legal system in the case of criminal acts. The family was the pre-eminent unit in Inuit society. Sometimes, Inuit families worked together during the winter hunt for help and reinforcement, but most of the time they were on their own. Yet there were some periods when they worked and lived together in a larger context. A family head might emerge as the leader of a group because of his personality, hunting skills, or wealth and prestige; he might, for example, own a boat or a team of fine dogs. Thus people would turn to him in cases of trouble. He would exercise his authority by gaining their respect and loyalty. If there was trouble he would hear the evidence and decide upon the punishment.[47] Restitution, reprimand, teasing, shaming, and, in extreme circumstances, ostracism, were used in handling misbehaviour and antisocial activities in Inuit groups. The death sentence was never given, even for the most heinous of crimes. That said, ostracism could be a very harsh punishment in the winter tundra.

One of the weaknesses of the system was that punishment for serious crimes, such as murder, wife stealing, or rape, was not always effective either in preventing recidivism or satisfying the offended parties. Blood feuds and vendettas could arise, leading to further murders and thefts. Usually, the dispute was finally settled by negotiation, for example, through the transfer of valuable property such as dogs or a sled to the offended family.

The Native Indian social structure was more or less the same, except that it had a more sophisticated political aspect. There was an elected or hereditary band chief and an elders' council. This council assumed the role of a criminal court when required, all those concerned in the case being given a chance to have their say. The members of the band were, therefore, more inclined to accept the decision, because it came from a group rather than a single person.

The superimposition of the white legal system on northern peoples created problems. It was completely alien to their way of thinking. They couldn't understand the formal written charge, a foreign notion to their oral traditions. From their point of view, there was no need for such a detailed charge. The offence would be fully discussed at a council hearing, and all the nuances and mitigating circumstances fully covered before a decision was made. Also they hated the long delays, and all the bureaucratic procedures of the white man's courts. The preliminary investigation, the hearing, and the trial, generally took place long after the crime had been committed, when it was no longer fresh in their minds.

The white magistrates tried to conform to the common-sense Native approach to justice as much as they could, especially in minor cases. However, there were those who went by the book to the point of absurdity. Obviously, it was much better to settle minor cases out of court by counselling and this was sometimes done. It was extremely important to explain the white court procedures in simple terms to the Natives, and make sure that they understood the rights of the accused. Even with an expert interpreter, it was difficult for this to be done. Consequently, the northern magistrates had an additional layer of difficulty to contend with. Successful magistrates needed to have considerable imagination, flexibility, and sensitivity as well as a good knowledge of the law, a combination not always found in the northern judiciary.

John Parker has written that there was another element in running Native courts, namely the difference between Indian and Inuit. He felt that the Native Indians were far too inclined to listen to the advice of white men, often at their own peril, and were not self-assertive enough. The Inuit, on the other hand, considered themselves superior to white people, although being invariably polite, they would never show this. There was some of this sense of superiority in the Native Indian too, when he commented on the ridiculous clothing that whites sometimes wore in the north, and the mess that they left around the landscape. In Parker's opinion, it was, therefore, very important to encourage Natives to speak out, particularly Indians, and not to let them be overawed by court procedure. Very few Natives spoke English at that time, and, though many were extremely skilled in their Native ways of living, few had received a formal white education.

One of the drawbacks of the Stipendiary Magistrate court system was its lack of total independence in awarding completely impartial judgments. A Supreme Court judge has this independence and can only be fired by a committee of his peers, whereas a Stipendiary Magistrate could be fired by his employer (the government) at any time without recourse to redress. R.A. Gibson, during his forty-one years service in the Territories (he retired in 1951), tended to interfere with the northern courts on occasion. In one instance, he wrote to Magistrate Perkins to find two men guilty and punish them severely. In the end, the two pleaded guilty and were given a light sentence of three months imprisonment. Perkins received a letter from Gibson "rapping his knuckles very, very, severely."[48]

By John Parker's time the court had some well-trained lawyers of independent mind who would not countenance this sort of conduct. Parker considered that, despite the inherent problems of a court of salaried officers without tenure and institutional autonomy, on balance, fair judgments were made in most cases during his time in Yellowknife. He didn't agree with Graham Price's conclusion that "NWT stipendiary magistrates were not impartial, and did not enjoy judicial independence, and, as a result, this lead to a 'cheapening' of their status as judges." Parker held that some of them may have been deficient in the law, but that all of them did their best to render fair judgments and mete out punishment that was not too harsh. He never heard of or saw any interference from Ottawa.

He considered that Price's view that the court's record in relation to the Magna Carta dictum that the accused receive timely, impartial, and uniform justice from a jury of their peers was chequered at best, was a little too strong. True, he conceded, there were delays — and some of them far too long — and the accused did not always have a qualified defence lawyer. Admittedly, Natives did not initially have a jury of Natives, but white juries always gave unbiased decisions. Price implies that white juries could be receptive to sometimes biased instructions from the bench. Parker disagreed with this; such instructions were not given and juries had enough sense to ignore anything that was out of order.

The first Indian juror sat on the Lamont trial in 1947 at Fort Smith, while the first Inuit juror was the foreman at the Alikomiak case in 1951 at Cambridge Bay. John Parker was involved with both these cases. Native people were called for jury duty as much as possible after 1955 with Mr. Justice Sissons's arrival. Parker felt that the use of Native jurors should have been initiated much sooner.

Ceremony has always been important in English courts. In Wales, for example, High Court judges were met at the town's boundary and escorted by trumpeters, the sheriff, and county dignitaries. In England there was a cavalcade, attended by pikemen and liverymen, with bells and music. Magistrate Lucien Dubuc (1921-32), first introduced this tradition to the north by insisting that an RCMP officer always accompany him up the Mackenzie River on his court circuits. This tradition was kept up. The magistrate, the prosecutor, and the defence counsel, in Parker's time, were always gowned and there may even have been the odd wig in the old days. This was the routine no matter how humble the courtroom. Justice Sissons made sure that the Canadian Red Ensign, and later the new Canadian flag, were brought along, and raised in a ceremony outside the court building. This was particularly important on our northern Arctic islands, to establish our sovereignty.

The procedure at these courts was that once the accused and his attorney and the prosecutor and witnesses were assembled, the magistrate would be escorted in by a Mountie and the court clerk. If it was a serious case, the accused would be allowed the option of having a jury. Parker once defended a man accused of murder who chose to be tried without a jury. After this, the clerk would read the charge, and the prosecutor and defence counsel would make their preliminary statements. The prosecution and defence would then introduce their witnesses, and the examination and cross-examination would proceed. After the prosecution and defence summations, the magistrate would then either explain to the jury the law as it pertained to the case and sum up the case, or, if there was no jury, give his verdict and sentence. If the accused did not take the stand, the prosecution had the last word, otherwise the defence could sum up last.

John Parker was guided by a number of principles in his relationship with clients. He never refused to act for the defence unless he disliked the accused so much that he thought he could not represent him fairly. Sometimes he refused to act for the Crown for various reasons (as we shall see later), and had no compunction in doing this because he knew that the Crown could always retain someone else. In criminal cases, if he accepted an accused client, he usually insisted that payment be made up front. He found, from bitter experience, that if he didn't do this he probably would never get paid. If clients were acquitted, they argued that they were obviously innocent and no service of consequence had been performed. If they were convicted, it was obvious that they had hired a poor lawyer who didn't deserve payment. If he was asked to act for a poor person, he didn't charge. If it was a serious case, the Department of Justice usually covered such defence fees in any case.

Once the matter of fees had been settled, he then told his clients that they were under no obligation to tell the truth, but if they lied it would be extremely difficult to conduct their defence. If they told the truth and it involved their being guilty, then they could not be called as a witness. The ethics of the legal profession prohibit a lawyer from presenting to the court evidence which he or she knows to be false. However, a lawyer may be very suspicious of the story which he is told, but that does not prevent him from calling evidence in support of that story. Suspicion is not enough: he must be absolutely sure. The lawyer must not call a witness whom he or she thinks might lie. Parker said that most clients apparently feel that they must persuade their lawyer of their innocence. He would explain to them that it was immaterial to him whether they had committed the offence or not since it is quite ethical for a lawyer to defend a person he knows to be guilty. According to him, the one group who almost invariably told him the truth were the Inuit.

Parker reminisced that it was remarkable how good a defence could be presented honestly for a guilty person. The chances were that Crown counsel had available to him a strong body of evidence implicating the accused, but almost always there were gaps in this evidence of greater or lesser importance. The trick was to fill in these gaps to the advantage of the accused. Witnesses, being human and subject to the ordinary frailties of observation and recollection, can be expected to make mistakes no matter how honest they are. The result is that the case of the prosecution may not always be perfect. If the defence lawyer is in complete possession of the real facts, then he is able to emphasize the mistakes of the Crown and possibly undermine the credibility of the prosecution witnesses. The chance of acquittal is sometimes there.

He said that the task of acting for the Crown was different. The RCMP would bring him cases which warranted prosecution. Usually the charge had already been laid. He would read the detailed investigation reports that backed up the charge, consult the police, and ask questions about points which didn't seem to be fully covered. Most lawyers would then talk to all of the prosecution witnesses to secure additional information, but he never did this. He would get the police to secure the additional information. It is perfectly proper in Canada for the prosecution to interview witnesses. While he always wanted to know what the witnesses were likely to say, John felt that he could usually get that information from the reports. By doing this, he avoided suspicion by the jury or the magistrate that there might have been collusion between him and the witness. Occasionally, a defence lawyer would ask the witness whether he had discussed the case with the prosecution in the expectation that the answer would be "yes." The purpose was to sow doubts in the jurors' minds about the prosecution's conduct.

Parker's first criminal case was a major one and concerned a murder committed by an Inuit woman, Martha Mafa, from Coppermine on the Arctic coast. Having shown his legal skills in several minor cases, he was asked by the Department of Justice in Ottawa to act for the accused. Andrew H. Gibson, a Stipendiary Magistrate from Fort Smith, a trained lawyer and a very experienced and capable magistrate, was to preside. Magistrate Cunningham was to prosecute. Ian Maclean was the recorder.

The judicial party with others flew up to Coppermine from Yellowknife in a Grumman Goose aircraft for the trial on 20 and 21 August 1946. The flight was 500 miles almost due north over barren, largely flat country covered with hundreds of lakes and stunted vegetation and trees. The treeline stretches almost to the coast at this longitude. About half way, the plane met the Coppermine River and followed it northwards, flying over Bloody Falls, where Matonabee had massacred the Copper Inuit nearly two centuries earlier. Coppermine is on the northern coast at the west end of Coronation Gulf, facing north across to Victoria Island, fifty miles away. The Copper Inuit think nothing of crossing this gulf by sled on the ice in winter. The village itself was an untidy spread of Inuit skin tents and small wooden buildings scattered about the scraggy flat shoreline.

The sun was shining and the weather was balmy but not hot when the legal party arrived. The Inuit wore light clothing with the women in colourful long "Mother Hubbard" dresses and the white people in heavy shirts and summer trousers. There wasn't a trace of snow. A clear blue sky with a few white clouds contrasted sharply with the blue-grey of the Arctic Sea. It wasn't quite what one imagined such a northern post to be and was so different from the cold bleak place it was in the long dark winter. There were about fifty Inuit and nine white persons living there then. Of the latter, two were in the HBC trading store, two were RCMP, three were in the radio station, one was a Roman Catholic priest and the other an Anglican priest. The wooden buildings housed the radio station, the police, the HBC, and the two clergymen. None of them was large. There were no telephones, one sometimes temperamental radio transmitter, no roads, and no vehicles, other than the ubiquitous dogsleds.

The Copper Inuit, like their other northern brethren, eked out a hard existence in this unproductive land. They lived in light skin tents or in igloos depending on the season. A few worked for the white man as special constables, guides, interpreters (very few of them spoke English), dog team drivers, and house servants. The rest hunted for seals out on the gulf ice in the winter. In summer they fished for whitefish, grayling, char, and tom cod, and hunted the Bluenose Herd of caribou. There was also white-fox trapping if the lemmings were plentiful, and blueberry picking in the fall. Interest was beginning to develop in the south in their soapstone carvings, some of which were sold to visitors or through the Yellowknife Handicraft Society.

The caribou migrated from the west in the spring and crossed the Dolphin and Union straits to Victoria Island. Coppermine had been a summer camping area for the hunt until 1928, when it became a permanent settlement. The main body of people had prior to that been at Bernard Harbour to the east near the caribou crossing, but the families there had been hard hit by a terrible influenza epidemic and had moved to Coppermine where a six-bed nursing station operated at the time.[49]

There was no school and the young Inuit children acquired their skills and culture from their parents. They learned to stalk caribou, drive a dog team, spear seals, jig through the ice for fish, clean and scrape skins, sew garments and tents, butcher a carcase, carve small sculptures, even make a drum. With the arrival of the white man, if times were tough, families could receive destitute vouchers, administered by the RCMP and redeemable at the HBC store.

This then was Coppermine when John Parker first visited it in 1946. He, along with the rest of the court party, stayed aboard the famous RCMP schooner St. Roche, which was anchored offshore and was used as a floating accommodation.[50]

Parker was given the RCMP investigation reports which were not too helpful to the accused woman's cause. They read like tragic and violent opera. The story began in the winter of 1945 when she came into Coppermine on her own after a hunting trip with her husband, saying that he had died of pneumonia and that she had buried him on the tundra. She was a good looking young woman who had several children and was well thought of in the community. Her husband had been a good provider and they had lived the normal Inuit life and appeared to be quite happy. The Anglican priest, the Reverend Harold Webster, liked to take winter trips in his dogsled to visit the Natives out on their hunting grounds. In a casual conversation with the RCMP, he mentioned that he was surprised to learn of the death, because he had seen the couple a few days before the husband's disappearance. They both had appeared to be in good health and in no difficulty. It seemed unlikely to him that the husband had died so suddenly.

The RCMP decided to examine the body, reported to have been buried about two days journey away. A police officer and an Inuit special constable set off and had no difficulty in finding it, since the Inuit buried their dead in winter by simply placing the body on the ice and covering it with skins weighted down with ice chunks or whatever else was at hand. Wolves and foxes would dispose of the corpse in the spring. A quick examination of the frozen body revealed that there was a suspicious leather tied around the neck several times. Murder was suspected so the body was brought back to Coppermine. When the clothing was removed, a bullet wound was discovered near the heart and another one in the back, indicating that a bullet had passed through the chest.

The body was sent to Edmonton by air for a pathologist's examination, and it was confirmed that the man had been killed by the bullet. A coroner's inquest was held in Coppermine and Martha admitted, under oath, that she had indeed murdered her husband. She explained in some detail how she had done it. After shooting him, she had tied the thong around his neck to make sure that he was dead, which as the autopsy revealed, he already was.

Not long after this incident, Webster came across a second tragedy on another of his dogsled trips. He saw an igloo in the distance and headed for it to talk to the inhabitants. As he approached, he noticed that nobody squeezed out to greet him. Normally, the barking of the dogs tied up outside would arouse someone, and strangers were always welcome company. It did not make sense that no one was there. Webster could not understand why the occupants, if they were away, had not taken their dogs with them. He called out but no-one replied. When he crawled inside the igloo, a gruesome sight greeted him, a man and a woman both dead. The woman had a large spike protruding from the top of her head and her body was cold, but the man's body was still warm. It was apparent that he had just shot himself, presumably because the barking dogs had alerted him to Webster's approach.

Webster lifted the two bodies onto his cariole (a dogsled with canvas sides) and brought them back to Coppermine. It was suspected in the community that Martha Mafa and the dead man had been having an affair, and had apparently agreed to a death pact whereby they would murder their spouses and then get married. The man had been the best hunter of the village, and was much admired by the women of the settlement.

With this amount of adverse evidence, Parker wondered whether he was going to be much help to the accused. However, a ray of hope began to shine as he read through the coroner's inquest and the preliminary hearing. The inquest had been conducted by a senior RCMP officer and had been extremely poorly handled. First, Martha had been called as a witness, which should never have been done as she was a prime suspect. A much more serious mistake, however, was also made. The coroner did not explain to her that anything that she might say might be used in evidence against her. It seems incredible that a trained police officer could make such a mistake. Maybe he thought that, as this was not a trial, the usual caution was not necessary. Adding fuel to the fire, he told Martha that it would be better for her if she told the truth. Also, there had not been a jury at the inquest, and this fact had not been recorded or mentioned in the report of proceedings. There was thus a possibility that the complete inquest record might be declared invalid.

Martha had not made a statement at the preliminary hearing, so her only admission of guilt had been made at the inquest. Parker planned, at an appropriate point in the proceedings to try to have the magistrate declare the inquest evidence inadmissible and thus break the prosecution's case.

He got a local Inuit to act an interpreter, and went to meet the accused woman. She was a quiet, shy person, with an attractive round face and appeared not to be the type to carry out such a frightful premeditated act. He said to her through the interpreter that it was his responsibility to protect her interests, and she could tell him anything that she thought might help him to do this. She merely smiled and said nothing. It seemed pointless to ask any further questions.

John Parker was very concerned about the composition of the jury. It would comprise six persons and would most likely be picked from the white people in the community.[51] This was a real worry to him as they knew the details of the case and might not decide only on the basis of the evidence. Inuit were not then used on juries because it was considered that they would not understand court procedures, and because the language problem would further complicate and delay matters. No direct questioning of prospective jurors from a panel is permitted by either the Crown or the defence. Questions have to be referred to the judge, who may or may not ask them. About the only permissible questions are those which concern any possible special relationship between the accused and a potential juror, the age of a juror, and whether he or she had ever been convicted of an offence. The defence has the right to reject a certain number of jurors without giving reasons, the number depending upon the seriousness of the offence. The Crown also has this right, but if all the panel have been called and a full jury has not been selected, it must accept those it has rejected. Neither the Crown nor the defence can inquire of a potential juror what he thinks about the accused, or about any matter connected with the forthcoming trial.[52]

It so happened that on the morning the trial was to begin an RCAF Canso flying boat landed on the bay for refuelling. The RCMP corporal in charge of the Coppermine detachment quickly drew up the necessary papers for the crew of seven and some passengers to be placed on the jury panel. The aircraft captain at first refused to comply, but after being warned of the consequences, he agreed. The trial was held in the RCMP building and the room was crammed with court officials and white and Inuit spectators. The first six prospective jurors drawn from the panel were five RCAF men and a doctor who had flown in with them. Parker accepted all of them and the prosecutor made no objections. He had met the doctor the previous night and had been impressed with him. The doctor had been flown to Coppermine to take part in another case.

Parker told Martha, through an interpreter, that she was to say nothing except to plead not guilty when he told her. She could ask him any questions she wanted at any time. Indeed, she said nothing throughout the proceedings except to plead not guilty. One interesting aspect to the trial, which might have helped the defence, happened quite spontaneously. Martha Mafa had a small naked baby with her, which, in Inuit fashion, she kept on her back in a pack inside her loose-fitting cotton dress. Parker told her that it was appropriate for her to have the baby with her for, he said, "How could anyone convict a young Inuit woman of such a crime when she had a small baby in her care?" Periodically throughout the trial, very quietly, she would somehow know that the baby needed attention, and would let it slide out of her dress and put it on an empty tobacco can to do its business. Then she would carefully put it back under her dress again.

The Crown introduced its witnesses and cited the accused's statement at the inquest as its key evidence. Parker didn't contest any of this, but when the final Crown witness took the stand, he saw that he might be able to score a point. This witness was the priest Webster, who testified about his encounter with the couple a few days before the husband's death. Parker was in two minds as to whether to ask his question, but knowing the clergyman to be a decent, fair-minded man, he decided to take the risk. Sometimes the questioning of prosecution witnesses by defence counsel with a weak case can lead to even more problems. John asked the witness to forget anything that he might know of the case, and give his opinion on the character of the accused. The priest thought for a few moments and then said, "I would say she is a sweet, gentle creature."

Parker called no witnesses. In his summation, he pointed out that there was no jury at the inquest — a major factor in a case where murder might be the cause of death. He also mentioned that this had been not been mentioned by the coroner in his written report thus invalidating the report in a court of law. He added that the accused should have never been called as a witness at the inquest in the first place, and that she had not been warned of her rights before she was questioned. All this made her statement at the inquest inadmissable, and it should not be considered as evidence in the current proceedings. Without this statement, Parker said, the Crown's case was entirely circumstantial. There had been no witnesses and no forensic evidence. There was, therefore, no admissible evidence that the accused had killed her husband.

The court was taken aback and magistrate Gibson pondered awhile in the hushed room. Finally, after adjourning proceedings for a short period, he addressed the jury. He agreed with Parker that the statement by the accused at the inquest was not admissible for all the reasons he had given. After a short deliberation, the jury pronounced Martha not guilty. The accused's expression did not change in the slightest, when the interpreter explained to her that the trial was over and that she was free. She rose to her feet and walked quietly out of the room with the baby still concealed somewhere in her dress. Her first display of emotion came about an hour later, when a group of Inuit were being taken in a launch to see the St Roche. A Mountie who had not heard of the verdict, told her she must remain on land, and then she finally broke into tears.

What the Inuit must have thought of the outcome was difficult to say. Under their law, Martha would probably been given some kind of punishment. John Parker was concerned about her, because an Inuit woman would find it very difficult to survive on her own. He asked Webster what would happen to her. He was told, "She is really quite a catch and this will all be quickly forgotten. I would expect that she will be married within six weeks." And so she was.

Parker prosecuted and defended several criminal cases in 1947 and 1948. He was appointed Crown prosecutor in 1948. In 1947, he defended a young Native Indian in Hay River of rape. Magistrate Gibson again presided over the court.

Hay River is located at the southwest end of the Great Slave Lake at the mouth of the Hay River. It called itself "the Hub of the North" because of the river traffic that reached it from Grimshaw. One of the first HBC posts in the Territories was built there in 1868. The settlement lay on a flat marshy estuary and was subject to periodic flooding. Don Stewart, in his later testimony to the Berger Commission stated that in 1946 Hay River contained a Native village, a runway with some Quonset huts left by the Americans, an Imperial Oil tank, five neat houses for the white families, two churches, and the HBC store. It was a tight-knit community based on trapping, fishing, and transportation. Fair control of credit by the HBC manager had led to efficient Native and white traplines and a relatively prosperous village.[53] Parker, however, didn't think too highly of the place. It was hot and dusty in summer and the buildings were somewhat run-down because of the flooding. In the spring, one sometimes had to get around in a canoe.

The young Native Indian was charged with raping an Indian girl in a house located in the middle of the Indian village. According to the plaintiff's evidence, the crime had happened around noon. Parker wondered if there were any people about at that time of day to whom she could have called. He cross-examined her on this point, and established that the window in the room where the offence was committed was open and she had heard voices outside. He then asked her "Why didn't you scream and get some help." Her answer was, "I was afraid that somebody would hear me." Her odd reply caught Parker completely by surprise. Before he knew it, he smiled, but Magistrate Gibson berated him with the retort, "That was a perfectly reasonable answer."The accused was found guilty of the lesser offence of assault.

On 11 July 1947, Parker appeared for the plaintiff in the first civil case tried by jury in Yellowknife. It concerned a suit brought by three prospectors, George Little, Ronald Ross, and Leonard Peckham against a mine called Diversified Mining Interests (Canada) Ltd. and David Lieberman of Toronto. These prospectors had sold their claims to the parties being sued on the basis of a signed agreement that they would receive a percentage of the company shares in addition to a cash payment. As far as Parker was concerned, it was an open and shut case, as the shares had never been transferred. Bruce Smith, who later became Chief Justice of Alberta, acted for the defendants. The evidence was led, and the jury found for the plaintiffs, awarding them $20,000, based upon the number of shares to be paid at their current value.

After the award was announced, Smith complained to the magistrate, Frank Cunningham, that the complete mining records office file had been given to the jury, instead of just the pertinent parts. He contended that this information was confidential and was prejudicial to his clients and might have affected the decision of the jury. Parker countered that the reason that the whole file had been given to the jury was because the records office clerk had objected to anything being removed from it, as it was contrary to government regulations. He said that some of the papers in the file were an important part of his clients' case, and therefore the whole file had to be given to the jury when they asked to see the evidence. In any event, the contents of the file concerned only administrative matters, had nothing to do with the case and could not be construed as being prejudicial to the defence. Much to Parker's surprise, Cunningham then reversed the decision of the jury, saying that the proceedings were invalid because of the revelation of extraneous material to the jury.

Parker advised his clients that, in his opinion, there was no question that the jury's decision would be upheld by an appeal court. He recommended that the case be appealed. His clients, however, were fed up with the proceedings and wouldn't let him proceed. He earned nothing for his efforts, as he was to have received a percentage of the award. Parker later said that this was the only time in his long experience of the north where an invalid decision was made by the judiciary. There didn't seem to be any logical reason for it, Cunningham may have wanted to avoid criticism from Ottawa for allowing the whole file to be shown to the jury.

Parker's first experience as a prosecutor was in a manslaughter case at Fort Smith in July 1947. Angela Branca, the Vancouver city prosecutor who later became Chief Justice of the BC Supreme Court, was brought in by the local Roman Catholic priest to defend the accused, one Lamont. Gibson was the magistrate. The accused had got drunk and into a vicious fight and killed a man. The jury decided to give him the benefit of the doubt and acquitted him, as the dead man had fallen during the fight. The case was notable because it was the first time that Native Indians had formed part of the jury.

In August 1948, Parker prosecuted in a murder trial of a Native Indian named Charlo, in the lower Mackenzie River village of Fort Simpson. This fort was the earliest white settlement on the Mackenzie, going back to 1804, when a Northwest Company trading post had been set up there. It is located about 130 miles down from Great Slave Lake, near the mouth of the Liard River.

The Charlo case was particularly dreadful. Charlo was an older Slave Indian who lived in a small community about eighty miles west of Fort Simpson. His first wife had died, and he had acquired a new and younger one with the help of a visiting Catholic priest. This young orphan had been educated at the Catholic mission school at Fort Resolution. She could only speak a little broken French and no English or Slave. She had never lived in the bush and was thrust into a strange environment with a harsh much older husband with whom she couldn't communicate. Experiences like this tended to jaundice Parker in his views of the Roman Catholic Church and their schools in the north.

In this small settlement there was a strange Indian woman who appeared to have an extraordinary hold over members of the little band there. From what Parker could ascertain; she abused her charismatic powers by putting the fear of God into anyone who thwarted her. From the start, she resented Charlo's new young wife. It was believed, although no-one would testify to this effect, that she influenced Charlo in his awful treatment of his young wife. He did not provide her with enough wood to keep a proper winter fire going, or enough food or warm clothing. Gradually, with the onset of winter, the poor woman became weaker and weaker.

This situation came to the notice of the RCMP at Fort Simpson, and a Mountie was despatched to investigate. He found the woman in dire straits, living alone in a caribou tent with no heat and very little food. She appeared to be on the point of dying of starvation, and she could not move because her legs were frozen almost to her knees. Immediately, she was taken out by dogsled, but died later in hospital at Fort Smith.

Charlo was charged with manslaughter and with failing to provide the necessities of life for his wife. Gibson was the presiding magistrate. Ken Conibear, a white trader who was well known and well liked on the Mackenzie River, acted as the accused's friend.

John interviewed two young Indians who disliked the old woman and suspected her of influencing Charlo. They agreed to give evidence for the prosecution, but, when the day of the trial came, they didn't arrive. The RCMP officer described the situation that he had found in the tent of the deceased woman. Conibear made a statement in support of the accused, saying it had been a harsh winter and trapping and hunting had been poor. He contended that no criticism should be levelled at Charlo. Gibson found the accused guilty and he was sentenced to two years imprisonment at the penitentiary at Prince Albert, Saskatchewan.

As a result of this case, John Parker wrote a strong letter to the person responsible for education in the Indian Affairs section of the Department of Mines of Resources. He described the case and the education that the young Indian wife had received at the Catholic mission school, which, he contended, had contributed to her tragic death. He suggested that Indian and Inuit children should be allowed to keep their own language, and should be taught English and not French in such schools. The children were already separated from their families and it was inhuman for them not to be allowed to use their own language. Later, the official to whom Parker had written sent a memorandum to the deputy minister supporting Parker's proposal. A copy was forwarded to Parker, but nothing was done about this important matter.

Immediately after the Charlo case, the court party went on to Fort Resolution on the south shore of Great Slave Lake, to try several further cases. Fort Resolution is another old northern settlement. The Northwest Company built a trading post here, near the mouth of the Slave River, in 1786.

The cases concerned two Métis, Mandeville and Lambert, who were charged with manslaughter in two separate trials. Lambert was a seventy-five-year-old trapper who lived in a tiny log cabin outside the town. He had bootlegged 50 cent home-brew beer for years. Mandeville and another Métis were drunk when they forced their way into his house at three in the morning demanding liquor. A fight ensued with Lambert's gun going off and hitting the Métis. Mandeville hit Lambert with the butt of his rifle. The Métis's wound became infected and he later died. The jury found the two not guilty, presumably believing that this was a case of justifiable self-defence.

In 1949, Parker prosecuted in a case concerning the theft of surplus equipment left at Fort Norman by the US army after the war. Paul Jacobs, who operated a machine shop at Yellowknife, was charged with break and entry and theft. With the help of some men, Jacobs had taken several old bulldozers and spare parts from a dump there, loaded them on a barge, and transported them to Yellowknife. Then he restored them to working condition. The RCMP got wind of the episode and found the equipment, and charged Jacobs because he was the leader of the expedition. He was awarded bail, and retained a lawyer from Edmonton, Neil Maclean, to defend him. Special arrangements were made for the Northwest Territorial Court to try the case in Edmonton to accommodate Maclean and some of the witnesses. Gibson again was the presiding magistrate.

A representative from the US army was flown in to identify the stolen property. Maclean argued that his client had thought that the equipment had been abandoned because it was not worth shipping out. It had been rotting in the open for many years, hundreds of miles away from civilisation, and was in very poor condition. It was well known on the river that people had helped themselves from time to time to anything there, and nothing had been done about it. Notwithstanding this defence, Jacobs was found guilty and fined $300.

Parker travelled throughout the territory seeing problems at first hand. In April of 1949, he went to Aklavik to prosecute in a case concerning the illegal slaughter of reindeer. The party comprised Parker, Ray Mahaffey, the defence lawyer, and the court reporter. They flew there in a Yellowknife Airways Fairchild 71 piloted by Mush Sharon, the "Duke of Malta," who had flown with Buzz Beurling in Malta during the war. He was tragically drowned a year later in the icy waters of Great Bear Lake, trying to rescue an aircraft which had broken free from its moorings.

It was 24° below zero when they landed at Fort Norman for the night. The weather was the same at Aklavik. The place was then in total darkness and had been for weeks. Although there was a hotel at the settlement, the party was billeted with various members of the white community. The locals longed for new company to break the monotony and were glad to accommodate visitors. Parker stayed with the Anglican minister, a priest from England, Canon Montgomery.[54]

Aklavik is located on the western edge of the Mackenzie River delta, about 150 miles north of the Arctic Circle and 70 miles south of the Beaufort Sea. The area around comprises thousands of islands, channels, lakes, and swamps, fanning out for a hundred miles to the coast. It was an attractive place for northern peoples because of the abundance of wildlife. It teemed with muskrat, beaver, marten (sable), fox, bear, and moose and, at times, caribou. Millions of birds migrated from the south to nest for the short hot summer. There were also white whales and seals in the open sea at the river's mouth. Aklavik itself is on low-lying land surrounded by meandering channels. In 1949, it was the third largest NWT community, after Yellowknife and Fort Rae, with about 150 whites and 600 Natives, mostly Loucheux Indians and some Métis and Inuit.

Belgian Oblate fathers, closely followed British Church of England priests to set up missions in 1919 and 1920. Two sets of schools and hospitals, both in competition, were built there by each denomination. An RCMP and a HBC post followed the missionaries a few years later.

Although the Mackenzie delta country is locked in a cold dark shroud for most of a long winter, in summer it is a completely different place. Mary Crocker Peters, a teacher working there for many years, wrote of muskrat and caribou hunts, blossoming trees, and colourful birds, and spring flowers. She noted that, in the fall, the village would suddenly empty when word came that the caribou herds were in the offing. These animals were of the Porcupine Herd from the Yukon and Alaska. With the coming of winter, the animals would migrate southwest from their calving grounds on the open northern coastal plains. Crocker Peters saw herds that stretched for fourteen miles.[55]

She also wrote of the Native children in the Anglican school where she worked. Though separated from their families, they received loving care and, apparently, some worthwhile education. Parker was very impressed with the Loucheux Indians, named because of the appearance of their eyes, after the French "loucher," to squint. They were a handsome, energetic, friendly people, and in his view were much more dynamic than their brethren to the south. They had a fierce, turbulent history, often fighting their enemies, the Inuit. They were known as great traders and travellers, traversing the rivers westward as far as the Alaskan coast.

The trial took place in April 1949, just after the muskrat hunt. Good pelts were then selling for $2.60 each and many Native and white trappers had taken 2,000 or more apiece, so the town was celebrating. But Parker had work to do and immediately entered into consultations with the RCMP, the government game warden Frank McCall, and a government biologist, Ward Stevens.

Reindeer and caribou belong to the same species of deer, originating in Northern Europe and Asia. Reindeer were domesticated centuries ago. They have slightly darker coats and shorter legs than caribou, and they run and stand differently; they tend to mill around in circles when rounded up whereas caribou try to disperse.[56] Reindeer were first introduced into North America in 1902, when 1,280 were brought from Siberia to

Alaska. In 1929, the Canadian Government arranged for 3,450 Alaskan reindeer to be moved 1,400 miles eastwards into the Mackenzie delta. It took the Lapp herder Andrew Barr five years to get them there after many misadventures. The idea was to provide work for the Inuit, who could manage their own herds and sell the carcases. Like so many of Ottawa's plans for the north, it was not successful. Conditions in the northern Mackenzie delta were different from northern Sweden and Lapland, and the Inuit didn't take to the sedentary life of animal herding.

However, a large reservation, about 150 miles square, had been set up for the reindeer. It overlapped the range of the Bluenose caribou who moved between Great Bear Lake and the Mackenzie delta. The herds were, therefore, well protected and it was illegal for anyone, even the Natives, to shoot them. Caribou could be shot by the Natives for their own use but definitely not the reindeer. Some small-scale selling of caribou meat was going on in most communities, but the RCMP turned a blind eye on the practice provided it didn't get out of hand.

In 1948-9, however, the RCMP suspected that some poaching was going on in the reservation, and had warned everyone to keep an eye open for evidence. It came to the notice of the police that a plane-load of butchered meat suspected of being reindeer had been delivered to Jimmy Jones, a white Aklavik fur-trader. Frank McCall, the district game warden, flew out to examine at the southern edges of the reservation, where it was thought that the poachers were operating. Flying in very cold weather and in relative darkness, he sighted what looked like the remains of some animals about 100 miles west. The land was open and flat so the plane was able to land. All they found were the heads of slaughtered animals and these were collected and taken back to Aklavik.

One way to prove that the slaughtered animals were reindeer was to examine their ears, because the ears of all reservation reindeer had been clipped for identification. Strangely these heads had no ears at all, a suspicious circumstance.

The RCMP questioned Jones and the pilot of the plane that had brought the meat in. They confirmed that McCall had landed in about the same spot that the shooting had taken place. According to their testimony, two Natives had been working their traplines, about seventeen miles south of the border of the reindeer reservation, when they encountered a herd of twenty-six animals. Assuming that they were caribou, they shot them. They butchered the carcases and took some meat to their camp, leaving the rest in a cache. Jones claimed that he happened to be fishing nearby to feed his dog team. It was then that he came across the hunting party and arranged to buy some meat from the cache. He bought the equivalent of three animals.[57] Later he made arrangements for Mike Zubko, who operated a charter plane out of Aklavik, to retrieve the meat and bring it back to Aklavik.

The Natives contended to the RCMP that they were outside the reserve and had thought that they were shooting caribou. The explanation for the absence of ears on the heads was that these, being frozen, were brittle and had simply broken off. It seemed an odd coincidence that Jones, so far from Aklavik, happened to be fishing so near the Native party. The Natives admitted that they were not too far from the reserve. They must have realised that these animals might be reindeer. There, therefore, seemed to be enough circumstantial evidence to convict Jones, and he was charged with possession of reindeer meat contrary to the Reindeer Protection Ordinance.

It was at this point that Parker arrived on the scene. He thought that more definite proof was needed. Accompanied by the RCMP, he flew out to inspect the spot where the cache was located to see if there were more witnesses. In the meantime, a wire was sent to Ottawa asking whether there was a way of identifying the heads of reindeer. Within two days a reply was received conveying some interesting information. Several known reindeer and caribou skulls in Ottawa had been examined and it had been found that certain differing jaw measurements were indicative of the respective deer types. The width of the reindeer jaw is greater at the back than at the front, whereas precisely the opposite was true of the caribou jaw. The jaws of the heads in question were carefully measured by Stevens and it was found that half were reindeer and half caribou. There was now direct evidence that some of the heads were from reindeer, and there was a good probability that some of the meat was from reindeer too. Parker felt that this new information plus the circumstantial evidence might be enough to convict Jones, and the trial would serve as a deterrent to future poaching.

The trial was held in the Legion Hall with Robert Bouchard, the resident magistrate, presiding. Jones elected not to have a jury. This was the event of the year for the small community and the room was packed with spectators.

The prosecution called McCall, Stevens, an RCMP officer, and others to give evidence and explain the circumstances of the case. Mikel Pulk, a Laplander who was chief herder at the reserve, was asked whether caribou ever mixed with the reindeer herds. His answer was that this happened only in exceptional circumstances. He was then asked whether he had ever lost any of his reindeer, to which he replied that this happened in very bad storms when some animals might become dispersed. Under cross-examination, Pulk said that the average loss per year from straying was about 300.

The defence elected not to have Jones testify, but brought forward the Native hunters who stoutly defended their actions, saying that it had never occurred to them that any of the animals could be reindeer. They considered that they had been outside the reservation. In any event, it was very difficult to differentiate between the two types of animals.

Mahaffey's cross-examination of McCall revealed that several people had the keys to the lock-up where the heads had been kept and he implied that someone could have tampered with the evidence. He also pointed out that, as the carcases had been butchered, it was impossible to identify any particular animal, so who could say if any of the reindeer meat had been purchased rather than caribou meat.

Bouchard, in his judgment, stated that the Crown had established beyond reasonable doubt that some of the meat that the trader had purchased was reindeer. Nevertheless, he dismissed the case because Jones had purchased the meat innocently, believing it to be caribou.

There appeared to be no intention, after the trial, of charging Jones or the Natives with purchasing or selling caribou meat. The community had had enough of reindeer and caribou, and no further action was taken. McCall believed that, although the trial deterred further poaching, human nature being what it is, some of it still continued.

Later in 1949, on 2 September, Parker was sent to Cambridge Bay on Victoria Island to prosecute a manslaughter case. It was his first trip to the Central Arctic, and he greatly looked forward to it The island was flat on its coastline with a mountainous interior.

The settlement had quite a long and notable history. It lay on a bay on the south coast of the island, separated by Dease Strait from the Kent Peninsula on the mainland, about twenty-five miles away. This was not far from where the Franklin expedition had disappeared. The strait was noted for excellent Arctic char fishing, and was called the "fair fishing place" in the Inuit language. The Inuit originally never had a settlement there, but periodically visited it to fish. Cambridge Bay settlement had been founded by Thomas Simpson and Peter Dease when they were surveying the northern Arctic coast for the Hudson Bay Company in 1836.[58] It had been named after the Duke of Cambridge and they had thought that it might be a good harbour. An HBC post was established on the island in 1923, and was moved to the bay area in 1934. A Roman Catholic mission soon followed. The Maud, later called the Baymaud, Roald Amundsen's famous three-masted schooner, had been moored in the bay in 1927. Amundsen had, then been trying to establish a chain of northern weather stations. The ship remained there for several years, finally sinking at her moorings in 1932. Her mast, superstructure, and part of her hull could still be seen in 1949.[59]

At the time of Parker's visit, the white population consisted of the HBC factor, a Catholic priest, an RCMP officer, and some Department of Transport personnel. About three-quarters of the 300 island Inuit population were elsewhere, spread over various coastal camps. A radio navigation tower had been built at Cambridge Bay at one time but had been found to be impractical and was not in use. However, the Inuit had helped with the construction of the station, and had appropriated the small tractors that had been left behind by the building contractors; practically every male Inuit in Cambridge Bay had his own tractor. When the judicial party arrived, they were transported from the beach to the settlement in a sled towed by a tractor driven by an Inuit.

The case concerned a young Inuit lad who had helped his aged mother to commit suicide. Inuit tradition allowed for this under certain circumstances, such as when a group was out on the tundra in freezing conditions and an elderly person felt unable to continue without seriously burdening the rest of the group. In this case, the Inuit family was well away from the settlement. The mother had asked her son Eeriykoot to help her to take her life. He thought about this for a time but he was understandably reluctant to accede. Finally, presumably at his mother's further urging, he steeled himself for the ordeal. However, he needed the help and support of his friend Ishakak. He used the traditional Inuit method. A rope noose was hung from the tent ridge-pole. Then the mother, with the help of the two young men, carefully put her head in the noose. They then pushed her head down sharply so that her throat was constricted and she was asphyxiated. The RCMP had uncovered this case because some of the Inuit in the settlement considered that the suicide had not been properly performed. Although it was perfectly proper for Eeriykoot to aid his mother, it was not right for him to involve someone outside the family in the task. For this reason the Mounties were told about the incident.

Although the old age pension had been inaugurated in Canada just after the war, its administration in the north was difficult. The Inuit didn't keep written records, and it was difficult for the RCMP to keep track of births, marriages, and deaths, although they tried to do so during their inspection trips to the camps. Most Inuit died early in their forties anyway, and so didn't qualify for a pension. Parker stated that the Inuit, in the early years of white control, didn't understand the concept of a social safety net at all and, in any case, would not have been interested in it. They were a proud independent people who preferred to look after themselves without outside help. In any case, Eeriykoot probably had no knowledge of the pension scheme which might have made it possible for him to refuse his mother's wishes.

Despite all the mitigating circumstances, it was decided that the two young men should be tried, and that an example should be made of them to stamp out the practice. Two separate trials were held, one for Eeriykoot and one for Ishakak. They were conducted in an empty shed of the navigation station. Magistrate Gibson presided, with D.T. McDonald of the Department of Justice in Ottawa, defending. Airforce personnel from a visiting aircraft and DOT personnel made up the jury. The facts of the incident were detailed and the accused did not take the stand. McDonald stressed that it was difficult for the Inuit to break with traditional practices which to them were indispensable, if distasteful. Whereas assisted suicide was totally contrary to white religious beliefs and sense of fairness, to the Inuit it was a question of one elderly family member suffering for the benefit of the rest. Notwithstanding these pleas, Eeriykoot was found guilty and sentenced to one year's imprisonment in Cambridge Bay.

This proviso was fairly typical of the northern judiciary which in practically every instance directed that sentences for Inuit be served in the north, as near to their homes as possible. It was considered inhumane to send them to a large penitentiary in the south. Parker was very firm on this point. Consequently, the prisoner would be kept under house arrest in the RCMP post and allowed outside daily to execute menial tasks.

Ishakak was found not guilty.

Parker had one last case in 1949. It was a strange one, a bank robbery in Yellowknife, the first one ever staged there and probably the last for a long time. One wonders how the robbers thought they were going to get out of town, given that there was no road out, the Mounties could easily control the airport, and it wasn't difficult to detect an escaping boat from the air. The robbery happened on Sunday, 2 October 1949, after three men had consumed a bottle and half of rum in five hours. Their defence was that they were drunk, but this availed them nothing because, as Magistrate Gibson commented drily, "Pretty hearty, but not an impossible ration." The culprits had then proceeded by car to the Rock, smashed a window and entered the Imperial Bank of Canada, physically removing the safe. They took it to a shack on the outskirts of town and started to jemmy it open with a crowbar. Unfortunately for them, someone had seen them and alerted the RCMP. Within minutes, they were rounded up. Silver to the value of $220 was found in their possession, and the rest of the loot consisted of about $200,000 in travellers cheques and money orders.

They pleaded guilty and appealed to the mercy of the court. Gibson, after lecturing them severely, meted out relatively light sentences. One man, an ex-policeman and a six-year war veteran who should have known better, was given three years, another, two-and-a-half, and a third, one year. Don Hagel, for the defence, pleaded in mitigation that one of them had come from an unhappy home, one was totally drunk, and the third had an excellent army record. The ends of justice, he said, would be better served by a lenient sentence rather than a sentence. He seems to have got the better of the argument because Parker, for the Crown, had suggested long terms for all of them on the grounds that breaking and entering was particularly reprehensible in the north.[60]

INUIT ART

Chapter 3 Notes

46. Price, <u>Remote Justice</u>, p 409.

47. Margaret Blackman, <u>Sadie Bower, Neakok, an inupiag woman</u>, (Douglas and McIntyre, Vancouver, 1989) p 150.

48. Price, <u>Remote Justice</u>, p 83.

49. <u>Northwest Territories Legislative Assembly</u>, Government of Northwest Territories, 1980, p 64

50. *St Roch* (104 feet long) was built in North Vancouver of douglas fir in 1928, especially re-inforced for Arctic waters. Under her famous captain, RCMP Inspector Henry Larson, She was the first ship to circumnavigate from the Pacific Ocean to the Atlantic Ocean via the Arctic. A voyage that lasted from 1940 to 1944. She became a national historic monument in Vancouver in 1965. Henry Larsen, <u>Big Ship</u> (Mclelland and Stewart, Toronto, 1967)

51. The juries of the Northwest Territories were composed of six persons, as did Alberta juries, whereas the rest of Canada had twelve.

52. To prevent a juror from being badgered, a juror must "keep the Queen's counsel" (not mention what happened in the juryroom).

53. O'Malley, <u>The Past and Future land</u>, p 30

54. He was Field Marshal Montgomery's brother

55. Mary Crocker, <u>Aklavik in 1943</u>, the <u>Beaver</u>, December, 1943.

56. <u>People and Caribou in the Northwest Territories</u>, Government of Northwest Territories, Yellowknife, 1989, p 171

57. <u>The News of the North</u>, 4 February 1949.

58. Peter Newman, <u>Company of Adventurers</u> (Viking, Toronto, 1985) p 299

59. The <u>Beaver</u>, summer, 1955, p 45

60. <u>The News of the North</u>, 21 October 1949

Trappers line hut, Firth River, NWT, 1950   Courtesy of Frank McCall

Aircraft & riverboats in front of the wireless
station & HBS Post, Aklavik,1937
(National Archives of Canada PA 130429

Aklavik from the air
(National Archives of Canada 447841)

Barge and tug on the Mackenzie River, 1950
Courtesy of Frank McCall

Inuit children with sled Courtesy of Eaon McEwen

Inuit girls at Aklavik Courtesy of Frank McCall

The Richardson Mountains which can be
seen to the Westward from Aklavik   Courtesy of Eaon McEwen

Michael Pulk,
Reindeer Station,NWT, 1949
Courtesy of Frank McCall

Left
Frank McCall in his office in Yellowknife
Courtesy of Frank McCall

Right
Flying over the Franklin Mountains
near the Mackenzie River
Courtesy of Eaon McEwen

Frank McCall's
Government House at Aklavik
(left of photograph)
Courtesy of Frank McCall

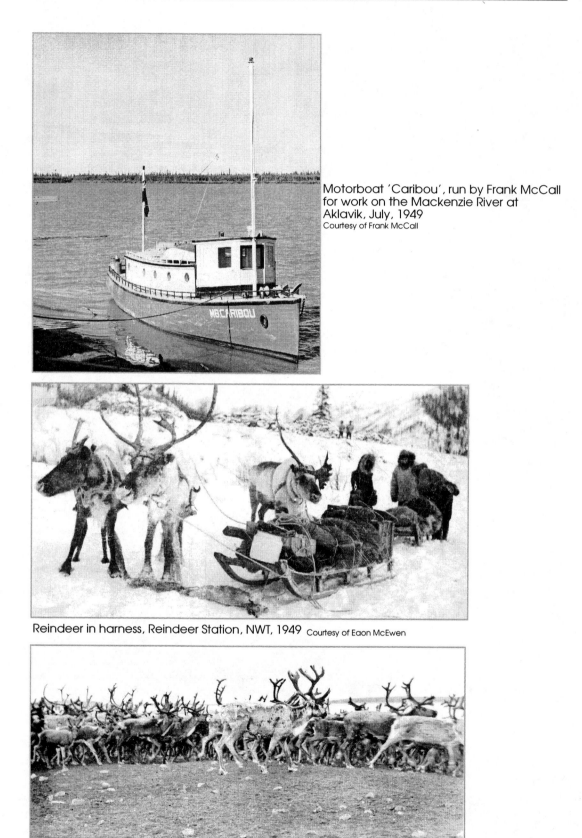

Motorboat 'Caribou', run by Frank McCall
for work on the Mackenzie River at
Aklavik, July, 1949
Courtesy of Frank McCall

Reindeer in harness, Reindeer Station, NWT, 1949 Courtesy of Eaon McEwen

Reindeer herd at Kidluit Bay, Richards Island, NWT. 1949 Courtesy of Frank McCall

Chapter 4
Friends and Personalities

Despite the growing pressures of legal work, John Parker and Claire led an active social life together and made many friends among the northern characters with whom Yellowknife was so richly endowed.

Pre-eminent among these was Vic Ingraham whose adventures had begun when he served as a GI in the US expeditionary force that had been sent to northern Russia in 1918 to fight the communists. There he made a name for himself by driving a railway engine all the way across the wastes of Siberia to the Pacific coast, which he reached unharmed after several exploits and adventures. Having arrived safely, he promptly sold the locomotive. This episode awakened his interest in the north and he came to Canada in 1924, settling at Fort McMurray where, with typical energy and enterprise, he started a small logging company.[61]

When serious prospecting began in the Great Bear Lake area in the 1930s, Ingraham and his partner Gerry Murphy, a polished ex-civil servant and another future friend of the Parkers, set up a transport company and a general store to provide goods and services to the local mines and miners. Among these services was the supply of liquor. Bootlegging may have been profitable, but it did place Vic in an awkward position in the summer of 1933 when no less a person than the visiting RCMP commissioner invited him to become a justice of the peace. It was only with difficulty that Vic wriggled out of this dilemma by successful persuading the persistent commissioner to select another candidate, a reclusive but allegedly well educated Englishman who lived in the bush. This character was duly appointed but, according to Parker, never presided over a case, fortunately.

Later that year, in October, tragedy struck Vic. He was bringing the last boat-load of goods of the season to Cameron Bay, the site of his store on Great Bear Lake, when he encountered foul weather.[62] To aggravate the situation, the straining engine of his vessel caught fire and he was burned on his hands and feet as he tried to extinguish the blaze. His efforts were in vain, and he and a surviving crew member managed to get away on a small life-raft just before the vessel erupted in a violent explosion. After further harrowing adventures, Vic found the party of passengers who had been in the barge that had earlier been cut loose from Vic's boat. He had intended at the time to press on in his craft to obtain help and assumed, correctly, that the barge would drift ashore unharmed. Now it was the stranded passengers who had to help him, for by this stage he was in very poor shape.

The fateful voyage had begun on 20 October, on 29 October an air search for the missing vessel was instituted, and it was only eleven days later that the survivors were found.[63] By now, Vic was feverish, and the smell of gangrene hung in the air. He was immediately flown to Aklavik where several of his fingers, and both his legs below the knee were amputated. But Vic was a man of astonishing grit and resilience. He made a good recovery, was fitted with prostheses, and soon had mastered the use of elbow crutches. The tale of his incredible escape, meanwhile, had been carried in press reports across the world.

In the mid-1930s, when the first Yellowknife gold rush began, he moved to the new settlement and into a new line of business, the hotel trade. Over the years, he built a succession of hotels, each bigger than the last and all amazingly tightly run and orderly.[64] Indeed the beverage room in one of them regularly did duty as a courtroom. Vic was generous with his credit, particularly to the town's drinkers, and his bad debts sometimes mounted alarmingly. He was also generous of himself, travelling extensively for the US War Department to demonstrate to badly wounded servicemen what could be achieved with artificial legs. John Parker remembered how Vic always loved to carry a wad of $20 bills around with him: during the war, when only $100 could be taken out of Canada, Vic would stash away an additional supply of bills in his artificial limbs.

Parker did work for him over the years and, in his jolly manner, Vic would always introduce Parker as, "my mouthpiece." You always knew when he was around because his artificial legs squeaked.

After the war, he added a GM car dealership to his stable of businesses. He even prevailed in person on the company president to guarantee him an adequate supply of vehicles for sale in the north — this at a time when waiting lists for new cars were the norm throughout North America. Vic finally left Yellowknife in 1951 on the advice of his doctor. He moved to Victoria where he bought a motel. He was in a bad accident in California and the highway patrol thought he was a goner when his two legs were found outside his vehicle. But in typical Ingraham fashion he was soon on his legs again and quickly discharged from hospital, He died in 1961.

His former partner, Gerry Murphy, had also moved to Yellowknife where he was very active in community affairs, being the first president of the Yellowknife Chamber of Commerce [65]. On the night of 3 October 1948, John and Claire Parker dined alongside him at the hotel, he having just returned from a trip to stake some prospecting claims. Next morning, they were dismayed to learn that he had collapsed and died shortly after they had left him. Not long before his death, he had requested that his good friend and bridge partner, Father Gathy, should bury him. This was a rather awkward request, since Murphy's sisters insisted that he be buried by Anglican rites and the good father was a

Catholic. But the priest was also an amiable man who duly did as he was bidden from a packed Legion Hall. Unfortunately, as John and Claire Parker later learned, the priest, who had once been a circus clown, got into serious trouble for being so obliging.

Father Gathy was also another very well-loved character of the town. He was Belgian and had been a clown in a circus in his youth. Various stories were circulated about his early life. The common one was that he had been captured by the Germans in the First World War and vowed that he would serve God if he was able to escape. Louis Audette, a member of the NWT Council for many years who knew him well, said that, as a lad of fifteen he had been forced by the Germans to watch his mother's execution by a firing squad. She had been harbouring allied prisoners of war. This lead to his decision to go into the church. He had a fine career working in the Canadian north respected by all. Even the miners liked him as he did conjuring tricks he had learnt in the circus.

Another of the town's great legends was Jock McMeekan, owner-editor of the Yellowknife Blade. He had first come to the area in March 1935 when the town was no more than a scattering of tents and the caribou still migrated through the mining camps in their hundreds in the spring. Initially, he worked at the Burwash Mine, but in 1941 he started the Yellowknife Blade which he produced more or less regularly — unless the lure of a yarning session in the beer parlour proved irresistible — until 1962, when he retired. At various times, the paper carried such grandiloquent or pugnacious mastheads as "The Only Newspaper in a Million Square Miles," "The Voice of Voteless Canada," and "We Demand Representation." But it was the editorials that were his real forte; they were an ideal vehicle for his overblown but amusing rhetoric which he regularly directed at the "comatose, swivel-chair" bureaucrats of Ottawa.

John Parker was associated with Jock through the Northwest Territories Association, whose objectives both men supported. These were the introduction of freehold property, proper parliamentary representation separate from the Yukon, elected representation on the NWT Council, and an elected municipal council. Late in 1945, a petition was signed by Yellowknife residents, including Parker, espousing these aims and, shortly afterwards, Jock and another delegate headed off to Ottawa bearing the petition with them. Jock was prepared to make a scene in the Commons to draw attention to his mission but had the wind taken out of his sails when the minister responsible for northern affairs, John Glen, agreed to meet with him and, moreover, listened to the demands in the petition sympathetically. It was years, however, before concrete action was taken to implement these changes. In the meantime, Jock had gone on to become an elected member of the board of municipal trustees in which capacity he continued his chequered career.

Not that relations between John Parker and Jock were always harmonious. On one occasion, Jock penned a piece that was far from complimentary about lawyers, recommending that potential clients should consult him first. To this end, he had recast himself as a notary public and a confidential consultant on "business, bills of sale, and wills." John did not agree with Jock's valuation of his skills and riposted that clients would be far wiser to see him, John, before consulting Jock. He also withdrew his advertisement from the Yellowknife Blade. Despite this, John Parker looked on Jock affectionately as a colourful personality and a hugely entertaining rascal.

One of the most amazing stories to come out of Yellowknife was how Tom Payne became a rich man. Like every great story it is hard to find the truth. Everyone in Yellowknife knew of it. Parker described Payne as a rough diamond cockney. Richard Finnie describes him a a bear of a man in a tattered shirt and torn flannel trousers.[67] He came north to make his fortune being grub-staked by the Ryan brothers of Fort Smith. They gave him a small income until he found gold splitting the profits on a 50-50 basis.

He came north to be near the mining action and hopefully get involved. The Mosher claim was well-known. It had been made by an eastern mining man who flew in and staked some property right next to the Con Mine to the east and left and proceeded to forget about it. There were various dates as to when the claim lapsed. Payne got his partners to find out about it at Fort Smith and they got the right date. It was 27 August 1936. The Con Mine experts thought it would happen a year later. Payne put posts out in the bush and dug the holes for them the day before so that they would be handy to carry out the stake at the stroke of midnight and beat the competition. One story states that McMeekan carried out a stake on the islands offshore to the Con Mine which were part of the overal claim, but they proved to be worthless. Price wrote that Payne found the gold when walking across the empty property. McMeekan wrote that he found gold after the staking had taken place.[68] According to Price, Payne borrowed McMeekan's canoe, indicating that McMeekan had nothing to do with the staking

The claimed property which became the Ryan Mine was sold to Cominco in September 1937. Payne received $75,000 plus part of future profits from this property and became instantly rich.[69] It was this amazing deal which set off the Yellowknife Gold Rush. Payne was one of the few out of thousands who made a killing.

In a small city like Yellowknife it was hardly surprising that John and Claire Parker should get to know Elsie and Wally ("Bury 'Em") Smith, the undertakers. Wally always impressed John with his uncanny ability to predict the precise number of deaths for the forthcoming winter. Admittedly, this was an invaluable professional skill, since graves had to be dug in advance of the winter freeze. On the other hand, it was also a social liability, since people grew uneasy if Wally began to pay too close attention to them. For all that, he was an engaging fellow, except when the demon rum possessed him, but this could have been due to the nature of his job! He was well-known for trying to hasten proceedings during the freezing conditions in the church in winter funerals by ostentatiously preparing to wheel the coffin out of the church while the ceremonies dragged on. John Parker was present at a particularly lengthy ceremony when Wally attempted this ploy not once but three times. On each occasion, Father Gathy interrupted the service to admonish Wally loudly to cease and desist. Luckily funeral parties could stop at a house on the way to the cemetery which provided hot rum.

Even more bizarre was another funeral service attended by Parker. This was for a Freemason, and the executive of the local lodge was present to perform the masonic rites. Unbeknown to these three worthies, they had taken post on a snow-covered sheet of thin wood which lay across the mouth of an open grave. At a crucial point in the proceedings, this flimsy foundation began to sag under the collective weight and they very nearly cascaded in unison into the open pit. Luckily they managed to jump clear just in time, but that was not the end of their ignominy — they later learned that they had honoured the wrong man!

Apart from friends and acquaintances, John also had some colourful clients. One such was Denis O'Callaghan. He and his wife Mildred came to Yellowknife in the spring of 1939 on a homemade barge. They hadn't been in town a few days before they both got jobs helping Glen Cinnamon haul equipment up the Yellowknife River to the Bluefish Lake powerhouse. Denis drove a truck over a short portage along the route and Mildred cooked meals for the crews at the stopover.[70] Denis had Irish charm and his wife was also very congenial and Claire Parker remembered them as lovely people, very talented, hard-working, and generous. The problem was that Denis had a habit of getting into trouble. When this happened he would immediately go to John, throw a $100 bill on his desk, and start explaining what had happened.

After the Yellowknife River job finished, Denis got work as a miner at Con Mine. After a few years, he developed signs of emphysema, so the two of them decided that they would start their own business — a market garden, of all things. But this is not as unlikely as it sounds because vegetables grow very quickly in the north, once the hot weather comes, and fresh vegetables were always at a premium. A few people had small vegetable plots of their own, but no-one had started a market garden. The O'Callaghan's worked like dogs, digging the ground and planting their crops. Eventually they made quite a success of it.

They also kept pigs on their leased property in the new town. Unfortunately, Frank Cunningham, the Stipendiary Magistrate, lived across the road, one lot down, and he objected vigorously to the presence of the pigs. Cunningham was not a man to be trifled with. He informed the O'Callaghans that pigs were not allowed in the new town and that they must be removed immediately. Denis refused to do this, so Cunningham had his lease revoked. As usual, Denis immediately consulted Parker and McMeekan took up the cause in the Yellowknife Blade. Parker informed Cunningham in no uncertain terms that there were no written regulations barring pigs from Yellowknife. His plea fell on deaf ears; Cunningham wasn't about to be pressured and replied that the order would stand.

What was to be done? All agreed that Cunningham must be taught a lesson, something dramatic. By this time O'Callaghan's pigs were a cause celebre and everyone in town had an opinion on the matter. Most were against Cunningham. A meeting was held at Parker's house, and it was decided that everyone would stop paying their property taxes until O'Callaghan had a fair hearing. This brought matters to a head and, after some prolonged wrangling, Cunningham backed down and reconsidered O'Callaghan's complaint. He said that the eviction order would be stopped if Denis would move his pigs back to his own property from the adjacent lot where he had placed his pig pen. This was agreed and the problem was solved.

It wasn't too long before the last pig died, and Denis lost interest in pig farming. He held a party at about this time and served pork sandwiches in abundance to an anxious group of guests who wondered what the pig had died of.

The vegetable business was successful but it only brought in an income in the summer months, so the O'Callaghans decided to start up their own grocery store and so have a year-round operation. They purchased a building in the old town and moved it to the new town. It was winter, so the building was transported on a makeshift sled towed by a Cat. Unfortunately the top of structure was higher than the power and telephone lines strung across the street. Denis couldn't find the appropriate official to have the telephone lines removed, so he climbed up on top of the house and cut them down with garden shears and leather work gloves. Even so, the building snagged a power line, and the sparks flew. The upshot was that part of the town was without telephones and electrical power. Once more Parker came to the rescue. He arranged for the costs of repairs to be paid so avoiding civil charges. Denis's long-suffering neighbours accepted the inconveniences with a shrug because his antics made people laugh and because Mildred and he were so good-hearted.

The grocery store was a success, for one could always get good service and a tall story. On one occasion, Denis asked Parker what he should do about a newcomer who had started visiting the store. This man would come in and buy only cigarette papers and O'Callaghan suspected him of stealing. Parker recommended that the next time he came in, he and Mildred should keep him under close surveillance. If they saw him take anything and put it under his coat, he was to be confronted immediately. He was then to be told to pay for everything that he had stolen in the past, under threat of being reported to the Mounties. This was done and they found that his bulky parka contained several cans of food. He quickly agreed to sign a cheque and was escorted to the bank to have it certified.

As their business grew and prospered, Denis and Mildred finally got an opportunity to get out of the Territories. They went on holiday to California. Denis was particularly impressed by a bank advertisement in a local newspaper. The bank had an Irish name and was offering low-interest loans. Denis took this to be a sign from God, so he decided to look into the matter. On the recommendation of a bank manager, he purchased a small apartment. The down-payment wasn't too high and the rentals more than covered the mortgage and maintenance costs. As a result of this investment and the success of the store, he was eventually able to sell out and buy a home in Summerland, British Columbia.

By this time, people in the Northwest Territories had become increasingly dependent on air transport, as John Parker well knew from his travels from one far-flung courtroom to the next. Not surprisingly, he befriended several of the pilots, including Ernie Boffa, a famous bush pilot flying out of Yellowknife in the forties and fifties. John Parker considered him to be the top pilot in the Territories during those years.

Born in the States, Ernie started work as an air mechanic in the twenties before becoming a qualified pilot. He joined a flying circus, travelling around the Midwest entertaining the public with aerobatics and short passenger flights. He also performed as a wing-walker. His wife, Nettie, was also a pilot. When the public lost interest in this type of spectacle, he came to Canada and got a job as a northern bush pilot. During the war, he was an RCAF instructor. He was discharged in 1943 and was hired by Canadian Pacific Airlines to fly a Norseman, a small two-passenger aircraft, out of Yellowknife on charter work. He flew with Jerry Buchan, Claire Parker's brother-in-law. Their mechanic was Bill Cormack who later became a senior executive of Pacific Western Airlines. He later flew the Yellowknife/Great Bear Lake scheduled run and he never aborted a flight on this route.[71] If the weather was bad, he would just land on a lake and camp overnight and wait until conditions improved. Later he talked CPA into building a cabin on a lake en route where he could land in case of trouble. He remembers discovering what a good bridge player Father Gathy was on one of these lonely stopovers.

John Parker recalled Boffa's extraordinary knack of finding a location from the roughest of maps. On one staking trip, John handed Boffa a small rough hand-drawn map depicting many lakes north of Yellowknife, with one marked as the destination point. Taking the map in one hand and using the other to fly the plane, Boffa shook his head and muttered, "I can't figure this out." Then he turned it upside down and a big smile lit up his face. He immediately knew where he had to go. This, he said, wasn't too difficult because most of the prospectors flew to locations within a thirty-mile radius of Yellowknife. With all the flying he did, he got to know the terrain extremely well. He knew every trappers' cabin and every mine property between Yellowknife, Coppermine, and Great Bear Lake. As one might expect, he took part in many air searches.

After the war, when the Yellowknife gold rush started, he was very busy flying charters. Everyone wanted his services because of his reputation for never crashing an aircraft or losing a passenger. He could not only fly an aircraft but knew how to maintain it; he was resourceful in difficult situations; and he always carried a sleeping bag, tent, sextant, shovel, flares, a rifle, two weeks supply of food, and a Geiger counter. Like all bush pilots, he was knowledgeable about mining and was always on the look out for a promising property.

His knowledge of the north extended to Arctic history and he liked to explore for famous historical sites. One of his regular customers was an amazing American woman, Margaret Oldenburg, a librarian and expert amateur botanist. She must have had a private income because she would hire Boffa every summer for a month or two. They would go on long expeditions all over the north to collect flora specimens.

After fifty years of flying and 20,000 hours flying time without accident, Boffa retired to California in the sixties.

Another fine bush pilot of that era who went on to achieve international fame was Max Ward. Parker knew him well although he never did any legal work for him. They were close friends, and Ward and his wife would in later years visit the Parkers in Vancouver, flying in in Ward's executive jet. Parker remembered Ward, even in those early days, as a person with a vision, and marvelled at his ability to think about the future of the airline industry while at the same time running a one-man operation — flying and maintaining the aircraft, booking passengers, and even sweeping the floors of the terminal!

Like many others in Yellowknife, Ward was extremely hard-working and extremely capable and thorough in the care of his aircraft. He was also a very friendly person and was always willing to talk to anyone, and, as a result, was very popular. His attractive personality and his friendliness must have motivated his staff to greater efforts. John Parker reckoned that he was one of the first to introduce preventive aircraft maintenance. He once had to change an engine in his plane in a remote lake, and while he was at it he checked the other technical systems as well. He was also very lucky, escaping serious injury or death on several occasions in freak air accidents.

He got his wings at the age of nineteen in 1940, after he joined the RCAF. He spent the war training pilots. After discharge, he flew for a while in the north, until, in 1946, he formed his own company, Polaris Charters. He purchased a new de Havilland three-seater biplane Fox Moth, and operated it out of Yellowknife. His first year was very busy and very successful, providing air services for mining companies, prospectors, and trappers. A year later the federal Air Transport Board informed him that he could not operate without an approved charter. As a result, he was forced to amalgamate with Yellowknife Airways, then run by George Pigeon. The partnership was never satisfactory, and, in 1949, he sold out owing $5,000. Before this, the old Fox Moth, on which Parker had flown on a number of occasions, crashed, while approaching Yellowknife from the south. Ward was not the pilot.

He left the aviation business for a couple of years but returned to fly for

Associated. In 1953, he started up a new company, Wardair, and never looked back. This time he got approval from the Air Transport Board. He got financial help from Discovery Mine and the Canadian Industrial Development Bank. With this help, he purchased one of the first de Havilland Otters for $100,000. Things were looking up, but as Marjory Ward once confided to Claire, her idea of security "was not owing over a million dollars to the Canadian Industrial Development Bank."

Max Ward recognised that this aircraft was going to revolutionize air transport in the north. It had a range of 600 miles and could carry fourteen passengers or, if the seats were removed, a greatly increased cargo load. It was a short take-off aircraft and it proved to be one of finest aircraft that Canada ever produced, and it sold around the world. The Otter also meant that mining development could be accelerated, because it could carry building materials and other heavy items never transported by air before. However, at first the mining companies were not geared to moving so much equipment at one time and it took him quite a while to convince them to change their ways.[73]

As business grew, he added more planes, and he also began to fly parties of dignitaries around the Territories. When Mr. Justice Sissons became the first judge of the Northwest Territories Court in 1955, Ward flew his court party all over the north. Parker accompanied Sissons on some of these trips. From these beginnings, Ward went on to national and international air chartering and world fame. Wardair, with its Jumbo jets, had a reputation second to none.

REINDEER

Chapter 4 Notes

61. Price, <u>Yellowknife</u> p 45

62. Price, Yellowknife, p 46.

63. Price, Yellowknife, p 49.

64. Price, Yellowknife, p 197.

65. Price, Yellowknife, p 231,

66. Richard Finnie, <u>Canada Moves North</u>, p 140.

67. Richard Finnie,<u>Canada Moves North</u>, p 144

68. Gould, <u>Jock McMeekan's Yellowknife Blade</u>, .

69. Price, Yellowknife, p 90.

70. <u>Yellowknife Illustrated History</u>, p 196

71. Florence Whyard, <u>Ernie Boffa, Canadian Bush Pilot</u>, (Alaska Northwest Publishing, Anchorage, Alaska, 1984), p 99.

72. <u>Yellowknife Illustrated History</u>, p 87.

73. Max Ward <u>The Max Ward Story</u>, (McLelland and Stewart, Toronto, 1991) p 314

Canon Webster, the Anglican Priest at Coppermine, travels in his dog sled (Courtesy of Claire Parker)

Ernie Boffa (above)
(Osborne/NWT Archives N90-006-0539)

Dennis O'Callaghan,(rt) with his son in a Yellowknife market garden
(Courtesy Mrs. D. O'Callaghan)

Father Gathe doing conjuring tricks, Yellowknife,1945 (Courtesy of Claire Parker)

Ernie Boffa, with his wife Jacqueline and son
(Osborne/NWT Archives N90-006-0539)

Right:
Father Gathe
(Gathe/NWT Archives
N88-036-0007)

Gerry Murphy
(Yellowknife Museum Society, NWT Archives, N79-053-0001)

Right:
Hottah Lake,NWT, 1934.
Thomas Payne far right
(National Archives of Canada PA 74752)

Left
The 'Speed II' at the
Fort Smith wharf, 1927

(NWT Archives)

Right:
Martha Mafa,
Coppermine, 1946
(Courtesy of Claire Parker)

Max Ward in a Fox Moth aircraft, Snare River, 1947
(National Archives of Canada PA 89954)

DEAR DOCTOR KEENLEYSIDE   FOR YEARS WE HAD THIS - -

Cartoon in 'The Yellowknife Blade'
on Mackay Meikle, Mining Inspector.
8 September, 1947   (Courtesy of Gladys Could)

- - - - - PLEASE, NO MORE !

Wardair's DeHavilland 'Otter' CF-GBY,
at Wardair jetty, Yellowknife, June 1953
(Courtesy of Max Ward)

Vic Ingraham, between two men, in front of Canadian
Airways Junkers aircraft, Cameron Bay, 1932
(National Archives of Canada C 25141)

WE SHALL HAVE THAT BRIDGE! IN SPITE OF
MISREPRESENTATIONS OF LOBBYISTS AND OBSTRUCTIONISTS.

Frederick the Great Fraser's farewell to Latham Island on leaving for Blunderville.

"Now that I have gone; they'll NEVER get a bridge! Latham Island will
be the slums of Yellowknife!"
To which we reply " That's what you think, Laddie!"

The famous cartoon in the 'Yellowknife Blade' on Fred
Fraser, 16th. January 1948
(Courtesy of Gladys Gould)

Chapter 5
Faith and Hard Work Rewarded

St. Laurent took over as prime minister from Mackenzie King in November 1948. Mackenzie King had won a slim majority of twenty-five in June 1945 and St. Laurent called an election in June 1949.

A bill was passed in early 1949 finally giving the Northwest Territories the right to vote in federal elections. The Yukon territory had enjoyed this right since the beginning of the century. It was hoped that with a representative in Ottawa, some of the outstanding problems of the NWT would be solved. This reform didn't totally meet the wishes of electorate because the Territories were not constituted as a separate riding but were merely been tacked on to the Yukon territory seat. This was probably a political ploy by the Liberals to keep the seat, because the Liberal George Black and his wife Martha had held it between them for twenty-three years. The official explanation was that there wasn't a large enough population in the Territories to warrant a separate constituency. There were 24,000 persons in the combined riding, probably not much fewer than in a small rural riding.

The move didn't make any sense because the territories were isolated from each other by the Mackenzie Mountains and had never had much contact since communication was north and south. Moreover, both had experienced a different history and a different course of development.

John Parker was a member of the Yellowknife Conservative party and some of its members had suggested that he run as a candidate in the 1949 election. He was well educated and understood northern problems and he was well-liked because of his warm and jolly personality. In addition, he was known around the NWT from his trial work. He decided against the move for several reasons, but mainly because he couldn't afford it. The riding was the biggest in the country and it would be very expensive and difficult to campaign in it. The riding association couldn't raise enough money to cover even minimum expenses and he wasn't prepared to go into debt.

There was also the question of whether he could win. George Black had finally retired and Aubrey Simmons, a Whitehorse resident, had got the nomination to take his place. Although he was new, it would probably be difficult to beat him. After some consideration, it was decided not to put up a Conservative candidate but to support Matt Berry, a sixty-one-year-old ex-bush pilot who was running as an independent.

Parker knew him well and very much respected him. He agreed to be his agent and campaign manager and the party put what few resources it had behind him. Berry had the support of many of Yellowknife's leading personalities, including Vic Ingraham, Ted Cinnamon, and Jock McNiven, a mine manager who was active in community affairs and was later appointed to the Territorial Council. Berry also owned his own plane, a Fox Moth, and could get around the riding easily. It made a lot of sense to support him.

He had reasons for running as an independent. Although he favoured private enterprise and leaned towards Conservative policies, he felt that the party might be a hindrance. It had not been too successful under John Bracken and the new leader George Drew was an unknown factor. He had gained some national prominence as premier of Ontario but had yet to prove himself. Also, he hadn't made a very auspicious start, having called an unnecessary provincial election in 1948 and then losing in his own riding. He was reputed to be anti-French and this might cause Native Indians, under the influence of the local French Catholic priests, to vote against Berry if he ran as a Conservative. Moreover, Northern Catholics tended to be pro-Liberal, so Berry was going to need every vote he could get. Even so, it was thought that with the necessary effort he might win. The Northwest Territories had twice the population of the Yukon so that if he could gain a substantial lead in the Territories, he could offset his weakness in the Yukon.

There was also another candidate, James Stephens, a Yellowknife prospector, running for the Co-operative Commonwealth Federation (CCF), but he was not expected to make much of a showing.

Berry was something of a hero and his name was well known, particularly in the north. He had started flying in the First World War and had begun to work as a northern pilot in 1928 when he joined Northern Aerial Exploration of Northern Ontario.[74] By 1932 he was working for Mackenzie Air Service on the route between Edmonton and the Territories. He made the first flight above the Arctic Circle, into Gjoa Haven on King William Island, in November 1934 to pick up furs. They were then rushed to the European markets by air, saving months and beating the competition. He had flown in the Yukon for a year and had friends there. The Trans-Canada Trophy had been awarded to him in 1936 for his air exploits, and this had given him some national prominence.

Like most bush pilots he had many adventures and took part in many rescues. On one occasion, he broke a propeller on landing in the bush. Not dismayed, he cut down a tree and fashioned a temporary one, bolted it back on, and flew to the nearest settlement. In 1936, he became famous when he found a downed RCAF plane above the treeline in the barren lands, 150 miles northeast of Yellowknife. Parker was always amazed by his uncanny knack of working out where a downed aircraft might be. He was active during the Second World War in the Commonwealth Air Training Scheme and in building airports for the American army up the Mackenzie. After the war he formed his own company, specializing in airport construction.

The start of the campaign was not too promising. Berry, Parker, and McNiven flew to Whitehorse and Dawson City to file nomination papers and try to set up a territorial campaign machine there. Unfortunately, the Yukon Conservative party was not very active and there wasn't too much interest in the Berry campaign.[75] Undeterred, Berry and Parker flew all over the Mackenzie delta, campaigning and drumming up interest. They didn't bother with the north coast settlements because the Inuit didn't yet have the vote.[76] Parker noted that Berry was getting an amiable reception and seemed to have a lot of friends, but he wasn't much of a speaker.

One thing the campaign couldn't be criticized for was a weak platform. It had been mostly written by Parker and was well thought out and comprehensive. Anyone reading it would immediately know what was happening in the Territories. The first item was a demand for a separate seat from the Yukon in the House of Commons. It was patently unfair for a candidate to have to cover two separate areas of such enormous size. Also listed was the "immediate appointment of residents of the Mackenzie to the Council of the Northwest Territories including representation for the trappers and labour." Probably trappers and labour were given special mention as a ploy to attract their votes. On the other hand, there was no mention of the Native population having a repre-sentative. Nor was any suggestion made that council members be elected, although this had been proposed by Jock McMeekan and others on many occasions.

Increased income tax exemption for all Canadian residents living north of the 60° was also indicated on the grounds that public servants working in the north got a generous allowance to offset the high cost of living, so an increased tax break was appropriate for the general population. Another plank was that restrictions on the sale of gold be removed so that it could be sold at its real value. At the time, all Canadian refined gold had to be sold to the mint at a fixed price of $35 per ounce. This had been done to support the price in a weak gold market. Since the measure had been brought into effect, however, the market price of gold had started to rise again and was above the support price. Several years later this was abolished and gold prices rose steadily over the years.

Improved water and road transportation systems were suggested and vigorous action was advocated to better the position of the Native population. Parker said that this suggestion arose from the lack of proper education, healthcare, and housing for the territorial Native population. An estimate of the Native population in the Northwest Territories in 1951 was 8,000 (there were 3,600 whites) and yet only about 400 Native children were being educated in the religious schools at Aklavik, Fort Rae, and Fort Resolution, and the public school in Yellowknife.[77]

There were small religious hospitals at Aklavik, Fort Smith, Fort Rae, Chesterfield Inlet, and Pangnirtung, and the forty-bed hospital at Yellowknife, plus nursing stations in several other communities. However, there were only about eight doctors and not many more nurses working in these facilities, which served twenty-three communities covering an area larger than most countries. Additionally, there was the Charles Camsell Hospital in Edmonton which had been built in 1946 to care for the northern Native population who had contracted tuberculosis. Influenza and TB epidemics had decimated some Indian and Inuit communities in the twenties and thirties. The diseases had been brought in by whites and were still a problem. In his day, Parker said, there were still Native Indians walking around Yellowknife with TB. Testing services in the north then were very limited. Even when Natives were diagnosed, many of them wouldn't go to Edmonton for treatment, so that more local facilities and staff were needed.

The seventh proposal was to extend the federal franchise to the Inuit. "They have been cruelly neglected except when it comes to tax collection," read the relevant phrase. Apparently a few who had made money trapping and fishing had been badgered for taxes, although they were receiving very few government services. A demand was also made that the baby bonus for Native Indians be paid in cash rather than through coupons redeemable at a HBC store. This was considered demeaning and an infringement on their rights. There were a few known cases where they had been duped into buying items that they didn't want. The important issue of the right of Yellowknifers to purchase freehold land was, of course, included.

The platform of the Liberals wasn't nearly as detailed and no extensive list of important issues and problems was published by them. Simmons's approach was that the Liberals were going to win the election and if the people of the north wanted government help, they should ensure that they had a Liberal representative in Ottawa. John Parker believed that, in reality, Simmons was not very knowledgeable about many of the key issues and was not particularly interested in them. Instead, he contented himself with three points which were an elected representative on the territorial council (a better proposal than Berry's request for an appointed representative), a division of the Yukon-Mackenzie riding, and a voice in government caucuses and councils.

In his campaign, Berry didn't tour the Yukon settlements but concentrated on the Northwest Territories. Simmons made a swing up the Mackenzie and around Great Slave Lake visiting various communities. This was in addition to his thorough tours of the Yukon, which was much easier to cover that the NWT.

On election day, the Conservatives didn't fare too well under George Drew, as Parker had predicted. The Liberals increased their majority from 125 to 190, capturing seats from the Conservatives and the CCF. Berry received a good vote but not enough to beat Simmons. In the Northwest Territories, he won 1560 votes as against 1177 for Simmons and 303 for Stephens. However, his 383 lead was quickly eclipsed by a 1,000 vote margin for Simmons in the Yukon. Indeed, Simmons had also done quite well in the NWT, beating Berry in Yellowknife, Aklavik, Fort McPherson, and tying with him at

Hay River. Berry's biggest majority was at Fort Rae, thanks to the Native Indians who had come through for him. Clearly, there was a lot of support for the Liberals in the Territories despite the past conflicts with the Ottawa bureaucrats.

But the election was not the only major political event of 1949 in the Territories. In that year, the territorial council set up a commission to inquire into the financial problems of Yellowknife. It was chaired by A.H. Gibson who had just been transferred from Fort Smith to Yellowknife as Stipendiary Magistrate, and for whom Parker had a great deal of respect. There had been complaints that Yellowknife taxes on rental property were too high in comparison with other communities. In addition, there were a number of other issues to consider. No local representatives served on this commission, and it didn't even hold open hearings. In its final report, the commission didn't agree that rents were too high. Nevertheless, it made several important recommendations on other matters, some of which had a profound effect on the future of the district.

Among its recommendations was one that future capital projects be financed by federal government loans or from the issue of debentures and not by outright grants. This would place the town board on a similar footing with other town administrations. It further suggested that the number of Yellowknife District Board trustees be reduced from ten to eight. Five were to be elected, three appointed, with the chair being elected by the board and not appointed by the government. In the words of the commission, "This will constitute a body, the dominating portion of which is elected by the district, and give reasonable representation to the principal investor, the federal government."[78] However, it considered that the board should not become an independent body, like other Canadian towns, until it could raise sufficient funds to cover all its expenditures.

Much to everyone's surprise, it supported the proposal that the board assume freehold ownership of all lands for resale to leaseholders. A suggested price of $115,000 for all the property in Yellowknife was mentioned. This was indeed good news. Parker later recollected that the rental arrangements had always been problematic. Initially, lots were rented for five years at $10 a year for residential lots, and $25 for business lots. Rents were later raised to $25 and $50 respectively. Lessees were required to build on an empty lot within eighteen months in the new town. The problem was that neither the banks nor the Canadian Mortgage and Housing Corporation would underwrite a loan because of the five year leases.

Despite the commission's findings on the rental market, it wasn't long before the attention of the government was once more drawn to this question. Robert Winters became the new minister for northern affairs in 1950. He was an outstanding member of parliament and it looked as though the Liberals were finally going to pay more attention to the north. Although Winters was a Liberal, Parker had the greatest respect for him. Within a week or so of becoming minister, he found out about the rental problem and was appalled. One of his first acts was to have this situation changed; leases were immediately extended to twenty years. Even then the banks remained hesitant. As a result, the chair of the Yellowknife Board, Fred Henne, asked Parker, as town solicitor, to work with Mr. Bates of the CMHC in drafting amendments to the regulations.

The Ottawa bureaucrats had opposed the sale of freehold lands because they were worried about profiteering. They feared that speculators would descend to make their fortunes. Yellowknife was prospering but not that vigorously, and they wanted the free market to be kept out as long as possible. Actually their fears were not realised. Some people made money but the Yellowknife real estate market wasn't that good. Parker, after seven years of ownership, made very little profit when he sold his property in the new town in 1958.

When the report of the commission had become known, a committee was set up by the board to study the sale of district lots. McMeekan and Guy Wheeler, two trustees who formed the committee, produced a proposal that was amended and submitted to Ottawa. It accepted the price of $115,000, this being close to a recent appraisal conducted by an outside consultant, and derived by subtracting $85,000 (rentals already paid) from a total evaluation of $200,000. A simple price structure was submitted. It was based on the premise that, if all lots were purchased, the monies received would cover the total purchase price of the land to be paid by the district board. Lessees were not to be forced to buy, but if they wanted to, they could do it by either buying outright or applying future rentals against the purchase price.

Dr. Hugh Keenleyside, the commissioner, objected on the grounds that the purchase prices were too low. He felt that an opportunity was being missed "to lay aside a little wealth for use for future capital expenditures."[79] Nevertheless, probably on the orders of the new minister, the report was accepted and the purchase of the lands by the district was approved. The sale of lots to the public began in April 1951.

Also in 1951, Robert Winters introduced amendments to the Northwest Territories Act, increasing membership of the council from six to eight, with five members to be appointed and three to be elected. Elections were to be open to Native and non-Native residents. The minister indicated that a fully elected council with an administration located in the north was the final goal, once the people of the Northwest Territories were able to bear the full cost of government.

The first election was set for 17 September 1951. The territories were split into three new constituencies: Mackenzie Delta, covering the area around Aklavik; Mackenzie South, including the river and the south shore of Great Slave Lake; and Mackenzie North, including Yellowknife, Fort Rae, Eldorado, and Coppermine. The sparsely populated eastern part of the Territories, known as Keewatin, and the Northern Arctic islands were not included. This area was directly controlled by Ottawa and did not come under the purview of the council.

The three contestants in Mackenzie North, all from Yellowknife, were Jock

McMeekan, who still had a following, Guy Wheeler, and M.A. (Merv) Hardie, a young Yellowknife shopkeeper who had been making a name for himself as an effective municipal board member. Parker had considered running but was still hesitant because of financial considerations. In the event, Hardie won handily and Yellowknife finally had its elected member on the territorial council. John Brodie, a Fort Smith merchant, won Mackenzie South, and Frank Carmichael, an Aklavik trapper, Mackenzie Delta.

Council conducted its first ever meeting in Yellowknife in the Capital Theatre on 11 December 1951. The meeting was open to the public and the theatre was packed. Major General Hugh A. Young, the new NWT commissioner, was in the chair. Frank Cunningham was now deputy commissioner, having replaced the legendary R.A. Gibson who had been on the job for more than forty years. Also present were Commander Louis C. Audette, an Ottawa lawyer and naval veteran, Air Commodore H. Goodwin, D.A. Mackay, Brigadier Wood, and the three elected members. The council seemed to be a little top heavy with four senior military officers. Possibly, the idea was to have action-oriented men on the job.

Some interesting items were raised, but a lot was ignored. It was reported that thought was being given to creating a Supreme Court for the territories. New restrictive regulations prohibiting the sale of liquor to Natives, under the Indian Act, were to be brought into force. No mention was made of splitting the federal seat.

The problems of the Native population were ignored. None of the points outlined in Matt Berry's platform on this issue were covered. At the time, the Indian Affairs Branch, which was not even in the Ministry of Resources and Development, was responsible for administering the Indian Act and the 1921 Indian treaty. This included provision for Indian welfare and issuing food coupons for indigents. The RCMP carried out similar duties for the Inuit and the Department of Health provided for Native health needs.

As the case of the Indians and the Inuit suggests, the council did not directly control most of the government funds going into the Territories. Unfortunately, it also did not have the staff, the resources, or the authority to coordinate affairs between the various departments.

Council made no reference to a fully elected Yellowknife District Board, despite the complaints of the locals. The matter was raised by Hardie, but no decision was arrived at. This was probably the major problem to sour relations between jurisdictions. Commissioner Young also pointed out that the government was against a fully elected council for the time being, ignoring the fact that the Yukon, with half the population of the Territories, had had a fully elected council since the Dawson City gold rush days.

The community was very interested in seeing how the council worked. The fact that it had met in Yellowknife and was open to the public was a step in the right direction. With the three new elected members, it was hoped that more would be done for the north in the future.

Another difficult issue of this period was the proposal for a separate Yellowknife Roman Catholic school. Parker became involved because he was legal counsel for the Yellowknife School Board. The new expanded Yellowknife public school had been opened in 1947. In 1951, there were about 250 students of whom about 20 per cent were Catholics. The school covered grades one to twelve, and was open to Indians as well as whites.[80]

The Roman Catholic Church started to consider the possibility of having a separate school at about this time. There were many problems to be faced, particularly whether sufficient funds could be found to build and operate it. Most of the townspeople were against another school. They feared that it would lead to increased taxes or a reduction in funds for the public school. Parker was opposed to it because he thought that it would lead to animosity between the town's two main religious groups, particularly among young students. Yellowknife had always been free of anything of this nature. In his opinion, there were not sufficient Catholic students to warrant the added expense. Also, he did not think too highly of the Roman Catholic native schools, and was worried that the quality of instruction might decrease. He must have felt this despite the Canadian tradition of having Catholic separate schools in all provinces.

After further discussion, the Roman Catholic diocesan Bishop Trocellier at Fort Smith made official application to the commissioner for such a school to be started. A revised territorial school ordinance was drawn up and discussed at the July 1952 meeting of the territorial council in Ottawa. Fred Henne, municipal trustee board chair, Ken Grogan, school board chair, and John Parker, acting as legal counsel, attended the meeting. The Catholic Church also had a lawyer representing them at the meeting.

Details of what went on at the meeting were published in the *News of the North* in the form of a lengthy report by Parker. The revised draft of a new school ordinance had been gone over clause by clause, he noted. Section 12 of the Northwest Territories Act clearly stated that a minority of tax payers, whether Protestant or Roman Catholic, could organise a separate school.

However, the touchiest question was the clause on the language of instruction. The draft laid down that all schools should be taught in English, but it would be permissable for any district board to allow a primary course to be taught in French. Commander Audette believed this matter should be dealt with by the Commissioner. He argued that it was wrong for English to be the only language because one-third of the people of Canada were French-speaking. Moreover, he suggested that it might be necessary to accord French equal standing with English in the future and even suggested that classes might be taught in Inuit.

Parker believed that Audette was trying to pave the way for the introduction of French as a language of instruction. He considered that discussion of the language clause was the most important business at the meeting.

The final vote on this point was in Parker's favour and the draft regulations were changed so that English was to be the only language of instruction without qualification. Brodie and RCMP commissioner Nicholson were absent. Harvie, a Catholic, abstained. Audette was the lone supporter.[81]

Parker, in his report, referred to Audette as a Roman Catholic who was presumably French Canadian. When Audette read this account of the meeting he was furious. He took it to imply that he was being pressured by the Roman Catholic Church and retorted that he always decided on council matters on his own, without pressure from any party.[82] So angry was he that he even thought of suing Parker for libel. On further consideration and after talking things over with other council members, he decided against it. The matter eventually blew over and, when Parker was elected to council in 1954, Audette wrote a letter to him offering his congratulations. He admitted he had been avoiding him when he had visited Yellowknife, but he was now prepared to be friends. This was a generous gesture, and Parker wrote back immediately thanking him for his kind consideration. From then on, the two got along and respected each other despite their differences. Parker said that Audette was a very capable lawyer with a quick mind and was a good debater.

Further political reform came to the north in 1952, when changes were finally made to the election of the municipal trustee board. The chair was no longer to be a government appointee. Elections were to be held every two years for the chair, and each year for members. In the fall election, Jock McNiven, probably the most experienced and knowledgeable person on territorial matters, got the greatest number of votes. He thus became the first elected chair, or mayor, of Yellowknife. The town now had almost complete control of its affairs. It didn't have to get every by-law rubber-stamped by Ottawa, although it would continue to get some financial help for operating costs. Thus, its budget was still subject to federal approval. Nevertheless, it was now close to operating in much the same manner as any other Canadian municipality in respect to its relations with its provincial government.

Canada had been making great strides economically in the early fifties and this was reflected in the slow and steady growth in Yellowknife. The Giant and Con mines were doing well though the price of gold had fallen to $34.20 per ounce. Giant reported its best year ever in 1953 with a profit of $2.4 million. Unfortunately, Negus Mine closed in 1952 because of lack of viable ore.

In early 1953, a new federal riding of Mackenzie, separate from the Yukon, and including all the Northwest Territories, was set up. St Laurent called an election in August 1953 and the Liberal Merv Hardie handily won the seat. The grandfatherly St. Laurent was very popular, times were good, and the Liberals only lost twenty seats, still retaining a good majority. Jean Lesage, a Quebecer, took over as minister of resources and development from Winters. St. Laurent was still according the north a certain significance, since Lesage was an important person in the cabinet.

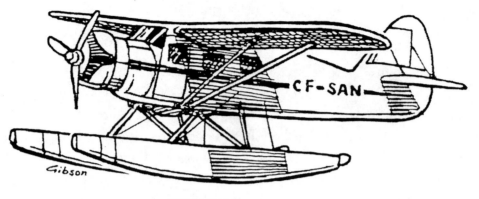

NORSEMAN

Chapter 5 Notes

74. Alice Sutherland, <u>Canada's Aviation Pioneers</u>,
     (Mcgraw Hill Ryerson, Toronto, p 92

75. Neilson, <u>The House is not a Home</u>, p 64

76. In 1949, The Yukon Inuit had the federal vote but not the NWT Inuit. Neilson
     introduced a private member's bill giving them the vote. It was passed which is
     unusual for such a bill.

77. L.C.Audette's papers, MG31, E18, Vol6 p 42 - Cdn Archives, Ottawa.

78. The speech of Major General H.A. Young, NWT Commissioner, to the NWT
     Council, 10 December 1951, in Yellowknife.

79. <u>Yellowknife Blade</u>, 23 November 1947.

80. <u>The News of the North</u>, 24 July 1952.

81. Trudeau insisted that French be made an official language for the NWT Legisla-
     tive Assembly. So now there are six languages used in the assembly - English,
     French, Inuit, Dogrib, Slave and Loucheux.

82. Interview with Commander Louis Audette, 27 June 1991

Fort McPherson, 1955 (Courtesy of Claire Parker)

Chapter 6
Improved Territorial Justice

In February 1950, Parker was Crown counsel in an appeal case involving a Yellowknife cab driver named Kostiuk who was charged with providing liquor to Native Indians. The RCMP were eager to prosecute to try to stamp out this practice. Native Indians were not allowed to purchase liquor and it was known that the town cab drivers were obtaining it for them.

This was not a jury case and the magistrate, W.G. Brown, upheld the decision of Magistrate Gibson who had found the accused not guilty at the original trial. Brown considered the prosecution evidence to be too weak.

However, he felt that one of the witnesses was lying and directed the police to investigate further. Two Native Indians had been found guilty of drunkenness, and one of them had testified that they had been given the liquor by a cab driver. Unfortunately for Parker, the other Native, under cross-examination, contradicted this. The defence lawyer, Don Hagel, pointed out that the only good evidence of the prosecution had been contradicted and was thus suspect. Parker responded that he had brought the witness forward because it was the duty of the Crown to lead all the evidence. He referred to the long-standing friendship that the prevaricating witness had with the accused. This was corroborated by another witness.

Native alcoholism, whether on reserves or in the towns, had been a problem since the arrival of the whites. Many white northerners felt guilt because they had brought this upon the Natives, and so wanted strenuous measures to protect them from it. Others felt remorse about introducing such restrictions. Universal prohibition had earlier existed, so restricting the use of liquor had not always applied only to aboriginal peoples.

This question recurred later, during Parker's term on the NWT council. Suffice it to say that his attitude towards the prohibition on Natives changed with his experiences in the north. He came to believe that, as Canadians, Native Indians were entitled to the same rights as anyone else, even if the use of alcohol was alien to Native culture and led to much abuse and misery. Natives had to learn to cope. Alcoholism was mainly due to their frustration and social confusion in adjusting to western ways, and could only be overcome by providing Natives with better education, health, and housing. In any event, in practical terms they were going to get drink whatever the regulations were, or, what was far worse, would poison themselves with lethal home brew.

This issue was grappled with at every meeting of the council that John attended. Members became obsessed with it, usually to the detriment of other important matters. The experience of these white men seeing drunken Indians and hearing of violent incidents brought on by alcohol upset them greatly.

That was in the future, however, and other matters demanded his immediate attention. In April 1951, Parker acted for the Crown in an attempted murder case in Cambridge Bay. The case was notable because it was the first time that an Inuit was selected for the jury. He was, indeed, made jury foreman. Magistrate Phinney presided and Don Hagel acted for the defence.

The case concerned an Inuit shaman named Alikomiak. Inuit shamans or "medicine men" were an interesting group. They were called representatives of the devil by some white clergy and were considered troublemakers by some Mounties. However, they were often the leaders in a group, usually good hunters, expert in Inuit practices, and knowledgeable about Inuit lore. They tried to keep the old Inuit practices and beliefs alive. Some were said to have very special gifts akin to those of white faith-healers. Dr. John Kelsall, a government biologist who had cadged a ride with the judicial party to visit the area, had heard of cases where shamans performed miracles, although in his many years in the north he had never seen any proof of this.

In the case in hand, two Inuit men were on a spring hunting trip, although there was some uncertainty about precisely when it took place. The evidence revealed that some of the caribou being hunted had antlers and others none. Kelsall testified that caribou do not have well-developed antlers from June to August. Bulls lose theirs in December or January and cows in May. After a few months the antlers start to grow again. It was his estimate that the hunt took place in the spring.

Alikomiak had found some caribou and gone back to camp to get a young Inuit man to help him. When they approached the place where he had seen the animals, he told the younger man to go forward to the rise of a small hill ahead to look for them. As the young hunter crept forward, Alikomiak removed the cover of his rifle and the gun went off, creasing the victim's head. The older man immediately went to the aid of his assistant, bandaged his wound, and took him back to camp.

A few days later, Alikomiak told the young man's wife that the spirits had told him in a dream that she must sleep with him. She refused. Later the Mounties learned of this incident, and, believing that this could have been the motive for murder, conducted an investigation. It was considered there was enough evidence to show that the shaman had tried to murder the young man, had missed, and had then lost his nerve. The jury disagreed and found the accused not guilty.

A few months later, in September 1951, Parker prosecuted in the most depressing case he had yet experienced. It concerned a particularly brutal murder by a man named Beaulieu. Judge John E. Gibben from Whitehorse conducted the trial in Fort Smith.

Don Hagel acted for the defence. Magistrate Phinney had committed Beaulieu for trial in June at a preliminary hearing in Fort Resolution. The case dragged on for four days with five experts giving evidence on the gunshot wounds.

Beaulieu had forced his way into a woman's house and raped her. While this was going on, two of her children awoke and tried to come to their mother's aid. Beaulieu shot them all dead. One child survived and was found cold and hungry by the neighbours.

Judge Gibben, according to his clerk, Jack Worsell, tended to become emotionally involved in his difficult cases.[83] In this instance, the accused was found guilty by a jury, and Gibben, in accordance with precedent, sentenced him to hang. Apparently because he was so upset, Gibben neglected to fix the date of the hanging and had to be brought back to Fort Smith for this purpose. Parker remembered this incident slightly differently; he left the date of hanging to the Justice Department in Ottawa, but should have set it himself. In any event, the hangman objected to the short notice. Ottawa informed Gibben that he should have suggested a time immediately after the trial had started, in case the accused was found guilty. Gibben replied, "This procedure offends the sensibilities and, from a judicial standpoint, I question the propriety or wisdom of following it." The deputy minister of justice answered that he should have followed orders, pointing out that there was only one executioner in Canada. The verdict was not appealed and Beaulieu was hanged.

Later in the year Parker was involved in yet another extremely disturbing case. The accused was a young Cree woman, Mary Paulette, who was charged with the murder of a baby and not with the lesser charge of infanticide, that is, ritual killing sometimes practised in the past in the north. The trial took place in Fort Smith on 19 September 1951 with Judge Gibben again presiding. Parker was the prosecutor and Hagel defended. Both had been present at the preliminary hearing held in Fort Smith on 25 June 1951 before Magistrate Phinney. Hagel waived the accused's right to a jury.

The woman had two young children by a husband who had died, and lived with her father in a small shack. Parker inspected the scene of the crime and found her living conditions appalling. Unknown to the neighbours — she had somehow kept her pregnancy a secret — she gave birth to a baby in the house and immediately killed it by suffocation. The local RCMP learned of the act and, in particularly gruesome circumstances, discovered the baby's body under the house. Paulette was taken to the police post and charged with murder. She was gently dealt with at all times, a police matron always being present.

The defence called upon a psychiatrist to prove that she had experienced the severe depression associated with childbirth. She had been so ill at the time, it was suggested, that she had not known what she was doing and didn't remember anything. Both prosecution and defence covered the psychiatric aspects of the case in great detail.

Certainly the defence was given every opportunity to deal with this issue.

Parker introduced the extremely damning police evidence. He referred to the mitigating circumstances of her living conditions and her earlier unhappy life. But, because of the heinousness of the crime, he asked for her conviction as a murderer.

Judge Gibben said in his summation that, while there was no direct evidence of murder, there was a great weight of circumstantial evidence to this effect. He did not think that the defence had proved its case that the accused had been temporarily insane and he found Paulette guilty.[84] Given his emotional sensibilities, he must have had a terrible time deciding upon the sentence — he ordered her to be hanged. Parker was shocked by the judge's decision and strongly disagreed with it. He knew the judge to be a fair, sensitive, and capable person, and couldn't understand what had prompted this judgment. He also knew that there were considerable mitigating circumstances — the youth of the accused, her unhappy life, and problems with her children — and he believed that a lesser sentence was appropriate. Consequently, he wrote at length to the Department of Justice arguing for a lesser sentence. In response, the department overrode Gibben and commuted her sentence to a term in prison. Paulette was released after about two years for good behaviour, and wrote several letters to Parker thanking him for his concern.

In June 1952, Parker had one of his few losses, another alcohol case. A white man charged with selling liquor to a Native Indian had been found not guilty by Magistrate Phinney, and his decision was appealed by the Crown. The defence imported a lawyer from Edmonton, A.W. Miller QC, to help Hagel. Parker and the police felt that the evidence proved beyond doubt that the act had been committed by the accused. The defence based their case on a technicality. They argued that the omission of the word "knowingly" from the charge sheet was not in accordance with legal usage. They didn't disagree that the liquor had been sold by the accused, but they claimed that he was unaware that the recipient was a Native Indian. The purchaser's dark complexion could have been due to a hot summer suntan.

Parker riposted that there could have been no doubt in the mind of the accused that the recipient was a Native Indian. He was a northerner who well knew how to distinguish between a Native and a white man. Parker further disputed the defence's contentions about poor wording in the charge sheet, quoting several cases where similar wording had been successfully used.

Judge Gibben felt the precedents quoted by the defence bore more weight, and confirmed Magistrate Phinney's original decision. Parker was not too happy with the outcome, a case of the law being an ass. However, the case only confirmed in his mind that the prohibition on the sale of liquor to Natives was wrong.

In the spring of 1953, he prosecuted in a case of fish theft before Magistrate Phinney in Hay River. It concerned two men, Morrin and Gardner, who were working under contract to a fish broker. This man provided them with nets, licences, and shelter in return for most of their catch. Evidence was led that they kept more fish than they were entitled to and they were charged with theft.

There was a lucrative summer fishery on Great Slave Lake. Several companies deployed fleets of small boats accompanied by a housing barge to various inlets on the lake. Long floating gill nets, about five feet in depth, were laid and anchored and were visited periodically by the boats to harvest the catch. The fish were taken to the barge where they were cleaned. Then they were stored in ice houses ashore. These houses contained ice blocks that were cut during in the winter and insulated with sawdust. The frozen fish would later be transported south. In 1952/53, six million pounds of fish, mostly white fish and large lake trout, were caught in the territories to the value of two million dollars.[85]

The case was straightforward and the two men were convicted and sentenced to six weeks in prison. However, the case was also unique in that the findings and the sentence were appealed to the Supreme Court of Alberta. The sentence was upheld but reduced to the time spent in gaol awaiting trial — a few days — plus ten days. The defence argued its case on a technicality, quoting from a section in the fisheries legislation dealing with the "theft of wild creatures." What was more odd was that immediately upon hearing the appeal court decision, the two men and their lawyer served notice that they were going to appeal to the Supreme Court of Canada, making this the first criminal case to be appealed from the Territories to the nation's highest court since 1905. It is believed the appeal was never actually made, the whole idea probably having been dreamed up after an evening's celebration over the reduced sentence.

Parker took part in a murder case that generated more publicity than any case in his time in the Territories. It concerned a Métis from Artic Red River by the name of Frederick Cardinal.

The village of Artic Red River is a tiny Loucheux community located in the far north, about fifty miles south of Aklavik. It is situated at a strategic point where the Artic Red River comes down from the Mackenzie Mountains and joins the Mackenzie River. The delta area of the great river begins at this point. A Roman Catholic mission had operated there since 1868. At the time of the trial, the population was about 200 persons.

Cardinal was educated in a religious school and spoke fluent English. He was well known in the community and on the Mackenzie River and had a good job as a special constable and interpreter for the RCMP.[86] Frank McCall, the government game warden, met Cardinal several times when he was in gaol in Fort Smith awaiting the outcome of his appeal. At that stage, he would work around the town under guard. Frank found him to be a friendly, polite, and well-groomed man, with a commanding bearing. John Parker observed that he was an intelligent person.

On 8 May 1953, a distraught Cardinal informed his neighbours that his wife had become very ill during the night and died. The prevailing custom among Christians in the north was for the wife's female friends to prepare the body for burial. Cardinal did not arrange for this but did the job himself. This raised some eyebrows but nothing more. He built a wooden coffin with the help of a relative. This proved to be a little too small, but he squeezed his wife's body into it, to the dismay of his relatives. The coffin was placed in the little Catholic church, famous on the river for being built on a hillock and for being visible from afar on the surrounding alluvial flats.

It was spring, so although it was freezing at night, the weather warmed during daylight hours. These weather conditions led to Cardinal's undoing.

The day before his wife had died, Cardinal had asked his boss, RCMP Constable P.F. Komache, if he could borrow the police dogs to take his family out to work on his trapline. As was usual, he was given the necessary permission. The next day, in the morning before his party was due to leave, he reported the death of his wife. He asked Komache to take pictures of the body in the house and in the coffin in the church. Each time the photographs were taken the head was covered with a cloth. Unfortunately the photographs did not turn out.

The constable thought this request a little unusual and for other reasons became suspicious. The local priest, Father G. Levesque, had told him that Mrs. Cardinal had been healthy the day before she died. She was active in church affairs and was in frequent contact with the priest. Also it was well known in the village that Cardinal had been having an openly amorous affair with another woman.

As the HBC post's radio wasn't working, Komache couldn't call his superior sub-division officer, Sergeant Mclaughlin, in Aklavik. He felt that the body should be examined as soon as possible. Flying was out of the question because of the spring thaw. However, the ground was still covered with snow, so Aklavik could be reached by dog team within about a day. Komache decided to set out immediately and asked Father Levesque to keep the body in the church until he returned.

The sergeant, after he had heard the story, decided to fly to Arctic Red River immediately. Flying was definitely risky but Mclaughlin, Komache, a physician, Dr. Schaeffer, and Mike Zubko, the pilot, decided to give it a try. They had a particularly perilous trip almost coming to grief several times. There were still large chunks of ice moving downstream in the river and there was not much open water for take-off and landing. However, prompt action was required in this case and these sorts of risk had to faced when working in the north.

The body was still in the church when they arrived, and it was taken to the priest's house for a post-mortem. Their attention was immediately caught when the body was lifted by the blood on the bottom of the coffin, under the head. The head must have unfrozen for a short period during the day and blood from an ear had oozed out. Doctor

Schaeffer found that he could probe the ear much deeper than was normally possible and he concluded that death was due to a head injury. Later, in the Aklavik Hospital, an X-ray and an autopsy revealed lead fragments from a .22 bullet in the skull.

Cardinal was arrested and charged with the murder of his wife, Mary Pace Cardinal, and taken to Aklavik for interrogation.

While in Aklavik he made several conflicting statements. One was that he had poked into his wife's ear with a stick to ease a pain. Another was that he hadn't used a stick but the magazine slide of a rifle. Later he came out and admitted that he remembered placing the rifle to his wife's ear. All these statements were made after he had been warned that they could be used against him in court.

Magistrate Phinney conducted a preliminary inquiry into the charges at Arctic Red River on 23 June 1953 and recommended that the case go to trial. This it did from 9 to 11 July 1953 in Aklavik, presided over by Judge Gibben. Parker was Crown prosecutor and Don Thorson of the Department of Justice was defence lawyer.

The story of how the body was found, the medical evidence, and the statements made by the accused, were elicited by Parker from the witnesses for the prosecution. A letter allegedly written by the accused's wife to Father Levesque before she died was also introduced. Cardinal had given the letter to the priest. In it, she had made some complimentary remarks about her husband and how loyal he was to her. Parker had his doubts about the letter. It seemed strange that such a flattering piece of evidence should appear at this point in the proceedings. He discussed his doubts with the police and it was decided to get a handwriting expert to examine the correspondence. Sure enough, the letter was found to be a forgery that had been written by the accused himself. Parker introduced this as yet another piece of evidence to show how carefully Cardinal had planned the murder and tried to cover his tracks.

He introduced witnesses to attest to Cardinal's long-standing infatuation with Josephine Baptiste. This, he argued, was the motive of the crime; Cardinal had found that looking after two women was becoming too costly.

The defence accepted that Mrs. Cardinal had been shot in the head and probably with the accused's gun, but it contended that Cardinal knew nothing about the matter because he had temporarily lost his memory during the period of his wife's death. He was put in the witness box — always a risky ploy in a murder case — to tell his side of the story. He said that he recalled picking up his rifle and placing it outside on the sleigh in preparation for the trip to the trapline next morning. Thereafter, he could remember nothing until he found his wife dead in bed after he had awoken next morning.

Parker tried to get him to change his story but he firmly stuck to it. He claimed that he had been confused when he had made his statements to the police, and that what he was now saying was the truth. The prosecution called a further witness, a psychiatrist, who argued that the alleged loss of memory did not fit any known pattern of temporary insanity.

Judge Gibben, in his charge to the jury, said that the evidence had shown that Cardinal had conducted an affair with another woman. The jury must decide whether this relationship "was enough to constitute a motive for the killing." He continued: "The question is: 'Did Cardinal have a sufficient degree of reason to know when he shot his wife through the ear and that what he was doing was wrong?" He concluded that the evidence must clearly show this to be so if the accused were to be found insane.

The jury spent very little time finding him guilty and Gibben once again had to agonise over the awarding of the death sentence which upset him so much. Parker never forgot the moment when Judge Gibben gave sentence. The people in the little room were tense with anticipation when he came in. As he started to speak and came to the dreaded words, a sudden clap of thunder reverberated across the lonely estuary flats. A great gust of wind rushed through the open windows, causing the floor-length curtains behind the accused to rise up above his head. Then the lights went out. Those present were frightened by this strange event, and even the judge stopped speaking for a few moments before delivering sentence of death.

Cardinal, because of his work as a special constable, was well aware of court procedures, and quickly asked for a lawyer to help him arrange an appeal. This was done and the case was reviewed by the Appellate Division of the Alberta Supreme Court. Mr. Neil Maclean QC, an outstanding criminal lawyer from Edmonton, was appointed to address the court on his behalf. He argued that the three statements alleged to have been made by the appellant and allowed by the judge, should not have been admitted as evidence. He maintained that the evidence about the relationship of the accused with another woman should also not have been allowed, since it had nothing to do with the case. If one accepted this, then the trial judge's statement that the relationship had been proven was misleading and incorrect, and was especially unfortunate in that it may have had a considerable effect on the jury.

He also referred to an infelicitous remark by Parker when he was questioning Constable Komache, which the judge had agreed with. Parker had asked the constable about the accused's state of mind and had said, "He is manufacturing his own evidence," whereupon the judge had said, "Yes." Parker later maintained there was nothing improper in his remark. The judge might have warned him to stop "leading" the witness, but in the context of the question, this issue didn't really apply.

Maclean also contended that Judge Gibben did not properly set out the essentials of the defence of insanity in his charge. He argued that he had misled the jury when he quoted from the Criminal Code by Tremeer. Referring to a precedent in this book, the judge had said that the defence must show clearly that the accused was insane not beyond a reasonable doubt, but by a preponderance of evidence. Maclean maintained that this placed too great an onus on a defendant who pleaded insanity, and was contrary to the appropriate section of Canadian Criminal Code. The Appellate Court agreed with

Maclean's complaints about the judge's charge on the defence of insanity and with other items and ordered a retrial.

This was conducted in Yellowknife because it was thought that a jury from Aklavik would be too close to the crime and would be unable to consider the case dispassionately. Mr. Justice Boyd McBride of the trial division of the Supreme Court of Alberta presided. Neil Maclean appeared for the defence and Parker was again the Crown prosecutor.

The public seating in the small Yellowknife courtroom was very limited, and Judge Boyd did not consider it big enough for the case. There was bound to be considerable interest and he felt the public must be able to exercise its right to view the administration of justice. Various buildings were inspected, and it was decided that the best place was the "Caribou Room," the bar in the Ingraham Hotel, which was by far the largest room in town. The jukebox was too heavy to be removed but was considered inappropriate to a court of law, so it was draped with a large Union Jack. Bar patrons were moved to another room in the hotel. The proceedings took two weeks, the longest case in the town's history up till then, and the courtroom was always packed with spectators.

MacLean conducted a very aggressive defence, arguing procedural matters at every point in the trial. First, he asserted that the accused, because his defence was insanity, should not have to plead either guilty or not guilty. Judge McBride, who conducted the trial very firmly, disagreed, saying that the accused was perfectly capable of taking part in his own trial and that the practice of not pleading was inadmissible in Canadian law. Cardinal therefore had to plead not guilty.

Next he argued that the trial should not be held in Yellowknife but in Aklavik, where the accused would have a better chance of getting a fair trial from a jury of his peers. Parker pointed out that Yellowknife was in the same judicial district as Aklavik and was the main town of that district. This was a major case requiring the best local facilities. The judge agreed.

The trial proceeded and the prosecution called its witnesses. When Sergeant Mclaughlin was being summoned, Maclean asked to address the judge in the absence of the jury. The jury was asked to retire and Maclean argued that Mclaughlin would no doubt give testimony concerning Cardinal's statements in Aklavik. These, he maintained were inadmissible because Cardinal had not been properly warned. With the judge's permission, and with the jury still absent, Maclean brought Cardinal to the witness stand and asked him about these statements. Cardinal stated that the sergeant had told him that anything he said would not be used against him. The sergeant was then called and contradicted this, saying that Cardinal had definitely been given the usual warning on each occasion.

It was a case of whose evidence the judge should accept. He took the word of the sergeant over the accused and ruled that the statements were admissible. The jury was brought back and the judge's ruling was read to them.

It is interesting that Maclean allowed his client to give evidence on his statements. A defence lawyer should never allow evidence which he considers might be a lie to be used in court. Perhaps in this case, although he had some doubts about its veracity, he reasoned that the accused should be allowed to speak before the judge, and in the absence of the jury who would know nothing about it.

The Crown also wanted to use a second RCMP officer to give evidence on another of Cardinal's statements. Maclean again disputed the admissibility of this testimony, and in this instance, Parker backed down and the witness was dismissed.

Witnesses were introduced to discuss the matter of temporary insanity. The question of possible epilepsy, which had been introduced by the defence in the first trial, was also covered.

Parker wanted to call several witnesses to give evidence on Cardinal's love affair. Maclean immediately objected and the jury again withdrew. Parker argued that the relationship would reveal motive. Judge McBride, however, ruled that it did not directly pertain to the case and could only be used in rebuttal if the defence referred to it.

Maclean had originally planned to call witnesses but at the last minute changed his mind and none was called. He must have reasoned that his major witness, Cardinal, would be of no avail and that he would argue the points of law pertaining to the plea of insanity without recourse to witnesses. He had covered this subject thoroughly during his cross-examination of the prosecution witnesses.

The prosecution and defence summations would therefore follow immediately the lawyers had prepared them. Parker went over the prosecution evidence in great detail. He emphasized the accused's incriminating statements which did not match the medical evidence. Moreover, he added, if the accused had been temporarily insane at the time of the murder, he could not have remembered what went on before and after it. Even more convincing was the evidence that the lead particles in Mrs. Cardinal's head matched the type of gun that the accused used. He then discussed a number of incidents that clearly showed that the crime was premeditated.

Maclean had the last word, a long eloquent speech, particularly dwelling on the question of temporary insanity.

Judge McBride's charge to the jury lasted two hours. He covered the question of the law in relation to the evidence in great detail. He also referred particularly to the crime of murder and to temporary insanity as a defence plea. The Crown must prove guilt, but Canadian law did not allow an unsupported plea of insanity to be an extenuation for a crime. This, he contended, would provide a convenient loophole for any criminal.

The jury retired and, in under an hour, returned to the court and gave their decision of guilty. A sentence of death by hanging was handed down and the accused was taken back to the Fort Smith RCMP goal to await punishment.

Cardinal again appealed the sentence and it was considered by the Alberta Appeals Court. On 7 May 1954, the court dismissed the appeal, saying that the proceedings were correct, the confessions of Cardinal were voluntary, the judge's charge was fair, and no jury of reasonable men could find any other verdict but guilty. Cardinal then appealed to the Supreme Court of Canada, but that court refused to hear the case.

On 4 June 1954 Cardinal was hanged at Fort Smith. Frank McCall noted that the hanging cast a pall over the little community. Wooden gallows were built behind the RCMP barracks, facing the Slave River Rapids and away from the road. The federal hangman — the only one in the country — named Ellis came to town. This was his trade name not his real name. There were three witnesses to the hanging, in addition to the police; the district medical officer, the local Catholic priest, and a government representative. Guards were posted around the post to deny access to ghoulish spectators. This was the last hanging to occur inthe north.

In October 1953, Parker prosecuted in four major cases in Yellowknife before Judge Gibben in the largest judicial docket ever in the north. One concerned a Native Indian who had set fire to a friend's house out of unrequited love. Although the evidence was circumstantial, the accused was found guilty and sentenced to two years imprisonment. Another was a manslaughter case concerning a serious traffic accident, a rarity in Yellowknife then. The third involved a Hay River man who was found guilty of assault with bodily harm because of a fight which resulted in a broken jaw for one of the participants.

The fourth, a three-day trial, concerned Alexis Fat who had returned from a prospecting trip saying that his brother-in-law, Antoine Marlowe, had been accidentally shot. He reported that he had buried the body in a portage in the Hearne Channel area north of Yellowknife. Fat, a Dogrib who spoke no English, gave several garbled versions of the shooting through an interpreter. The police began to suspect foul play and visited the site. They dug up the body and from bits of wood, a canoe, and ore samples that had been found near the scene, built a case. The stories that Fat had told did not correspond with what they had found.

Fat was charged with murder. Marlowe had been shot in the head from the back and detailed evidence to support this was led. Other prosecution evidence highlighted the discrepancies between conditions at the scene of the crime and Fat's statements. The motive for the crime was the division of the gold ore samples. Ironically, later assay revealed that these contained some gold mineralisation but nothing that was really promising.

Fat was put in the witness box by the defence and proved to be a very confused witness. Hagel, his lawyer, argued that he was "almost a primitive." He did not understand court procedure and was very upset by the death of his brother-in-law. Hagel contended that he had been thrown into a panic and had become confused in his statements. He argued that Marlowe had been killed in an accident. After two hours, the jury decided that he was innocent.

The Department of Justice had been studying changes to the justice system in the Territories for some time and the new Liberal minister of northern affairs and national resources, Jean Lesage, was actively interested in the matter. The NWT council had also discussed the question and so a new territorial court was finally inaugurated in 1955.

The population of Territories had slowly increased to 12,184 (White 3,666, Inuit 3,829, and Native Indian 4,689).[87] Court work was increasing and major cases were taking up more and more of the time of Mr. Justice Gibben from the Yukon. The Territories would continue to increase in population and there would be more court work. Furthermore, more responsibility was being given to territorial local governments. There was by now a small bar of qualified lawyers in Yellowknife and the northern population was entitled to the same standards of justice as other Canadians. The stipendiary magistrate system had worked quite well but was not perfect and the time had come for it to be replaced and for the Territories to have the same justice services as the Yukon had enjoyed for years. Consequently, Mr. Justice Jack Sissons, a very experienced and qualified judge was appointed to the newly established Territorial Court of the Northwest Territories on 15 October 1955.

Sissons was born in 1892 in Orillia, Ontario, of Scottish Presbyterian parents. He graduated from Queen's University and took his legal training at the University of Edmonton. He practised law from 1921 to 1940 in Grande Prairie in the Peace River district in Northern Alberta. During this period, he was active in the Liberal party and made a name for himself as a fierce proponent of western interests. He was elected to the House of Commons as a Liberal in 1941 for the Fort Vermilion (Peace River) riding. In 1945 he was not re-elected and he was appointed a judge of the District Court of Southern Alberta in 1946.[88]

Parker was extremely pleased at the formation of the new court, feeling it was long overdue, and with the appointment of Sissons. He regarded the judge as knowledgable in the law, extremely fair, and well versed in northern matters because of his time at Grande Prairie and Fort Vermilion. "Sissons changed everything and ran the courts properly," was his last word on the matter. Besides which, Sissons was a very affable person and a good travelling companion on the long territorial court circuit. He was interested in everything in the north, especially northern history and flora and fauna. Above all, he was concerned to safeguard the independence of the territorial court and threw himself into his new job with great vigour and enthusiasm. In fact he became a bit of a thorn in the side of Ottawa.

When he arrived in Yellowknife, an Inuit, one Allan Kaotok, had been languishing in the RCMP lock-up awaiting trial for murder. Parker had been designated as defence lawyer.

This was a novel role for Parker but is explained by the fact that he had recently been relieved of his duties as Crown prosecutor. He had been elected to the NWT council in September 1954, and the Justice Department had used this as an excuse to appoint a Liberal lawyer, Robert Bouchard, in his place. Parker had considered his replacement improper. It certainly was not due to his record.[89] Be that as it may, he decided to have some fun with the department by complaining in a letter and having the correspondence published in the *News of the North*.

The letter that John had received from the then minister, Stuart Garson, relieving him of his duties stated, "It is a well established principle elsewhere in Canada that persons who, as elected representatives of the public, have a voice in the enactment of the law, should not be charged with the responsibility of enforcing these laws." John's reply was to the effect that he could have no part in the enactment of the criminal law as he was not an MP. He continued that, "It is well known that the Department of Justice maintains a list of barristers who are faithful to the Liberal party, and when a lawyer is required to perform some government work a person from this list is selected for the job." David Fulton, BC Member of Parliament and Conservative justice critic and later minister of justice in the Diefenbaker government, took up his cause in the House.

When Sissons arrived, he found that arrangements had already been made for the Kaotok case to be tried in Yellowknife with witnesses being brought in and accommodated at government expense. He was uneasy about holding the trial 600 miles away from the accused's home and felt that the trial could have been held at Cambridge Bay, not too far from the scene of the alleged crime. Justice, he strongly advocated, should be brought to every person's door, where a jury of peers could be chosen. He decided, however, not to make any change as preparations had already been made, but said that he would never agree to such a thing again.

The case concerned an incident in April 1955 in the Central Arctic. Several Inuit families were seal hunting far out — sixty miles — on the ice on Queen Maud Gulf between the mainland and Victoria Island. They were operating from Perry River, a very small community located on the south shore of the gulf.

Kaotok, the accused, did not get along well with his seventy-three-year-old father Kitigitok, although they both had to hunt together for the family. The unpleasantness between them arose from the unhappy marriage into which Kaotok had been forced against his will by his father. The marriage had never worked and his wife had eventually left him for another man.

On about 25 April, he and his father returned to the coast to get some food from a cache. On his return he reported that his father had died and had been buried. Later the RCMP received a report about the incident from the priest at Perry River, and Constable Heapy from Cambridge Bay was sent to investigate. He found the burial site with the body placed under a caribou skin and a pile of snow in the traditional Inuit way.

Beside the body, he found a rifle with a piece of string tied to the trigger. Strangely, the deceased had a cigarette holder in his mouth, and his sunglasses on. The constable took the body and Kaotok with him back to Cambridge Bay. Kaotok now changed his story, saying his father had committed suicide.

The body was sent on to Yellowknife for an autopsy and inquest. An Inuit interpreter, Sam Carter, and Kaotok were also flown in to attend.[90] It was revealed at the autopsy that the bullet had entered the body from the back and lodged in the front of the deceased's parka. The coroner, H.J. Mitchell, found that death had been due to a bullet wound. Kaotok was charged with murder and held in custody pending a preliminary hearing.[91]

Magistrate Phinney conducted the hearing with Bouchard acting as Crown prosecutor and Parker as defence lawyer. Kaotok was arraigned and continued to be held in prison. He proved to be a very good prisoner, always cooperative and friendly. Each day, he was given various chores to do. The Mounties fitted him out with more suitable clothing. He was given a pair of uniform trousers and shown how to remove the stripes from them. Unfortunately, he got carried away when, in the absence of the duty constable, he went through the lockers and cut the stripes off all the trousers he could find. Watches fascinated him and a kind Mountie lent him a wristwatch to wear.

The trial was held on 15 December 1955 in the basement of the Elks Lodge. A number of witnesses from the north were called. For the Inuit witnesses, this was their first trip outside the Arctic and it was great adventure for them to see new country and a modern North American town. They were fascinated with everything and spent their time wandering around the streets, gawking at the buildings, and even inspecting the merchandise in the stores. Their presence in town, with their colourful decorated parkas and mukluks and smiling faces, made quite an impression on the local whites and Native Indians. They took a liking to taxi rides around town and were amazed at the voices coming over the their radio telephones.

Apart from the colourful witnesses, the trial created a lot of interest in the community because it was being conducted by the new Territorial judge, and the courtroom was packed with spectators.

Olakatah, the accused's former father-in-law, was the first Crown witness. He testified that Kaotok had left the camp with his father and returned without him, entering his igloo without a word. Angulalik, a prosperous trader and boat owner, testified that the father was a good hunter who was always happy, and he had never seen him angry at anyone. He said that he was still a very active man despite his age — very great for an Inuit. In a meeting he had with Kaotok after Kitigitok died, Kaotok had said to him, "I am all by myself now as my father has shot himself."

Alex Komaciuk, another witness, was described by Parker as "a delightful old Eskimo of colourful appearance and clothing." Komaciuk was deaf, could not speak, and knew no sign language. Amazingly, however, he had been taught to read Inuit syllabics — a written language developed for the Inuit.[92] The trial took a comical turn as a convoluted system was set up to question him. The only person in the court who could read the syllabics couldn't speak English. So an English-speaking questioner would ask the Inuit interpreter the question in English. The interpreter would then repeat it to the syllabic-reading Inuit, in Inuit. This person in turn would write it in syllabics and show it to the witness, who would read it. The answer then threaded its way back through the same complicated procedure. The Inuit couldn't keep straight faces as this technique proceeded and after about four questions, counsel let the witness stand down because of the effect the questioning was having on the court. Fortunately, his evidence was not that important.

Parker, in his summation, pointed out that Bouchard had not used in court the interpreter who had been present when Kaotok had made his original statement. This statement could have been construed to mean that Kaotok had assisted in his father's death. Parker therefore contended that the statement was inadmissible. Judge Sissons agreed with this in his charge. Parker's main argument was that there was no direct evidence that a crime had been committed. The only evidence was, therefore, circumstantial.

The all-white jury was out twenty minutes and returned with a verdict of not guilty. When the verdict was read and interpreted to the accused, he showed no emotion and did not move. Even when Sissons explained to him through the interpreter that he was free, there was still no change in his demeanour. His later explanation for this was that even if he had been found guilty he would have acted in the same way. Parker understood his reaction to be innate Inuit politeness — it was not up to him to be the first to leave. Finally, he got up and walked out of the prisoner's box, took a pack of cigarettes from his pocket, and handed them around to bystanders.

After the trial, the sheriff, as was usual, invited the jurors and the court policemen to have dinner at a nearby cafe at government expense, because of the lateness of the hour. During the dinner one of the jury men asked why the accused had handed his wristwatch to the constable. When the officer explained that it had been lent to him, all those present took up a collection and asked the sheriff to buy Kaotok one.

Unfortunately, the story ended on a sadder note. Kaotok caught TB when he was in Yellowknife and had to be sent south to recover. He was never able to go back to hunting. If the trial had been held in the Arctic this might never have happened.

Chapter 6 Notes

83. Graham Price, <u>Remote Justice</u>, p 309. "Gibben's court clerk, Jack Worsell, offers this revealing comment on him - Gibben was temperamentally unfit to be a judge. He felt strongly for people and, through sympathy, became deeply involved emotionally. Sentencing in criminal cases was very much an ordeal. He choked up and tears were not far off. At the end of a day's seating, he would shower interminably, as though to wash away the stains.

84. Court Record of Stipendiary Magistrate Court of NWT. His Majesty versus Mary Paulette.

85. Commissioner R.G.Robertson Opening Address to the NWT Council, 17 January 1955. Louis Audette papers Canadian National Archives, Ottawa.

86. It was brought out in the trial that Cardinal's father had had a similar job working for the RCMP detachment at Dawson city in the Yukon during the gold rush.

87. L Audette's papers. The population figures for the 1986 NWT population (*Focus on Canada, Stats Canada Cat 98-120 and 98-120.* The white population had increased proportionately. The results were; Inuit 15,451, Indian 13,847, White *21,940, Total 52,238.*

88. Jack Sissons, <u>Judge of the North, (McLelland & Stewart, Toronto, 1968)</u>, p 52

89. John Parker's personnel file in the Canadian Archives. Parkers was paid $3,678 in 1949 and 50. . The RCMP commissioner was asked by the Justice department to assess capabilities. Replies from northern RCMP officers were - "Services from Parker were extremely valuable and justify continuation," "Parker very cooperative, the interests of justice foremost in his mind,'" Should be appointed to the Queen's Counsel in the 1951 honours list."

90. Jack Sissons, <u>Judge of the North</u>, p 65

91. <u>News of the North</u>, 27 May, 1955

92. Inuit syllabics are a hieroglyphics of Inukituk, the Inuit language. In 1841, Rev. James Evans, a Wesleyan missionary in northern Manitoba, who knew Pitmans shorthand, invented Cree syllabics—a system using symbols to make written words, based upon syllables rather than letters or figures. The language had never had a written form before this, being only used orally.

  In 1865, Rev. E. A. Watkins and John Horden, two missionaries, devised a similar syllabic script for the Inuit, based on the Cree version. It has been extremely successful and has been taught and used throughout the Canadian north since it was devised.In the 1950's. The Department of Northern Affairs developed a Roman Alphabetical writing system for the Inuit language, which is now also in use.

A language is unique and reflects a people and its environment and type of life. For instance; there are many Inukituk words for types of snow. The Inuit speak carefully about the future. They don't say, "when it gets light," but "if it gets light." There are no words in inukituk for "guilty" It translates, "Did you carry out the killing?"

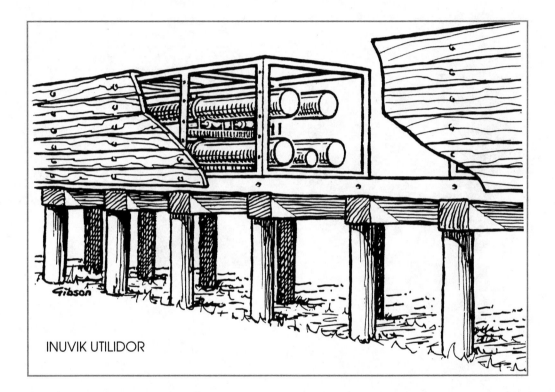

INUVIK UTILIDOR

Cambridge Bay, 1949   (Courtesy of Claire Parker)

Cambridge Bay, September, 1949. (L - R)
RCMP Inspector, Don Hagel, Magistrate Laurie Phinney,
John Parker, Rev. J. Webster, Ken Robson, unknown.   (Courtesy of Claire Parker)

Cambridge Bay, September, 1949. Court part, Eeriykoot murder case.
(L - R) Don Hagel, Laurie Phinney, Ken Robson and John Parker   (Courtesy of Claire Parker)

Above - Ishakak, Eeriykoot (Rt) with
Mountie and friends   (Courtesy of Claire Parker)

Right
Judge Sissons with two Indian Chiefs,
Old Crow, Yukon Territory
(Watt/NWT Archives N90-005:0690)

Inuit constructing an Igloo,
Cambridge Bay, 1949
(Courtesy of Claire Parker)

John Parker and Don Hagel unable to
get through the Igloo entrance.
(Courtesy of Claire Parker)

ᐃᣄᒥ ᐃᐅᐃ ᓄᐊᑲᔅ ᑕᒋᐅ ᓴᓇᓂ ᑭᓯᐊᓂ ᓄᐊᐁᑦ ᑭᒧᐢ
ᑐᐧᑐᐧᑐᑎ. ᑐᑦᒐᔪᐊᒐᒥ ᑭᒥᓄ ᑭᒥᐸᑕᐸᐁᑦ. ᐃᐅᐃ ᐅᑎᐁᑦ
ᔅᓇᐢᐧᐊᑎ ᐊᒥᓂ ᐊᐃᐧᐊᓂ .

Ilangit inuit nunakasot tagiok sinani kisiani nunakvaktut kimuksikut
tuktusiuktutik.   Tuktugaluagami kingminit kingmikautauvaktut.
Inuit utivaktut sunakasiagatik amingnik aisianik.

Many of the people live by the sea but they travel by kamutik far
inland to hunt deer . The dogs eat most of the meat from the hunt .
When they return they have gained almost nothing .

Innuit Syllabics, Roman Script and English from -)), Tuktut, Caribou.
(issued by the Department of Northern Affairs and National Resources)

Chapter 7
Emerging Northwest Democracy

The new St. Laurent government introduced a bill on the Northwest Territories in the summer of 1953 and it was given royal assent in December of that year. St. Laurent, in his speech to the House on this auspicious occasion, said:

> *"Apparently we have administered these vast territories of the north in an almost continuing state of absence of mind. It is time more attention was focused upon the possibilities of this area and what it will mean to this Canadian nation.*
> *The population has increased greatly in the last ten years. The potentiality for mining, fisheries and water power need examination, as do the problems of northern sovereignty, defence of the north and the needs of the Eskimo population."*

Gordon Robertson, who was appointed deputy minister of the new territorial department and became the new NWT commissioner in 1953, tells of the reasons for this new interest. In his distinguished career, he had been secretary to Prime Minister Mackenzie King from 1945 to 1949, and says, "King showed absolutely no interest in the north. He thought everything in Canada was in the provinces. Like most people, he thought it was inhabited by a few picturesque Indians and Eskimos, missionaries, HBC people and miners. The Canadian public too, like him, showed very little interest. The Northwest Territories never caught their imagination."[93]

Later on, he was instructed to report to St. Laurent in his office in the east block of the parliament buildings. The great man told him that the government wasn't satisfied with the way the country regarded the north. After all, it comprised 45 per cent of the country's surface area. There were no positive long- or short-run policies for the region. New, preferably young people with new ideas were needed to bring a fresh approach to the subject and to prepare recommendations for a new northern policy. He had decided to appoint a new minister, Mr. Lesage, and a new deputy minister, Robertson, to take this on.

Robertson responded that St. Laurent, whom he described as "a very marvellous man," couldn't have picked a department that he, Robertson, knew less about. The reply was, "Well Gordon, you're young and can soon learn."

From personal observation, Robertson knew that the government had been embarrassed when it had allowed the Americans to come into the country during the war and build the Alaska Highway, the Canol project, and the Northeast staging route for aircraft. At the time, Canada didn't have the economic capacity to carry out such major undertakings, but by the end of the war the country had become a significant power and its northern policy needed to take account of this fact.

When asked if it had anything to do with the complaints coming from the northerners, Robertson replied, "Being a new Commissioner, one supposes one did not know of the pleas and criticisms coming from the Territories over the years.. The new approach had nothing to do with the complaints being received from Yellowknife." As far as he knew, the whites were an itinerant population, mostly gold miners, fur-traders, and missionaries. He felt they had neither the interest nor the experience to bother with development problems. Nor did the Natives, who were uneducated. The two northern MPs, Hardie and Simmons, he regarded as good constituency men, who raised problems from to time.

The act changed the name of the relevant department from Resources and Development to Northern Affairs and National Resources. This new department now had authority to coordinate the activities of all government departments (education, health, social services, welfare, Indian affairs, and other matters) in the Territories; to promote economic and political improvement; and encourage northern research and development. The "Resource" side covered country-wide mining, oil and gas exploration, and national transportation.

The Gordon Commission on Economic Possibilities for Canada, which started its work in 1954, visited all the major centres in the Territories, talking to government, business, and local groups. No public hearings were held.[94] Its activities in the north further showed the government's interest in the area and it helped promote the region to the general public. It pointed out the great possibilities for major new northern mineral and oil finds in the Territories and discussed the difficulties in marketing these resources to the world at competitive prices because of high construction and transportation costs. There was no mention of environmental factors in the report, since these were not considered in those days. In other respects, the commission members showed considerable foresight.

This was particularly true of its recognition of an important issue which is with us to this day. This was the question of providing a livelihood for northern Natives. With better education and health services, their population was expected to increase. Yet fur prices were down and the caribou herds were decreasing. Would they be able to continue with their traditional hunting, trapping, and fishing way of life? Would there be any jobs in the business sector for them and could they be trained for them?

It was against this general background that John Parker became prominent in the political affairs of the Territories. He later asserted that some of his most rewarding experiences in the north derived from his tenure as a member of the NWT council. Robertson strongly agreed with him, even though his exciting and distinguished career spanned forty years, from1940 to 1980, and involved Canada's leading politicians: Mackenzie King, St. Laurent, Pearson, Diefenbaker and Trudeau.

The council at this time was breaking new ground. It was dealing with a particularly interesting and difficult problem, the imposition of modern society on a vast undeveloped region where two different aboriginal peoples were having to cope with the onslaught of western culture and technology.

The Canadian political parties, noting the success of the Yellowknife gold mines, the Territorial fisheries, and the Norman Wells operation, and the interest of the St Laurent government, were slowly starting to take notice of the north. The general public and the Canadian press, however, were still apathetic. So it seemed that the federal government would have to provide the initial leadership and funds. This approach continued with the Tories under Diefenbaker. Indeed, the development of the north formed one of his populist political planks, the "Road to Resources." Lester Pearson called it :"building trails from igloo to igloo."[94A]

In the spring of 1953, Parker decided to run for a seat on the NWT council that had been vacated when Hardie resigned to run for the new NWT seat in the House of Commons. At that time there were ten members on the council, six being appointed by the government and four being elected. The four elected members came from the ridings of Mackenzie Delta, Mackenzie River, Mackenzie South, and Mackenzie North. These covered the area from the Yukon border to a line north from the east end of Great Slave Lake. It was Mackenzie North that was now vacant, and it included Gros Cap on Great Slave Lake, Yellowknife, Fort Rae, Eldorado, Bathurst Inlet, Coppermine, and intermediate points.

The area to the east of this, which included the barren lands and all the Arctic Islands, was called Keewatin and was not included. Its population was too small and the distances too great for polling stations to be set up. Keewatin came under the direct control of Ottawa, but the council still had jurisdiction over it. The problem was that there was no direct participation from people living there. Communications were poor, so elected members had no first-hand knowledge of local conditions.

Council members did not have the powers of an elected MP. A majority vote could be ignored by the chairman, the NWT commissioner. The council was merely an advisory body, although, in most cases, the government accepted its wishes. Parker said that, contrary to what one might expect, there was no rift between the elected and non-elected members. Votes were always split within each group. He could not remember a vote which directly divided elected and appointed members. Nevertheless, debates were lively and there were sharp differences of opinion.

Some insight into the spirit and substance of council proceedings may be gleaned from the correspondence that passed between two of its members, Louis Audette, an appointee, and James Brodie, elected from Fort Smith. Brodie complained that the current commissioner, Young, dominated meetings and would not let elected members have their say. Brodie implied that this conduct might provoke a walk-out of elected members.

Audette replied that Young's conduct at the meeting had not been domineering, but stressed that elected members had every right to speak out against anything that was bothering them. He did not agree that elected members should form themselves into an official opposition, since this would be counterproductive. He had probably made more objections to measures than any other member. However, once council had made a decision, often a compromise that the majority could accept, he would go along with it even if he had argued against it. This was the way that council should operate. It ensured that the work got done and it was quite a different method from that used by a legislative assembly.[95] Parker agreed with Audette's ideas. However, it should be added that Robertson, who was chairman during his time on council, was a completely different person from General Young. Parker had nothing but praise for the way he conducted meetings.

Nominations were not to be made until August, but Parker decided to set his campaign in motion early. Although he was well known throughout the Territories from his legal work, he felt he should concentrate on Yellowknife where 70 per cent of the votes were. Ever one to do things a little differently, in May he started a paid column in the *News of the North* with his picture above it. This was a way of getting his name before the public, as well as of forcing himself to master the issues. He ran these columns every two weeks until the end of August. Nothing had been done like this before; certainly major issues affecting all of the Territories had not been discussed in this way. McMeekan had aired purely Yellowknife concerns, but had not covered such broad subjects as health services, education, welfare, and transportation. Parker's articles provide an invaluable synoptic view of the state of these services at the time.

His first column dealt with voting qualifications and voter registration for the voters' list. The next two covered education, a subject he was familiar with, being legal counsel to the Yellowknife School Board. In them, he listed the government expenditures and grants for the various types of northern school. Broadly speaking, the federal government paid for Native education and the territorial council received federal funds to cover the education of non-Native students. Day schools for non-Indian children were operated by the Department of Northern Affairs and National Resources at Fort Smith, Hay River, Fort Resolution, and Fort Simpson. Indian day schools were run by the Indian Affairs Branch of the Department of Citizenship and Immigration at Rocher River, Jean Marie River, Fort Rae, Lac La Martre, Fort Norman, Fort Mcpherson, Fort Good Hope, Fort Franklin, and Arctic Red River. The Roman Catholic Church ran residential schools at Aklavik, Fort Providence, and Fort Resolution and day schools at Fort Simpson and Fort Smith, while the Anglican Church operated a residential school at Aklavik. These schools were for Native students but some white students attended them. Federal day schools for Inuit children were operated at Aklavik, Tuktoyaktuk, Coppermine, Chesterfield Inlet, Coral Harbour, and Cape Dorset. Non-Inuit children could attend these schools. The only organised school districts in the Territories were at Yellowknife with the new Yellowknife Public School and the Yellowknife Separate School. Several mining companies outside Yellowknife operated schools for their employees.

Parker believed that a new grant for vocational training in Yellowknife should be increased. With the sharp drop in fur prices, he felt this trade would no longer support young prospective graduates. Vocational training would enable them to fill other types of jobs.

He also wrote that the education of Native children was not doing a proper job and needed great improvement. Many of them in the small settlements still did not receive formal instruction. Only 100 Inuit children were receiving full-time schooling at this time. With the growing Native population placing more pressure on the supply of game, he argued that other sources of employment must be found for them, thus highlighting the need for education. The religious schools were run on very tight budgets, so their student/teacher ratios were high.[96] Many northerners doubted whether the subjects being taught in these schools were suitable for Native students and whether the staff were properly qualified.[97] Parker pointed out that there was no government inspection or supervision of these institutions and felt that there needed to be more uniformity in school curricula.

His next column was on health and explained the financial arrangements and services available. Health services for Native Indians were funded by the Department of Citizenship and Immigration, for Inuit by the Department of Northern Affairs and National Resources, and for whites by the NWT council. There were four hospitals in the Territories; the 50-bed Catholic establishment in Aklavik; the 120-bed Anglican one also in Aklavik; the 72-bed Red Cross Stanton Hospital in Yellowknife; and the 50-bed Catholic one in Fort Smith. These hospitals received very little financial assistance from the government.[98]

There were also a number of small nursing stations with a handful of beds operated by the Catholic church or the Department of National Health and Welfare at Cambridge Bay, Coppermine, Fort Norman, Fort Simpson, Hay River, and Fort Rae. The federal government employed four doctors at Aklavik, Fort Norman, Fort Simpson, and Fort Smith. They acted as public health officers and had other non-medical duties. Two were Indian agents.

The NWT council had a budget of $171,000 to cover health services for the white population, embracing such items as hospital operating costs, free TB treatment, free cancer treatment, hospital costs for indigents, medical treatment in outlying settlements, and other items. This was before the federal Hospital Insurance and Diagnostic Services Act was passed in July 1958, so people had to have health insurance or pay full physician and hospital costs.

As was the case with education, the religious hospitals were on tight budgets and needed more staff and equipment. Having two hospitals in Aklavik was wasteful; their occupancy rates were low [99]. There were only eight physicians in the Territories in 1950, which was too low for such a huge area. The ratio of hospital staff in the Territories to the average number of patients was one-quarter of that in the provinces. It didn't come up to national standards until 1961.

At the time that Parker was writing, Native infant mortality was shockingly high: 200 per 1,000 births for the Inuit, 150 per 1,000 for Indians, compared with the Canadian rate of 35 per 1,000. Gordon Robertson noted that Native shelter was mainly very poor, adding that igloos and skin tents were almost a sentence of death. The smoke from the fires in them caused a sooty build-up in the lungs, and the Native population was very susceptible to pulmonary diseases.[100]

The next column concerned welfare. There was no comprehensive territorial welfare organisation then. Relief for indigent people was covered by council for whites and by federal departments for Natives. In Hay River and Yellowknife the municipality paid twenty per cent of welfare costs with the balance covered by council.

As far as Natives were concerned, the church, the government, represented by the RCMP, and HBC posts helped if people were in dire straits. When the situation was beyond the power of the Native family or band to solve, these organisations stepped in and did the best they could. HBC trading posts would give credit to trappers who were having a bad season. There had been occasions when the Bay gave out rations with no prospect of payment.

There was a government fund available to help in very serious situations such as starvation or loss of property or for a serious epidemic. On several occasions, caribou carcases were flown from another area to a starving band. This fund also covered relief food-vouchers which could be distributed to Natives in distress for dry staples such as flour or rolled oats, dry beans, tea, and sugar. These vouchers were distributed by the RCMP for redemption at HBC posts.[101]   The problem was that Native bands and families were spread over the Territories and it was hard to keep track of them and know if they were in dire straits. Family Allowance ration chits for food, fuel, and clothing, issued by the RCMP, certainly were a godsend for families with children.

A government health study at that time revealed that, by national standards, a great proportion of Natives were suffering from malnutrition. This made them very susceptible to disease.[102] The problem was particularly acute among the barren lands Inuit who depended almost entirely upon the caribou herds for their food and clothing.

There was only one HBC post in their vast area, at Padlei.

The Territories Indians also received payments under the Indian treaties. No treaties were signed with the Inuit. Treaty 8 was signed by the Mackenzie Indians at Fort Resolution in 1899 "in the interests of future white settlement." Under it, all band members — men, women, and children — were paid $5 a year and money for ammunition. They were allowed full rights to hunt, trap, and fish in their traditional lands. Later, in 1921, a more restrictive treaty was signed with other Native bands. It did, however, include a promise of payments for education and relief assistance.[103]

Parker had seen the deplorable housing conditions of many of the Natives, their poverty, and the harshness of their lives. He was impressed with the cheerfulness with which they faced the world and felt that they must be given much more encouragement and help.

In this column, he mentioned that council had met in Yellowknife in June 1954 discussing aspects of Native policy. He agreed with their recommendation to abolish the ordinance prohibiting Natives from purchasing liquor. "It does not, in my opinion, make any difference whether or not you are in favour of anyone having liquor. What is important is that there should be no discrimination against Canadians on race, religion or any other grounds."

In his next column he dwelled on the plight of the Natives at Fort Liard on the BC border and at Wrigley on the Mackenzie River above Fort Simpson. Noting that neither settlement had a school, he observed that his comments about Fort Liard were derived at first hand. In the summer there were over 100 children of school age at the settlement and, although that number diminished greatly in winter, enough children remained to justify a school. Only a handful of children could speak English.

He wrote that "the standard of living in Fort Liard is pitifully low. Exploration for oil has been going on in the area, but the Indian people living there cannot take advantage of the opportunity for work because they cannot speak English. The shocking thing is that their children are going to be in no better position. They are receiving no schooling of any kind whatsoever.

Where does the responsibility lie in this matter? In fact, it lies with the Indian Affairs Branch. This is a situation where council can achieve a satisfactory result by calling it to the attention of the federal government. It is late in the day to do much to help the adults but we cannot permit the children to be victims of this continuing neglect. We have a duty to speak out."

In his next two columns he discussed the question of transportation in the north. He wrote that "no one doubts that the Territories will be wonderfully developed two hundred years from now and the people living here then will probably enjoy every convenience. My concern is for the people who are here now and for those who will join us in the next few years." Among these concerns was a winter road from Hay River to

Yellowknife and a large car ferry in the summer. The latter, he thought, would provide passenger and car transportation much more cheaply than the existing smaller vessels.

In this context, he mentioned the exciting recent discoveries by Cominco of large lead/zinc deposits 100 miles east of Hay River. A proposal was being mooted to extend the railway from Peace River in northern Alberta to Hay River and beyond. If this eventuated, Parker suggested that the ferry should operate from Pine Point.

Parker had covered a great deal of ground in his newspaper columns. Ranged against him were three other candidates: Charles Crate, a union business agent; Neil Huchins, a carpenter at Giant Mine and a Pentecostal minister in Yellowknife; and Peter Baker. Baker was a colourful character who was nicknamed the "Arctic Arab" because he had come north from far-off Lebanon in 1921. He was in his fifties, and claimed to be the oldest old-timer in the Territories. He made his living mostly as a trader, having started with soft drinks, chocolates, and oranges. His trading posts had been at Fort Smith, on Great Bear Lake, at Fort Rae, then at Thekulthili Lake northeast of Fort Smith, which he had operated for many years. He could speak Dogrib and was on good terms with the Native Indians and was concerned about their plight. They nicknamed him "Oranges" because he was the first person to bring this fruit to the north.

Parker observed that "we were indeed an oddly assorted lot and it was apparent from the beginning that the votes would be fairly evenly divided amongst us." He therefore determined to visit every part of the constituency. His first trip was to Gros Cap, a Native Indian summer fishing base on the north coast of Great Slave Lake, about fifty miles south of Yellowknife. It would be a pleasant day's trip by boat, or so John thought.

His friend and supporter Walter England, who ran Yellowknife Hardware, offered to take him in his old motor boat and they took their families along for the outing. The weather was good on the the way south. On arrival they were greeted by the manager of the local fishing company and shown the plant and the crews' quarters. There John met a bright and friendly young Native Indian who spoke English and who agreed to be his local agent, publicist, and voting scrutineer.

So far, the day had gone well. The party's departure was delayed because repairs had to be made to the boat. Getting back was expected to take about four hours but, unfortunately, after an hour the engine broke down. The after-tank was empty and the feed-line from the forward tank was plugged so that gas wasn't reaching the engine. It was decided to pump the gas by hand using a bilge pump and pails, a risky operation because of the danger of fire. Nonetheless, this was achieved without mishap.

England then pressed the starter but nothing happened. Generator malfunction and a dead battery were suspected. By now it was late in the evening and even at that latitude it was starting to get dark. Unless they could start the engine, the north wind would drive them south from Yellowknife Bay out into the open lake which is about 100 miles wide at this point. There was very little chance they would sight another boat and no-one was likely to search for them until the next morning. The boat was quite old and Parker doubted that it could stay afloat in the rising swells.

Everyone remained calm but the adults were naturally concerned. The children, of whom there were six, were quite happy and soon went to sleep. England hoped that they would drift towards one of the many little rocky islands further offshore. Some floor boards were taken up and used as paddles but this did very little good. The lights ashore to the north continued to recede as the hours passed and the waters got rougher. Then someone suggested that the skipper try the starter again and by some miracle the engine fired. They headed north and at two in the morning went alongside the Con Mine jetty. The children were put up in Dr. Stanton's house and Parker and his wife took a taxi home. Despite his efforts and adventures, John Parker received no votes from Gros Cap.

After this little episode, John thought seriously about going to the far north, despite the cost. It was essential that he receive a large part of the Inuit vote because he felt that Baker would win most of the Indian vote. Parker was an open Conservative and he knew that the Dogribs, following the advice of their chief and the Catholic priest, were Liberals and wouldn't vote for him. His decision to oppose the Yellowknife Separate School was coming home to roost.

It was therefore imperative that he visit the Central Arctic. Max Ward's Beaver plane was chartered and Parker set off with his wife and some friends, bound for Coppermine on the Arctic Sea. The trip was made in August so the weather was fine. Two days earlier, the Duke of Edinburgh had visited the community, so there was an air of residual excitement about and most of the residents were still wearing their finest parkas and dresses.

The Anglican clergyman, Canon Jack Sperry, who spoke Inuit, and another Inuit interpreter agreed to assist him. The party visited every white home, every office, and every Inuit tent. Everywhere he went he was received most cordially. Parker wasn't sure whether this was genuine admiration or just inherent Inuit politeness. He arranged a public meeting, knowing that the Inuit enjoyed such occasions and feeling sure that he would get a good turnout. What he could accomplish for them as their member on council, he had no idea, since he was more familiar with the problems of the Native Indians to the south. However, he had tremendous admiration and sympathy for the Inuit and wanted to learn about their concerns. At the same time, he was firm in his belief that he would not make promises he could not keep.

Before the meeting, he had a word with the local Mountie, asking him what he could reasonably say to them. He was told that it would be a good idea to distribute the little campaign photographs of himself to them. Also, cash was short at this time of year and many of the Inuit still had some good soapstone carvings left over from the Duke's visit. He would make himself very popular if he bought what was left, crediting the purchases to the HBC post where the Inuit could buy what they wanted.

Parker's first reaction was that this was a morally questionable ruse, but the more he thought about it, the more he realised he was doing something worthwhile in helping them to market their excellent works of art. Moreover, Didi Woolgar from the Yellowknife Handicraft Society had accompanied John on this trip. She was a leader in helping the Inuit to market their art to the outside world. In fact, she had come hoping to make contact with the local Inuit carvers and artists.[104] She thoroughly approved of the plan and was prepared to value the carvings at a fair price and arrange for their further sale.

When the people had assembled in the school building he told them through an interpreter something of the purposes of his visit and of the function of the NWT council. The advantage of making a speech in this way was that there was time to decide what to say next while the interpreter was speaking. John always spoke from a few notes and not from a typed speech. Indeed, he was an excellent speaker, with a commanding presence and a quick sense of humour. He used colourful phrases, sometimes just a little overblown, to make his point, and he always kept the attention of his audience. He was a brilliant raconteur, the life and soul of the party. Gordon Robertson said of him that he spoke with colour and verve and never held back, going directly to the point.

He must have made quite an impression on the Inuit, despite the fact that they probably didn't understand much of what he was saying. His address was concluded with praise for Inuit craftsmanship and an offer to buy anything they wanted to sell. When this was translated their enthusiasm was obvious and they were all wreathed in smiles. The crowd quickly dispersed and soon returned in ones and twos carrying quantities of soapstone carvings. Some people did not come back for an hour or more and John had the feeling that they were putting the finishing touches on some unfinished masterpiece. Prices for Inuit art were much lower in those days and Parker paid about $1,000 for all the carvings he purchased, and suffered a net loss of $50 after they were resold.

The party also visited Discovery Mine, north of Yellowknife, and Eldorado Mine on Great Bear Lake. He shook hands with as many people as he could at these places, on the premise that, all things being equal, a voter would usually cast his ballot for someone he or she had met rather than a complete stranger.

There were some 700 eligible voters at Fort Rae and Edzo (across Great Slave Lake) and he felt that he had to do something there to get just a few votes, so close was the overall race expected to be. However, he was at a disadvantage in that Baker spoke Dogrib and he didn't. He decided to visit the community the day before the vote. After arrival in the afternoon, he would walk around the community and then he hoped to speak at a meeting. He would spend the night in a tent to show that he could live out in the bush with the best of them. He would pause to check on the voting the next day and then fly back to Yellowknife to cast his own ballot.

Somewhat to his dismay, he discovered that Baker had arranged to speak on that night thus ruling out his own intended meeting. All he could do was attend Baker's address meeting where he found virtually the entire community present. Although Baker spoke in Dogrib, his speech was translated. Parker wrote that it was an excellent speech: "He explained to them that he was not a white man and he was glad he was not one. It was the white men who had invaded the area and introduced commercial fishing, so that it was now difficult for the Indian to feed his family. The white men had destroyed the caribou herds. In fact, the white men had caused only loss to the Indians. He, Peter Baker, deplored the activities and behaviour of the white men and blamed them for every misfortune which the Indians had suffered." Parker added, "There was a good deal to be said for Baker's position and certainly it was what the Indians wanted to hear. I knew I was in trouble."

His friends at Fort Rae kindly organised a party after Baker's speech where food and tea were served. The Natives tucked in and some of them came over and spoke to him. He wondered whether there was any real interest in him or whether it was just the food.

Next morning an opportunity arose which he thought might help him. A plane landed on the lake and tied up at the jetty. A nun disembarked carrying a heavy bag. Gallantly he offered to carry it for her. She accepted his offer and he toted the burden about a quarter of a mile to the hospital. He liked to think he would have done it even if there hadn't been an election.

At the polling station, the Dogribs waited patiently outside until the chief and elders had gone in to vote. There was something quite different at this polling booth; scrutineers knew who people were voting for. Practically all the Native voters couldn't read, so the polling clerk had to mark their ballots for them and anyone could see who they were voting for. When he left to go back to Yellowknife, his scrutineer told him he hadn't got a single vote yet.

In the event, however, Parker beat Baker by 44 votes, 3.7 per cent of the total vote of 1206. He claimed that he wouldn't have won if a rumour hadn't started in Fort Rae that there were caribou in the area, so that a lot of the Natives took off. It turned out that there were no caribou. Parker hastily added that there was no suggestion that he or his friends had anything to do with the rumour.

The final results were: (over page)

	Baker	Crate	Hutchins	Parker
Old Town YK	95	53	55	53
Con Mine	8	11	30	55
Village	20	2	1	0
Discovery Mine	2	6	22	13
Snare	1	1	2	2
Giant Mine	1	13	31	58
Con Hydro		1	2	1
New Town YK	30	59	133	140
Eldorado Mine	9	15	15	12
Fort Rae	147	6	8	3
Coppermine	1	1	4	32
Boreal	1	0	0	4
Bathhurst	0	0	2	9
GrosCap	23	5	8	0
TOTAL	338	173	313	382
TOTAL VOTES CAST	1206			

Parker received 30 per cent of all eligible votes. Baker was most generous in defeat, immediately calling him and offering his warmest congratulations, saying that if he could not represent the constituency himself, there was no-one he would rather see do it than Parker. Baker was later elected to council in the sixties and became a legendary Yellowknife character. Parker sat for three years and was re-elected by acclamation at the next election. He said he tried to be an outspoken advocate for the rights of the people of the Territories, no matter who they were.

Before he attended his first council meeting in January 1955, John Parker already knew on the basis of his own experiences, researches, and travels, that there was a lot wrong with the Territories. In particular, he regarded Native education and healthcare as scandalous and there were other problems facing Council and he was determined to speak out on these subjects and call for immediate attention.

But first he had to learn something about his fellow council members and their backgrounds. The chairman of the council and commissioner of the Northwest Territories was, as has been noted, R. Gordon Robertson whom he already knew quite a bit about. He had received his Bachelors degree from the University of Saskatchewan and his Masters from the University of Toronto, before entering the Department of External Affairs in 1941. Between 1945 and 1949 he was secretary to the Prime Minister Mackenzie King. Later he served on the cabinet secretariat and became assistant secretary to the cabinet. Parker knew he would be dealing with one of the stars of the federal bureaucracy.

One of the appointed members was his old adversary, Louis de la Chesnaye Audette, the scion of a distinguished Canadian family. His father was a French Canadian judge and his mother was a Scottish woman, the daughter of Sir Andrew Stuart. He was a lawyer living in Ottawa and was obviously a good Liberal as he had been appointed to a number of federal boards, including the Canadian Maritime Commission and the Court Martial Appeal Board. During the war he had served very successfully in the Canadian navy, ending up in command of several ships with the rank of Commander RCNVR. He was a Canadian who kept the two ethnic elements of his background equally balanced.

Jean Boucher was another French Canadian appointee. A classically educated lawyer, he worked in the Department of Citizenship and Immigration as special assistant of the deputy minister. He was presumably appointed because the Indian Affairs Branch fell under his department. The other appointed members were Cunningham, the Yellowknife magistrate who was now deputy commissioner; C.M. (Bud) Drury, deputy minister of national defence and another distinguished war veteran; and the RCMP commissioner who was always a member, the incumbent then being L.H. Nicholson.

Frank Carmichael, an old trapper, was the elected member from Aklavik in the far north. He had lived in the north for thirty-five years, having first moved there in 1919, and was a tough independent northerner who knew the vicissitudes and hardships of a trapper's life. He and his Loucheux wife, Caroline — the daughter of a chief — brought up and educated two fine children largely on their own. It was through the Mackenzie Delta Trappers Association that he had learned to develop his speaking and organising skills. Parker liked him for his rough-hewn common sense and the two of them became friends. It was these two who were so outspoken in outlining the real problems of the north at Parker's first meeting of council.

The other two elected members were typical of many of the white settlers in the Territories. Robert Porritt, although born in England, was educated in Edmonton. He had worked in various jobs at Fort Rae, Fort Resolution, and Yellowknife, before finally establishing a successful trading post and store at Hay River. He had been active in local politics. The other man, J.W. Goodall had been educated as a teacher in England. He came to Canada in 1911 and drove north in a covered wagon through Edmonton and over the old Athabasca trail, homesteading at Athabasca Landing. He served in the First World War and he was one of the unsung trail-blazers who had migrated to the Territories in the Depression. A two-month trip with his small family in a motor scow had brought him to Great Slave Lake. Settling in Fort Simpson, he raised potatoes on the Liard River flats in the summer. Like Carmichael, he cut firewood in the winter for wood-burning steamers. Both he and Porritt were well read and scholarly.

Parker said that these men would have known each other through the "mocassin telegraph," carried by the Mackenzie tugs and paddle-steamers up and down the river. Goodall had seen Fort Simpson change from a fur post with dog teams and oxen and five mails a year to roads, motor vehicles, mechanical equipment, an airport and weekly mail service. Mrs Woodall, who accompanied her husband to the Council meeting, told reporters that she had taken only three trips out of the north in 27 years.

After Parker and his wife Claire arrived in Ottawa for the meeting which started on Monday 25 January 1955, he immediately got on the phone to the newspapers to make sure they attended the meeting. He contacted the *Ottawa Citizen*, the *Ottawa Journal*, the bureaus of the *Edmonton Journal*, the *Toronto Globe and Mail* and *Daily Star*, also the *Canadian Press* and even the *New York Times*, telling them they were going to be some interesting speeches. The press had been allowed to cover the meetings of Council a few years before but interest had been poor and coverage skimpy.

Council meetings of late had become more formal to conform with an elected assembly like the House of Commons. After members had assembled with an RCMP officer present acting as Sergeant-at-arms, the Chairman (the NWT Commissioner) would bring the group to order. A prayer would be said by one of the members and the proceedings would start. There would then be an opening address by the chair similar to the throne speech in the Commons. The chair would report on what had happened in the Territories since the last meeting and mention matters which were under consideration. Proposed new ordinances would be briefly explained.

After this address, a motion of appreciation of the speech by a chosen member would follow. Then a general debate would ensue on the speech and members could say what was on their minds. There was no limitation on what subjects they would like to cover. This part of the proceedings could take two days or more.

After this, individual items would be submitted by the Commissioner for discussion in detail and approval. These included the budget, new capital projects, troublesome problems (e.g. reduction of caribou herds, relief payments to indigents, etc.). Also new and to be amended ordinances. The procedure was somewhat akin to the House of Commons going into "the committee of the whole" after the opening throne speech for detailed discussion of the departmental estimates or new bills. Members were advised to stick to matters under the authority of Council, although passing remarks could be made to subjects concerning the north which had been discussed in the commons. John Parker's first session lasted nine days[105.] At night, entertainment and dinners were organised for the members and their wives. Members paid for their spouses' travel and accomodation costs. Members were paid transportation costs and a $50.00 per diem stipend.

Robertson commenced his speech by referring to recent mixed northern economic trends. Gold production in 1954 had increased slightly to $9.9 million and petroleum production was also slightly up at $297.000. Exploratory work in both fields had been good. The fisheries were slowly recovering from a slump[106.] He also alluded to the explorations at Pine Point, near Fort Resolution on a large lead/zinc deposit which looked extremely promising. A possible uranium find on the Marian River north of Fort Rae was reported, later called Rayrock Mine.

Mention was made of the difficult time fur-trappers were experiencing as a result of a drop in international fur prices, particularly muskrat pelts which dropped from $2.01 in 1951 to 70 cents in 1954. New synthetic furs were having some effect on demand. He said relief payments had been made to trappers in distress, particularly those in the northern Mackenzie delta area. The problem was aggravated by the increase in the native population and there were more in the trade. A study was being conducted to find out how to alleviate the situation.

Reference was made to an on-site study being conducted to move Aklavik and Coppermine to more suitable sites. Parker said it all started as a result of a study conducted by a sanitory inspector from Ottawa who looked at health conditions in the Territories—always a difficult problem. The inspector was shocked to find how bad things were in the various settlements. What with no central water or sewage systems because of the permafrost, water was being delivered by truck or sled and "wet garbage" was being carried off in tank vehicles.

Matters were particularly bad in Aklavik which was built on low-lying land about two square miles in size surrounded by lakes and swamps, The land was a thin layer of alluvial silt above frozen permafrost. Its highest elevation was only a few feet above the high water mark at the time of the spring run-off. The inspector thawed out some of the permafrost and found that a high percentage of it was water. He reported to the Department of Northern Affairs that if the Aklavik population were to increase much more, "before long the town would disappear into the primeval ooze," which was surely an exaggeration

Some of the poorer built houses without good foundations had problems of flooding and shifting during the spring thaw. Frank McCall says every four or five years there would be a serious flood in the spring. The place would be covered in a foot or so of water, as the river backed up because of downstream ice blockage. Drainage was negligible and very slow. The better houses had sump pumps. Another problem was the weak perimeter being eroded by strong river currents.

There were no gravel pits around to get land fill to build an airstrip for year-round air communication. Thus there were just too many problems for the development of a major far northern communication, military and transit centre. This was going to be needed for expected growth and expansion. There could well be future oil, gas and mineral exploration. Even then it was known there was a good chance of large oil and gas deposits being discovered in the estuary.

McCall agrees the move was needed, but, at the time, most people were against it. Very few of the locals, other than the government employees, moved when the new alternate site was built. They didn't like Ottawa bureaucrats coming in and telling them what to do. They were quite happy to put up with its inconveniences from time to time. The religious authorities had made a considerable investment in the place. However, much later as we know, it turned out that there was tremendous exploration in the area, and the government planners, in this instance, were proved to be right.

Arrangements were going to be made for the settlers and the natives to be given every opportunity to be trained to build the new town. This was a bit of pie in the sky. It did happen to some extent. Whilst the decision to build was right, the execution was another matter.

The new site was called initially East Three, one of three areas investigated, the other two being West One and West Two. Later the name was changed to Inuvik meaning the "Place of Man", Aklavik means "Place of the Bear."

Bent Sivertz, who was then Director of Northern Administration—he was later NWT Commissioner after Robertson, says he was the person who recommended the study be done. He said the main reason for the move was because of the poor port facilities at Aklavik. It could take only shallow draught ships because the water around it was not deep enough. More open water was also needed to ensure an early ice thaw and a late freeze-up. He preferred the sites on the west bank of the Mackenzie River because they were higher and firmer than the ones on the eastern bank. However, he bowed to the advice of the experts who said the western sites were like Aklavik and were only accessible up long sloughs. An inspection of Coppermine revealed no move was necessary.

Another matter which would have an important effect on northern enterprise and the life of the Inuit was tabled. This was the agreement between the Canadian and United States governments to build an early warning system of radar stations across the north to detect Soviet bombers. This was later called the Distant Early Warning Line (DEW line). It was hoped that it would boost the economy and provide jobs, which indeed did happen to some extent.

Referring to education, the Commissioner said much needed to be done. More government-run schools were needed. As native families were continually on the move it meant hostel accomodation as well as classroom space was necessary. Care had to be taken to ensure the curriculum covered native skills as well as the three R's. Native children must be prepared to go back to their Native way of life. The native training was never taught in sufficient detail leading to difficulties. It was expected there would only be limited possibilities, for the time being, for them to get salaried work. It turned out that many natives who were technically trained could not get a job. A Coordinator of Vocational Training had been added to the staff at Fort Smith.

Robertson has said that "the religious schools were teaching damn little." He felt native children should be given a "Canadian" type of education, although possibly to a lesser extent, as well as learning native skills. Otherwise, those who could not support themselves in their traditional manner would end up on welfare. He also said the rights of Indians under the Indian Act and Treaty Eleven to hunt and fish anywhere was sacrosanct, and that all policy must be based on this.[107]

It was an enormous challenge, fraught with difficulties; to give a balanced education to children from totally different cultures, spread over a huge isolated area, in difficult conditions. There was also the problem of dealing with the religious mission schools who had put such a lot money and energy over a long period into this work. Due to the slowness of government to take action and the difficulty in finding out what needed to be done, there was hesitation on the part of federal authorities to provide proper services. It was assumed the churches were doing a good job and not too much was needed.

Frank Carmichael led off the general debate in forthright terms saying he was disappointed that no mention had been made of "a permanent cure for the ailing fur trade."He wanted some kind of financial support for trappers. He also called for better education for Natives. He referred to a proposal he had submitted for Inuit to be allowed to purchase liquor.

Parker started off his speech by telling the story about how the Dogribs took off after caribou allowing him to win the election. Then he lit into the education problem by saying, although Yellowknife had a satisfactory school system—there were twenty applicants for every teaching position, there was a crisis in northern education. Something had to be done about it as soon as possible.

He charged, "Indian and Inuit children were going without adequate teaching and federal authorities had utterly failed to meet the need. Until day schools and hostels were established interim emergency measures should be taken to meet the needs of 4,000 Inuit and 5,000 Indians in the Territories. It is difficult for elected members to come before Council and say they represent the most disease-ridden, illiterate, poverty-stricken people in Canada. But this is true and I would be ashamed if the situation was allowed to continue longer than necessary". [108]

He said it was shocking that a number of children at Aklavik of the Anglican faith could only get teaching at a Roman Catholic mission school if their parents agreed for them to be given lectures in catholicism. This was because the Anglican school was full.

He strongly recommended a single government-run school system without discrimination as to race, religion or "anything else." He wanted a system of day schools with hostels to house the children where necessary. He said young native children should not be separated from their families. There should be no discrimination on any grounds and religion should be kept out of the classroom. "Ecclesiastical authorities" he said, "have no right to tell us what to do, though their advice would be welcome."

He also ranged more widely than this. He asked for a special $10.00 increase in the Old Age Pension (then at $40.00 a month) for northerners to offset the high cost of living—everything had to be shipped in by very expensive transportation. Special provision was needed for the Inuit, not one of whom had yet received the old age assistance. " Also, we shouldn't be sticky with them about proof of age," he said, " because their average age was much shorter than the white man."

He said many more roads were needed in the territories to open up communications and benefit the economy, as was a new car and passenger ferry for the Great Slave Lake for the summer months. This would promote tourism. He urged a year-round graded road be built from the south to Hay River instead of the temporary winter road and that it be extended to the Pine Point project when it got started. Later it could be extended to Yellowknife via Fort Rae. He pointed out that automobiles in Yellowknife had increased from 2 to 214 in the previous ten years, even though you could drive only four miles or so around town and to the mines—that was all the half decent roads there were in the Territories. It wasn't worth buying a car and getting a licence, although he himself drove a small truck.

He proposed that any company which paid for power lines to bring in electical power, get a 50% refund on power consumption until their power line had been paid off.

Another one of his items caught the imaginaion of the press which had turned out in force to the Council meeting. It concerned the clarity of the Radio Moscow signal being received all over the north and the difficulty of receiving anything from Canada. The Russian programmes were in English with good music, slanted news and propaganda. Whereas the reception from CBC Edmonton, which was supposed to look after the north, was very poor. He suggested that this was "a dangerous situation!"because the natives when they learned English would get the wrong idea about Canada . A special federal grant should be approved to build the necessary radio-relay towers to boost the strength of the Edmonton station.

He finished by castigating the Northern Transportation Company (a crown company) for its unreasonable profits which he estimated at 168 per cent[109]. "It was scandalous," he said, "that a federal company should charge rates giving it such a profit, unduly increasing the already high charges which the north has to accept. We are a patient long-suffering people but believe me this percentage is just too much for us to stomach."

This was certainly a new strident voice which had arrived on Council. The old civil servants must have wondered what hit them. This was somebody who wanted action and a breath of fresh air was probably what Council needed. One of the interesting things about this speech was that several proposals were quite new and came from the mind of Parker or from the Board of Trade in which he was an active member. The press picked up on his speech and it was carried across Canada. The Ottawa Citizen cartoonist, Johnston, drew a picture of a HBC post with a trader, a mountie and a Inuit listening to a Radio Moscow broadcast.

A motion was submitted by Carmichael, seconded by Parker, to allow Inuit to purchase liquor. Carmichael said it would only apply to the Inuit who lived in and around Aklavik for 18 months and given up their native way of life. He said only about 100 Inuit would be involved. He said it was unfair that his native trapper associates and other workers who lived a similar life to himself should be deprived of the rights which he had. He referred to the Inuit living in Manitoba and Quebec having full liquor purchasing rights..

This triggered a heated debate. C.M. Drury said he favoured giving NWT Indians and Inuit the right to consume alcohol. Depriving them of this right lead to the view that "the law was an ass." Parker said he strongly supported the motion, pointing out that "prohibition has never worked, never will and should be ended." He said natives living in the settlements were getting it anyway through bootleggers at $20.00 a bottle or making their own brew which was sometimes lethal. He was in favour of all natives having access to liquor, maintaining they should have the same rights as other Canadians. He said he would ask for full liquor privileges for the 6,800 Indians and 3,800 Inuit population at the next meeting.

Audette said that it would be an administrative nightmare having to decide the case of an Inuit living in an igloo and making money on the stock market.

Chairman Robertson was in favour of extending the right to natives but he was not required to vote except in the case of a tie. Audette was strongly against it, arguing that it was unfair to give the right to a small group of so-called "civilised" Inuit. He pointed out the same argument could be applied to the NWT Indians who were not allowed such rights. It had been suggested before but the Indian Affairs administration were firmly against it. The Indian Act only allowed provinces to grant Indians access to beer parlors. Only Ontario, Nova Scotia and British Columbia had done this. The department was watching what the experience of these provinces would be before it would proceed further. One member pointed out there were only two beer parlors in the Territories anyway, in Yellowknife and Fort Smith and many natives lived away from the settlements, particularly the Inuit. "In any event," Audette said,"Council only has the right to legislate for the Inuit." He said,"We are leading the Inuit away from his native way of life and the bait is a bottle of brew."

The RCMP Commissioner spoke out strongly against the proposal, saying it would increase Native drunkeness and lead to more problems for the police. He said, "The main concern of the Inuit is survival in a harsh environment and liquor has no place in the Arctic." Porrit and Goodall took the view that nothing should be done until the Indians were given the same rights. The vote passed passed five to four—Porrit, Goodall, Audette and Nicholson voted against and Parker, Carmichael, Cunningham and Drury voted for.

The Council then considered a proposed bill to allow natives and some special white permit holders[110] to be allowed to shoot game regardless of the hunting season rules or protective laws. The proposal was submitted because of a sharply worded Indian Affairs Branch complaint that Council was not honouring Indian treaty rights. With the opening up of the north and the arrival of more whites, hunting laws were being tightened up and game wardens were being hired to enforce them. In the twenties and thirties Metis and white hunters and trappers had moved into Native Indian hunting areas and some had ignored trapline rights and over-hunted to the point of causing hardship for the Indians who were already having a hard time. This had been clamped down on but was still present.

Except for the hunting of caribou, Natives were put under the same restrictions as the White man. This was something new for them and they resented it and complained to their Indian agents. Certainly the rules, as they applied to the natives, needed to be clearly stated and explained. A long discussion ensued, unfortunately without an Indian having a chance to participate.

The proposal would have meant that all fur-bearing animals such as mink, beaver and muskrat woul be fair game for Natives as well as wolves or moose. The regulations allowed Natives to shoot these animals only if they were facing starvation, but they were to report such incidents to the game wardens. The old trapper Carmichael said any Native, worth his salt, would reject a breakfast of fried mink. He said, "even a dog won't eat mink." He asserted, "The proposal is dynamite. In five years there wouldn't be a beaver left in the Territory. It would do the Indians more harm than good." He said it was all very well for appointed members of Council and civil servants to make such proposals. They were fine conscientious men, who even admitted they were not familiar with northern affairs, so why would they put forward such an outrageous idea.

Carmichael and Goodall said that restrictions could be lifted on moose and caribou. Goodall said black bears should be deprived of protection. He said they did more damage than wolves. Others suggested there would be no problem if the lifting of restrictions only applied to coyotes, wolves and wolverines. Parker said that allowing Natives to shoot fur-bearing animals for food would be like "brushing your teeth in champagne." These animals were very valuable and provided a living to many white northerners as well as Native trappers.

Council agreed there be open season on wolves, coyotes and wolverines. Natives and a few white trappers were allowed to hunt big game and non-migratory birds for food throughout the year. All other hunting rules would remain in effect.

There was some discussion about improving Native health care but little about Native housing. Two new doctors, one an eye specialist, a dentist and a public health nurse were to be hired for the Mackenzie River area. Funds for them to be split between Council and the federal government. These professionals would assist the medical staff coming under the Indian Affairs Branch and were to be the forerunners of a new northern health service under the Department of Health and Welfare.
This was good news.

The report of the meeting in *The News of the North* said that, despite strong differences, the meeting ended on a harmonious note[111]. There was no division in the voting along elected and appointed lines. The report noted Parker had said that everyone was striving for what was best for the north and it was only to this end there was disagreement.

Parker's speeches had been in the strongest possible terms, but they were made in his typically amusing, ironic, lively provocative style. There was no rancour or ill-will in his voice. He had achieved his objective of ensuring that the views of the northerners were forcibly conveyed to an apparently genuinely interested government. He also wanted the Canadian public to become aware of what was happening, and this had been achieved. The Council got the biggest national newspaper coverage it had ever achieved.

He had found the meeting fascinating. It had opened up a much broader view of the north to him and he had got some sense of the restrictions under which the Ottawa bureaucrats operated and how they looked upon problems. He might disagree with them but he found that they were interesting, intelligent and friendly. This was only natural because he always generated this kind of reaction from anyone he met.

FAIRCHILD 71C

Chapter 7 Notes

93. Interview with Gordon Robertson, 26 June, 1991.
94. John Hamilton, Arctic Revolution - Social Change in the Northwest the Northwest Territories, (Dundurn Press, Toronto, 1994), p 93.
94 A. Barbara Hunt, Rebels, Rascals and Royalty - The Colourful North of Laco Hunt , (Outcrop Press, Yellowknife, 1982) p163.
95. Louis Audette papers.
96. Report on Aklavik dated 1955, NWT Council background paper.
97. R.A,J. Phillips, Canada's North, p 229.
98. Report on Aklavik dated 1955, NWT Council background paper.

99. Report on Aclavikv dated 1955, NWT Council background paper.

100. Robertson interview.

101. There were no banks in the Territories in 1954 except in Yellowknife and Fort Smith. All transactions in the trading posts done by barter or credit.

102. R. Phillips, Canada's North, p 229.

103. The wording of the most important section of the treaty reads, "Indians shall cede, release, surrender and yield to the government of the Dominion of Canada all rights, titles and privileges whatsoever to the land which they and their ancestors have always regarded as their own. In return they have the right to pursue their usual vocations of hunting, trapping,and fishing throughout the tract surrendered, subject to such regulations as may be from time to time be made by the government of the country......and saving and excepting such tracts as may be required or taken up from time to time for settlement, mining, lumbering, trading or other reasons." Richard Furnie, "Treaty Time at Fort Rae," *Beaver* magazine Summer 1975. "The Indians saw the treaty as a way to retain their customs and to govern themselves in the future." Thomas Berger, Northern Frontier, Northern Homeland, p 213. *Note. There were no reserves in the NWT except at Hay River.*

104. James Houston, an Ontario artist, author and northern service officer, first encountered Inuit carvings in 1948 at Port Harrison in Northern Quebec. In 1950, with the help of the Canadian Handicrafts Guild, he set up an Inuit Art Centre at Cape Dorset on Baffin Island. Here he introduced Japanese print making and soapstone carving to the local Inuit. This spread throughout the Arctic Inuit communities. NWT Commisioner Bent Sivertz paid for him to go to Japan to study Japanese woodcuts

Charles Gimpel, an English art dealer and photographer played a major role in promoting Inuit art. He visited the Artic in the fifties and sixties buying art and then selling it in his London, Zurich and New York Galleries. He considered the best of Inuit art as comparable to the best art being made elsewhere in the world.

Northwest Assembly booklet November 1979 p 3, Maria Tippett, Between Two Cultures - A Photographer (*Charles Gimpel) among the Inuit*, (Viking, Toronto, 1994)

105. *Calgary Herald,* January 1955.

106. Gordon Robertson's address to NWT Council, 17 January 1955, Audette's papers

107. Interview with Robertson

108. *Ottawa Citizen, Globe and Mail, Canadain Press, Edmonton Journal, Calgary Albertan, Vancouver Province.*

109. A study on Northern transportation by C. Herbert, 1953, recommended no reduction be made for northern transportation rates. Audette's papers.
110. White trappers and hunters living in the bush in the twenties were given the same rights as the natives.
111. <u>News of the North</u>, 4 February 1955.

Gordon Robertson
(Courtesy of Gordon Robertson)

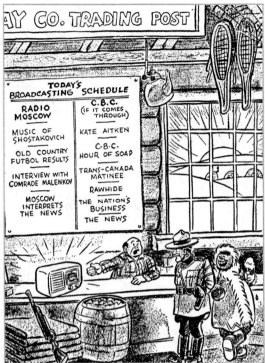

"If It Wasn't For Radio Moscow We'd Never Have Known About All The Starvation In The South"

Left
Cartoon from the 'Ottawa Citizen' on USSR broadcasts to the Canadian North
(Ottawa Citizen)

Below
Laying the Yellowknife Hospital Cornerstone, 28 July, 1947.
(L - R) Sandy Scott, Alan Lambert, Governor General Alexander, Frank Cunningham, John Parker. (Courtesy of Claire Parker)

Left
Yellowknife General Hospital opened 1948, facing Frame Lake
(Courtesy of Claire Parker)

NWT Council Meeting in the Railway Committee Room, Parliament Buildings.
January 1955   (L to R) J. Goodall, L. Nicholson, R. Porrit, Jen Boucher, C. Drury,
Gordon Robertson (Chairman), F. Carmichael, L. Audette, John Parker (standing),
F. Cunningham   (Courtesy of Claire Parker)

NWT Mace Presentation, Government House, Ottawa, January, 1955
Commissioner reding the citation before Govenor General Vincent Massey with
Council members and Lionel Massey looking on.   (Courtesy of Claire Parker)

Chapter 8
Worrying Northern Problems

The next meeting of the NWT council was held in Fort Smith in September 1955. Robertson, in his opening address, said action had been taken on the high northern transportation costs. Substantial reductions were to be made to the Northern and Yellowknife Transportation Company charges and discussions were being held with Canadian Pacific Airlines concerning their air freight and passenger charges from Edmonton to Yellowknife.

The proposal to set up a ferry service from Hay River to Yellowknife was being considered as one of a number of ways of improving northern transportation. Discussions about upgrading and extending NWT roads had occurred in the House of Commons. Mr. Lesage, the minister, had been in contact with Cominco regarding the construction of a railroad from Peace River, Alberta to their Pine Point property via Hay River. It appeared that the discoveries there were the greatest known ore body of lead and zinc in the world and they seemed to warrant the construction by government of the railroad. The cost was expected to be about $50 million and the project would need long and careful consideration.

Robertson then turned to less encouraging news, namely a recent disturbing report, sent to all members, concerning the barren lands caribou. Dr. John Kelsall of the Canadian Wildlife Service had just completed a survey of the Mackenzie caribou herds and Alan Loughrey had covered the Keewatin area. Both men had produced reports of their findings.

The great caribou herds of the Canadian north are one of the wonders of the natural world. The four major herds and their calving grounds were the Bluenose of Bluenose Lake, north of Great Bear Lake; the Bathurst of Bathurst Inlet on the central Arctic coast; the Beverly at Beverly Lake on the Thelon River; and the Kaminuriak at Kaminuriak Lake in the eastern barren lands. The Beverly and Kaminuriak herds came south into northern Saskatchewan and Manitoba in the winter. For centuries they have provided northern Aboriginals with food, clothing, and shelter. In fact, without these animals, there probably wouldn't have been a northern Native history. The earliest explorers marvelled at the enormous herds moving past them for hours on end, their hooves clicking mysteriously.

It was known the herds moved to winter ranges in the autumn, and then in the following March or April would start their long journey north back to their calving grounds. Caribou can move very fast, about forty miles in a day and hundreds of miles in a two-month period. Spring migrations begin when daylight and temperatures are increasing and the snow is melting, thereby creating bare lakes which make for ease of movement. There are no insects, and sedge and lichens are increasingly available under the melting snow. The pregnant cows lead, followed by the young animals and males. They move in endless single files and, sometimes, where the terrain is open, in wide columns. Leadership changes constantly and direction is uncannily direct. Sometimes they pass through the last winter storms, protected by their long body hair which is buoyant in water and always warm even in the coldest of weather.[112]

Early calculations of their numbers were inaccurate and far too high.[113] The first survey was conducted from 1924 to 1926. From 1948 to 1950, Dr. A. Banfield of the Canadian Wildlife Service carried out the first aerial survey in response to United Nations criticisms that Canada was neglecting its caribou. The migration patterns of the herds were established for the first time and the population of NWT caribou was estimated at 668,000. This was considered adequate to the needs of Native hunters and their families provided strict hunting regulations were enforced. Hunting was limited to Natives and a few whites only and there was to be no selling of caribou meat. These rules were in force at the time of the council meeting in late 1955.

In the years following 1950, reports were received of caribou scarcity. It was thought the reason might be that herds had changed their migration routes for some inexplicable reason. There were also reports of wolf attacks on herds and of wasteful hunting practices.[114] An experimental poisoning programme for wolves was initiated in 1951.[115] Kelsall conducted a further aerial survey using more sophisticated sampling methods in 1955. This revealed a sharp drop in the population to 279,000. By modern standards, Kelsall's survey is not considered too accurate. However, herd populations were definitely down. With no caribou, remote Native bands, especially the barren lands Inuit, faced starvation.[116]

The reasons for the decline in the herds were difficult to pinpoint. The 1955 Kelsall report considered human hunting (for eating and feeding dog teams), weather, predation, and accidents, in that order of importance, as the primary cause of the caribou decline. After much discussion, council agreed there should be further study of the problem, that action should be taken to reduce the wolf population, and that more education and surveillance of white and Native hunters be instituted. More coordination of effort between federal and provincial agencies was needed. This was going to present many difficulties bearing in mind the size of the Territories, its terrain, and weather.

The task was also complicated by the fact that every man in the Territories considered himself to be an expert on caribou and Kelsall would be obliged to sit through council meetings without being asked a single question and would have to listen to all sorts of misrepresentations of his reports. Although Kelsall said that this was to change when Commissioner Nicholson was appointed to the body

Council also considered many bills of an administrative nature before adjournment. Little discussion was held regarding Native problems such as education and healthcare, although it was known action was being taken by the bureaucrats.

In November 1955, Parker went to Edmonton to present a brief on behalf of the city of Yellowknife to the Gordon Commission on Canada's Economic Prospects. Firstly, he pointed to Yellowknife's economic dependence on gold production. The average price of gold was $35 an ounce, compared to $39 before the Second World War. It was difficult to operate mines at a profit at these prices and the smaller marginal mines had ceased operation.

Once again he took up the cause of better and cheaper ground communication with the south. Practically no roads had been built in the Territories in the past five years. There was only communication by steamers and barges in the short summer and air transport year-round, cut back in the spring thaw and the fall freeze-up.[117] A year-round highway was recommended from Alberta to Hay River and thence to Yellowknife with connecting car ferries at Fort Providence and Edzo in the summer and ice roads in the winter. The exorbitant charges of the Northern Transportation Company, a subsidiary of the Crown-owned Eldorado Mining and Refining Co., was mentioned in great detail. The envisaged railway from Grimshaw to Hay River and Pine Point would obviously greatly improve northern land communications. Such a railway, Parker suggested, would lead to cheaper air-freight services from the northern rail terminal to Yellowknife.

Strong dissatisfaction was expressed with northern air services. CPA had a monopoly on flying into Yellowknife. It operated much larger aircraft than other northern airlines. There was no competition to bring down prices. A CPA DC3 flew into Yellowknife daily from Fort McMurray via Fort Smith. This aircraft carried twenty-five passengers and had an air freight compartment. There appeared to be a reluctance on the part of the Air Transport Board to approve more aircraft for the north. "We are not happy with Canadian air policies — every decision made by the Air Transport Board in recent years has cost us money," stated Parker to the Gordon Commission. It was contended that air passenger and air freight charges, although just reduced, were still too high. They contributed to the high cost of living in the north which was a burden on the average person not in receipt of the generous northern allowances paid by government and the larger corporations.

The NWT council next met in January 1956 in Ottawa. Governor General Massey presented it with a carved mace made by Inuit craftsmen using a narwhal tusk, Native copper, and whalebone. After this pleasing ceremony, Commissioner Robertson reported on his own brief to the Gordon Royal Commission. What he said was very much in line with John Parker's thinking.

Roberston had stressed the great potential for new major mineral, gas, and oil discoveries in the NWT, although prospecting and exploration was being impeded by costly transportation. At the same time, more economic development was needed because of the precarious economic state of the northern Native population. This was being exacerbated by population increases, the poor condition of the fur trade, and the declining caribou herds. Relief payments in the north were increasing; a sad commentary on the life of northern Natives in contrast to the general prosperity in the south. He added "the only effective policy is one that will fit these people into wage earning activities in an expanding economy."

Roberston had made three suggestions for solving the northern transportation problems: road building into resource areas, a network of commercial air services, and the construction of a railway to Great Slave Lake.

Parker heartily agreed that there was a great future in the north. He recognised the urgent crisis in Native education, Native healthcare, and Native housing, although he felt that present problems deserved as much attention as long-term proposals. With the need for roads, improved air service, and the construction of a railway, he agreed. These were ideas that he had covered in his own brief to the Gordon Commission. However, he didn't want to see a huge wasteful bureaucracy built up in the north. Being a Conservative, he didn't support interference in the economy — the success of Yellowknife had been largely due to private initiative. Yet he agreed that the federal government must provide funds for some capital projects until the area reached provincial status and had the economic base to look after itself. Canada was doing well, exports were up, the national debt was low, so the federal government could afford to help the Territories.

After reporting on the progress of the construction of the new town near Aklavik, Robertson turned to the plight of the caribou. He said an intergovernmental advisory committee on the caribou consisting of experts from Manitoba, Saskatchewan, Alberta, the NWT administration, and the Canadian Wildlife Service had been set up. Bounty payments were still available to wolf hunters and the wolf poisoning programme was being intensified. With the latter policy, Parker was in disagreement, believing it to be dangerous and ineffective. He supported $25 bounties for hunters because it was a way of augmenting their income. By contrast, Kelsall later reported that, "bounty payments were not an effective way to reduce the wolf population, but poisoning was. It did lead to the death of other animals but only in a minimal way. 1,700 wolves were killed per year from 1953 to 1959. The programme was stopped in 1962," Later bounty hunting and trapping were stopped. The wolves were left alone and nature was allowed to take its course.

A major job for council at this meeting was to review all NWT ordinances going back to 1898. That done, Parker and Carmichael proposed a price support system for furs to enable trappers to make a bare living. There had been a 40 per cent drop in fur prices since 1937, most of it in recent years. Yet the Canadian economy continued to boom. Almost 50 per cent of the 16,000 NWT inhabitants depended upon trapping for all or part of their income. Carmichael said floor prices were provided for agricultural products yet the trappers were forgotten. Furs should be sold to a pool for set prices per type of fur, with the prices being raised and lowered as market conditions fluctuated.

Parker added that if this could not be done, then a crash programme must be initiated to stimulate northern economic conditions. Robertson agreed the situation was serious and deplorable, especially when the rest of the country was booming. His advisers, however, had told him that floor prices for furs would be too difficult and costly to administer.

Parker also supported Carmichael on another issue, this one very controversial. Carmichael charged that government employees responsible for Native affairs in the Aklavik region were unfit for their jobs. He said relief rations provided for destitute Natives were niggardly and should be doubled. These agents were not interested in the problems of the Native Indians or the Inuit; they were more interested in keeping their jobs.[118]

The regulations for the relief vouchers then were vague and out-of-date. Natives would go to the government agent or Mountie and ask for help. A voucher for any amount was most welcome to them and they were very thankful for anything. The agent might give them a voucher, say for $10, to take to the HBC post. Often, he hadn't taken the trouble to find out what the living conditions of the recipients were like. There were funds available for such eventualities. Some of the agents were probably of the old school and went strictly by the book.

Cunningham was highly upset by these remarks: "Carmichael is slandering a class of civil servant with a keen sense of duty and obligation." He said the Northern Affairs Department was studying the rations provided for unemployed and sick Natives and would increase them if necessary. Carmichael retorted that "everything seemed to be under investigation." Parker supported Carmichael by saying that officers could be more flexible in their handling of relief vouchers. He pointed out that half-starved Native school children were sickly and unable to learn. Perhaps he had read the report in *The News of the World* of 29 June 1955 of a speech made by Merv Hardie, the Yellowknife MP. "I am telling you that the relief the Native gets from the Department of Indian Affairs is not worth the powder to blow it to Hades. These people are interested in working and making a living if they are provided with work. There is no work in this part of the country, even if they have received training." Parker had always held that it was the white man who had attracted the Natives to built-up centres, so he had some responsibility to educate them, help them get work, and provide them with relief if necessary.

In response, Robertson observed that "the provision of rations was a most serious difficulty in the administration of the Territories. If it was too luxurious it might encourage Natives to remain unemployed. Some may not work if they can get relief sufficient to maintain even a minimum standard of existence." As to the suggestion that relief rations be doubled, he described the idea as "fantastic." However, he agreed there probably should be an increase.

The conditions of the barren lands Inuit, living south of Padliuk, 100 miles west from the shores of Hudson Bay, were particularly bad. These Natives, because of their location, couldn't hunt seals in the winter so relied on caribou which were scarce in that season. A few of these people were dismissed as "post loungers" by the whites, but staying close to a post was probably better than trying to eke out a sparse existence in the bush, since the HBC would never turn away someone close to starvation.[119]

One problem was that there was no-one elected to council from the Keewatin region who could tell what conditions were like there. However, six northern service officers had been appointed to work with the barren lands Inuit in 1954 and keep track of them.[120]

There seemed to be a difference of opinion among council members and MPs about how the Natives were adjusting to the new circumstances caused by the onset of white culture. Some council members even advocated that the Inuit be kept away from DEW line installations. This was something that Parker strongly opposed.

The conflicts and confusion among the men on the council is hardly surprising, since they were dealing with a most difficult and complex problem, much more difficult than their southern counterparts had to face. This was human engineering on a vast scale. One can sympathize with the bureaucrats. They were being asked to do so much and weren't sure what they were dealing with and what the consequences of their actions would be. They needed as much advice as possible from people on the spot and not just from their own field employees, who often didn't remain in the north very long. In retrospect, what was lacking was a Native voice. Certainly the elected members of council served as a very useful sounding board, and no doubt the appointed members appreciated this.

While Parker was in Ottawa for the meeting, he was diverted from the knotty problems under discussion when he received a call to meet John Diefenbaker, the Conservative leader of the opposition. John and Claire Parker had already met and been entertained by Diefenbaker several times. They found him and his wife Olive to be unfailingly friendly. The two men had similar personalities — both were good speakers with a flair for the unexpected and both were full of fun. On this occasion John suspected that Dief had something momentous in mind, something to do with the general election which the Liberals, who had won the last election in August 1953, could call at any time.

The Liberals at that point seemed to be running out of steam. They had been in power for twenty-two years and, while they were still governing soundly, there was a feeling in the country that perhaps a change was needed. St Laurent was still popular but his chief lieutenant, C.D. Howe, was becoming hated for his dictatorial ways. The House was at that moment in the middle of a debate to force through a bill to construct a natural-gas pipeline across the country.

The Conservative party, on the other hand, were showing signs of regeneration. "Dief" was making his mark with his populist outbursts. He was a good stump speaker with a flamboyant manner. Behind him he had some good men who had been harassing the government relentlessly in debate, men such as Davie Fulton and Howard Green from BC, Doug Harkness from Alberta, Alvin Hamilton from Saskatchewan, Walter Dinsdale from Manitoba, and George Hees and Donald Fleming from Toronto.

When John Parker arrived at the opposition leader's office, he was met with a broad smile from this obviously strong personality. The niceties completed, Diefenbaker came right out and asked him to run as the Conservative candidate for the Mackenzie riding against Merv Hardie in the anticipated election.

This was the critical decision of John's life. Diefenbaker added that Erik Neilsen, another lawyer, would run in the Yukon, and the two of them would make a very strong team for the north. He, Dief, was interested in the north and knew of its promise, and Doug Harkness, one of his chief lieutenants, was very knowledgeable about its problems. Indeed, it was during that election that Diefenbaker coined the theme "Roads to Resources." He may have borrowed it from Robertson's speech to the NWT council in January 1956, in which he said "the federal government should adopt a program of building development roads into mineral or other resources areas."

Parker replied that he would think about this proposition. Back home, he discussed the matter with his wife. Many other people had suggested that he should run, so he was under a lot of pressure. He knew he could win the nomination and he had enjoyed his work on council and felt that he had done a good job. There was little doubt that he could do a similar job in Ottawa and, with some luck, make a name for himself. On the other hand, he felt he could do as much for the north on council as he could as a backbencher in the House. Also, he had to support his wife and children. He had no partner to keep his law practice going, the salary of an MP was not that high, and he would have the expense of supporting two households.

The thought of living alone in Ottawa and spending most his time there was not a happy one. He would be separated from his children at an important period in their young lives. As it was, he was kept so busy with his practice, his council duties, and his activities with the Yellowknife Board of Trade and other organisations, that he saw little enough of them.

There was also the high cost of running the campaign in the largest riding in the country. Erik Neilsen, being a wartime pilot, had his own aircraft and wouldn't have as much territory to cover.

The Liberals also seemed to have a firm hold on the constituency. The critical

Native Indian vote would not go in his favour. At that time, the Inuit, who had proven to be good supporters, did not have the federal franchise.[121] Merv Hardie was a likeable man who had plenty of support, although he had not created as much interest as Parker.

After much soul-searching, John decided not to run and wrote to Diefenbaker accordingly.

Before long, he was once more caught up in the demands of his daily life, which did not always run as smoothly as expected. Like everyone else who worked in the north and did so much flying, Parker had his share of stories about aircraft adventures and near-misses. A trip that he took at about this time was one of them.

The morning after the 1956 annual RCMP ball in Yellowknife, Parker and several others took off in a Wardair Otter to attend to some judicial business in Hay River and Fort Smith. Six Mounties went with them, returning to their stations after the previous night's festivities. Everyone was travelling light with no sleeping bags or extra clothes. It was a fine clear day with the temperature at about 30 below zero.

The flight was proceeding smoothly when suddenly the engine started to make alarming noises, as if a rifle had been fired. Then it sounded as if a bucket of bolts were being shaken about vigorously. The engine cut out and smoke began to pour into the cabin. At this stage, the aircraft was at about 3,000 feet. Paul Hagedon, an ex-Luftwaffe fighter pilot and a very careful and methodical flier, calmly called to them that he was going to attempt a landing. He quickly picked out a suitable lake and skilfully and smoothly brought the stricken aircraft down onto its frozen surface. One advantage of flying around Yellowknife was that you were rarely out of the sight of water.

Hagedon sent out a distress signal over the radio just before touching down and it was almost certain that the message would be picked up by either the charter company or an army signal station, since the bush-plane wavelength was monitored without interruption. Also a flight plan had been filed before take-off, so even without the distress signal, alarm bells would ring within an hour or so, the time it would normally take for the plane to reach Hay River. The advantage of the radio signal was that it would much reduce the search area.

On landing, everyone evacuated the plane as quickly as possible in case of fire. The large lake that they were on was south of Edzo. The area had been burnt by a forest fire, so there was an abundance of smaller dead trees lying around. A young Mountie, who obviously hadn't had much wilderness training, tried to cut a frozen tree but broke the only axe. The survivors then had to struggle to gather some small dead trees in order to start a fire. Parker, who had some experience living in the bush, selected a spot on the beach to start it. It was a nice open space well away from the undergrowth — they didn't want to start a muskeg fire. Also the smoke from a fire in this place could be seen at a much greater distance from the air. They soon got a huge fire going, and a plume of smoke, enlarged through vapourisation, rose slowly upwards.

Parker knew that one could survive in the bush in such circumstances for a long time if one didn't panic. Water is abundant and animals and birds can be snared with wire or shot if one has a rifle. The party took inventory of what they had and it wasn't too promising. It amounted to one large chocolate bar, a bottle of whisky, and a few sleeping bags. They had no rifle or fishing gear. Parker vowed that this was an oversight he would never repeat. Ernie Boffa would never have made a trip, no matter how short, without proper survival equipment, for he knew how very unforgiving the north could be. In future, John Parker always asked the pilot what equipment he had aboard.

Court clerk Tingley, who was in the party and who had done survival training, took charge. The sleeping bags were attached to poles and provided a windbreak near the fire. Everyone was in good spirits, confident that they would soon be rescued. But after two hours clouds started to roll in, gradually filling the sky. They were low, an estimated 200 feet, thus making it more difficult for a rescue plane to spot them. The party stoked the fire furiously to give more height to the smoke and get it through the clouds. Three watches were established: one sleeping, and two awake to collect wood and attend to the fire.

The days at that season were short and darkness would soon descend. As dusk was just fading, they heard the sound of a distant aircraft, and their mounting tension began to drain away. They still couldn't see the plane, but, miraculously, its sound didn't fade. It seemed to be circling, and then they heard it flying nearby at much lower altitude. They assumed that it had spotted them through the clouds and was trying to reassure them before returning to Yellowknife to come back in the morning. Then it suddenly burst through the clouds, landed easily, and taxied over the ice towards them. Don Braun, the chief pilot for Wardair, was their rescuer. The plane was a four-passenger De Havilland Beaver, so the whole party couldn't be retrieved in one flight. At their insistence, the RCMP were left behind for the second trip, so Parker was one of the lucky ones on the first flight.

Normally these aircraft didn't operate in the dark but, in this emergency, everyone was evacuated that night. This was fortunate because the temperature dropped to 56 below. What's more, the fire burnt its way through the ice-cap, dropping with a last hiss into the water below. Parker had been wrong in assuming that they had built it safely on the beach. Luckily, no-one got wet, and even more luckily it was a moonlit night and the clouds began to clear, so that Braun had no problem in mounting his second rescue flight. The damaged Otter was rescued later after the engine had been repaired on-site. A blown cylinder head and an ejected spark plug were the cause of all the excitement.

This was not Parker's only close shave in the course of his professional duties. Another time he was flying with "Rowdy" Rutherford, an ex RCAF fighter pilot, from Aklavik to Fort Norman, a distance of about 500 miles. Normally pilots followed the Mackenzie River for safety, which added about 100 miles to the trip, but Rowdy decided to take the direct route. Unfortunately they ran into a heavy snow storm and visibility was reduced to about 100 feet, so they quickly lost their way. Rowdy decided to drop down and find a lake, flying as low as he dared.

They located a small stream with low hills on either side of it, and decided to follow it to the west. This, they later found out, was the Rabbit Skin River. It had no straight stretches and was really a succession of hair-pin bends. Weaving left and right at 100 mph in a blinding snowstorm, with cliffs flashing by outside at a great rate, was distinctly hair-raising for John. Rowdy was in his element, reminded of his wartime experiences.

He was heading in the right direction because the plane suddenly shot out over the broad Mackenzie and everybody could relax. A few months later he and a passenger, a geologist, were less fortunate when they were tragically lost over Baffin Island. The plane and a note were only found fifteen years later.

On another occasion, in the middle of winter, Parker was flying from Fort Liard down the Liard River on the edge of Mackenzie Mountains to Fort Simpson. It was an extremely cold day and halfway down the river the engine began to cut out. This had nothing to do with the switch from one tank to the other, since the engine subsequently stopped completely. The carburetor had iced up and the pilot decided to descend to where the air was warmer in the hope that the ice would thaw.

Their situation was dangerous as they were in mountainous country without any lakes. They couldn't land on the frozen surface of the Liard River because it was covered with large ice blocks. The pilot dropped down as low as possible over the river to search out for level patches of ice or a sandbar. Unfortunately, there didn't seem to be any in sight and the passengers, the pilot, and the engineer prepared for the worst. When they were about twenty feet above the river and gently floating down at much reduced speed, the engine suddenly started to splutter and then, wonders of wonders, it fired up and kept a steady beat. They waited with bated breath for more trouble but none came, and they proceeded safely on, flying low over the river in the warmer air, to their destination.

Thus spared, John Parker was able to attend the eleventh session of the Northwest Territories council in as yet unnamed Inuvik on 23 August 1956. This was the first time the council had met north of the Arctic Circle; at last Canada was taking its northern territories seriously. In the words of Gordon Robertson in his opening address to council, "The council meeting this far north is a testament of faith for the future of the north. It demonstrates a conviction that the present economic problems of the area, serious as they are, can be overcome and an active future achieved.[122]

The final decision to move Aklavik to a nearby safer site had been announced by Minister Lesage in October 1954. C.L. Merritt, a geographer and veteran of northern exploration who worked for the Department of Northern Affairs, had carried out the search for prospective sites near Aklavik from a small Bell helicopter. On the current project, he had to coordinate the activities of all the other departments involved: the

National Research Council, Mines and Technical Surveys, Public Works, Transport, and National Health and Welfare.[123]

During the summer of 1955 a jetty had been hastily built at the new chosen site, seventy miles north of Aklavik. Trucks, tractors, bulldozers, cranes, steam drills, pile drivers, and loads of building materials were barged up the Mackenzie River and unloaded there. Thousands of wooden piles were towed north in log booms, and hundreds of workers poured in. The whole enterprise was like a large military exercise. A great deal of Canadian expertise, economic activity, and money went into the project, the likes of which had not been seen in the north since the wartime Canol project or the building of the new Yellowknife townsite in 1946. No other country had built a modern city from scratch this far north before, not even the Russians. Little was known about construction on the Arctic permafrost and problems had to be overcome on a trial and error basis.

The town was planned to house 1,300 people with a possible increase to 5,000. Its site was just inside the treeline atop permafrost 900 feet deep. To prevent heaving and buckling, larger structures were built on a mass of wooden piles driven deep into the permafrost. The piles protruded four foot above the ground. They were so close together that they stuck out like the columns of some ancient Egyptian temple. Buildings had to be this high above ground so that the floor heat would not melt the permafrost beneath. Smaller houses were put on gravel mounds.

The Inuit and Loucheux Indians must have been dumbfounded at all this construction and activity. The buildings were not particularly attractive and the water and sewage systems had to be put inside an above-ground insulated wooden structure called a utilidor. Raised, gravel grid roads were quickly built and a runway, able to take larger aircraft, was to be laid over the next few years about three miles from the town. In the interim, a small airstrip was quickly commissioned.

To encourage Aklavikians to move, the government offered them the price of their houses against a new place in Inuvik. The locals were even threatened that government services would be withdrawn if they didn't move. This was like waving a red flag at a bull; very few accepted the offer or moved. Aklavik continued to be a trapping centre. In fact, over time its population increased and a bigger school was needed. However, Inuvik did become the new centre of government and health services.

An organisation to help Natives adjust to modern city life was planned and a vocational training centre to encourage Natives to become building tradesmen or helpers was instituted. Contractors were urged to use as much local labour as possible. Some Natives took advantage of this programme and got work.

Parker had long been sceptical about the Inuvik project. Like most northerners then he basically opposed it as impractical and costly. Moreover, he liked Aklavik and thought it worked well. The whites, the Métis, the Indians, and the Inuit cooperated together and air communications were reasonably good. He was worried that Inuvik would become an expensive civil service haven, which indeed it did. However, it had been planned long before he had been elected to council, so there was nothing much he could do about it.

According to Parker, the initial estimate was $1.5 million to move all the buildings. However, it was soon discovered that government buildings in Aklavik could not be moved or were not worth moving or had to be dismantled, thus greatly increasing costs. The Roman Catholic and Anglican churches, which had a substantial investment in Aklavik and whose bishops had the ear of the minister, had to be placated. They wanted new buildings on the Inuvik site. A new cost estimate had to be made.

During the 1956 January council meeting in Ottawa, Parker met the deputy minister of finance about an unrelated matter. He was asked what he thought of the new estimate of $40 million to carry out the move. He replied that it would not be nearly enough. The DM merely laughed. At this point, it was not known that all the buildings on the new site would have to be built well off the ground and a that utilidor would have to be put in. Later the estimate was raised to $100 million. Parker recalled that about ten years later he stopped keeping track of the project. By then, spending had got completely out of hand and had risen to $300 million. What really pushed the cost sky-high was the airport runway.

But hopes were still high when the council had its historic meeting at the new site in August 1956. Many journalists were brought in for a briefing and an inspection of the new site. Parker said Cunningham gave a comprehensive description of the project and described, in glowing terms, all the facilities that the new town would have.

He pointed out that small houses would be built for very low rentals for the Natives. However, these houses would not be on the utilidor system and therefore would have no water or plumbing. In time, the delta Natives did congregate at Inuvik. The rents on the houses were far too high for them and a nasty slum of tents and lean-tos sprang up and Inuvik was no different from other northern communities — so much for the plans to have a wonderful new modern far northern community. These developments were not foreseen in August 1956. However, Parker did complain bitterly at the council meeting about Native housing not being on the utilidor system. A newspaperman described it as "an organised slum."

Indeed, Native issues featured prominently during the session. Parker introduced a motion that Natives, both Indian and Inuit, in the Territories be allowed the same privileges for purchasing liquor and beer as whites. He urged no half measures. All the arguments in support of this proposal were cited, and a vigorous debate ensued.

Porritt felt that a more cautious approach should be taken. He suggested that a commission be set up to study the proposal. Natives, in his opinion, did not understand how to handle liquor and needed time to learn more. Other opponents of the move in council noted that in Aklavik Native children were coming to school "under the influence."[124] "Already we are starting to see a drop in the Native characteristic of hardy independence and a rise in drunkenness, petty thievery and even some prostitution."[125]

The "pro" members reiterated that the Natives must be given the same rights as all other Canadians. They were given the right to vote so why shouldn't they be given the right to purchase liquor. They were getting it anyway. As to the problem of drunkenness, good counselling services would help them.

Finally the motion was voted on and it was agreed that legislation and regulations be prepared to give NWT Natives this right. Amendments would have to be made to the Indian Act, and this could take several years. It was agreed that it would be unfair to allow this concession to the Inuit and not to the Indians.

On another matter, Native Indian bands and government biologists had been complaining that fish stocks in Great Slave Lake seemed to be diminishing. Lake trout were not as prevalent as they once were. It appeared there might be overfishing by the Slave Lake fishing companies. Council proposed that a study be undertaken to investigate the problem, and if necessary, regulations drawn up to limit commercial fishing of certain species. At about this time, too, a study was being conducted into the effects on Yellowknife of arsenic fall-out from the smokestacks of the Con and Giant refineries. Since 1950, residents had been warned every spring that standing pools of water left after the freeze-up could be contaminated with arsenic. However, it was only in 1960, after studies had shown that deposits were indeed above safety levels, that regulations were passed to enforce mines to install scrubbers.

Among other things, council was told that relief rations for Natives had been increased. This was a positive step, but there was still a long way to go. Parker was all too aware of this need; on 30 November 1956, long after the council session had ended, he requested that a social worker be hired for Yellowknife as soon as possible. The need for this appointment was suggested all too vividly soon afterwards in a report in The *News of the North* of 4 January 1957 on living conditions in Yellowknife.

A group of young people had decided to call themselves "Santa's Helpers" and bring Christmas cheer to the underprivileged children of Yellowknife. All classes, white, Métis, and Native were visited. The "Helpers" were shocked at the living conditions they found, describing them as "appalling." Showing a lot of initiative, they wrote a report on their observations. Among other things, children were not properly dressed; slops lay about on the ice; wood piles were inadequate; and the interiors of the relatively new houses were extremely untidy and dirty. In some cases the men were only part-time workers and in others they had no work at all, so their families were in very bad circumstances. The helpers felt that many recipients believed that society owed them a living. They concluded by reiterating Parker's plea for a case worker to be hired by the town. This officer should by suggestion, persuasion, and, if necessary, by legal means, bring about change in the living conditions of the people concerned.

At root, the problem was largely one of the urbanisation of hitherto nomadic Native hunters. They were not used to spending time in one place and leading a sedentary life. If a campsite got dirty they would move on. They didn't understand banking, having to pay utilities bills, and modern hygienic methods. They needed help in making the huge adjustments that confronted them. In retrospect, McCall, the government game warden, felt that government administrators could have been more imaginative and flexible in dealing with these problems.

Be that as it may, from this time on these problems started to be addressed, as the Northern Affairs Branch expanded and more attention was paid to the north. Also influential in this regard was the advice of the elected council members. Social and case workers were hired in the next few years, and, as we shall see, a great deal was achieved.

INUVIK WOODEN CABIN

Chapter 8 Notes

112. John P. Kelsall, <u>The Caribou</u> (Department of Indian Affairs and Northern Development, Canadian Wildlife Service, Ottawa, 1968) p 100.
113. <u>People and Caribou</u> (Government of NWT, 1989) p 95.
114. Joe Robertson, <u>From Prairie to Tundra</u> (J Robertson p 359. Robertson, a provincial wildlife officer, describes coming upon 450 caribou carcasses at the narrows of Duck Lake in Northern Manitoba in 1955. He had found such waste in previous years, but this was the worst. Frank McCall says he heard the Cree would cut the tongues out for a delicacy and leave the carcass. In 1954, Dr. A. Banfield reported finding 113 carcasses in the wake of a large herd near Ghost Lake, NWT. An Indian said that they were being left to be a frozen cache for use in winter.
115. A wolf poisoning programme was recently reintroduced in the Yukon and Northern BC. A new idea is to capture wolfpacks by air and inject the females to make them infertile. The public will now not accept wolf poisoning.
116. The caribou population of NWT was 805,000 in 1989, <u>People and caribou</u> p126. Now it is known that if calves were born on the migration they were picked off by wolves up to the time they could outrun them which was about two or three weeks after birth. Even bears could do this so this is a critical time in the migration.
117. The rough winter road from Hay River to Yellowknife was only opened to traffic in the fall of 1957.
118. *Edmonton Journal*, 20 January 1956.
119. Richard Harrington, <u>The Face of the Arctic</u> (Thomas Nelson, Toronto, 1952) p 244.
120. Farley Mowat, <u>People of the Deer</u> (Atlantic-Little, Brown, Boston, Mclelland and Stewart, Toronto, 1952). Mowat wrote in 1952 which created a sensation because of the plight from starvation of the Barren Lands Inuit. His book was full of errors and strongly criticised by A.E. Porsild, a Canadian government biologist in the *Beaver*, June 1952 p 47. Richard Harrington photographed the starvation and terrible conditions of the Padluk band in his book. Parker knew Harrington well and admired his work. Parker said nothing of this situation had been reported to the NWT Council. Harrington's photographs are now regarded as Canadian treasures and his book on the Canadian north a classic. He is still alive and has finally received the recognition that eluded him all his life
121. Erik Neilson, <u>The House is not a Home</u> p 125.
122. Speech of G. Robertson to NWT Council meeting on 23 August 1956. Audette's Papers
123. Irene Ward, <u>Inuvik, Place of Man</u>, *Beaver*, Spring, 1959
124. <u>The News of the North</u>, editorial, 27 January 1956
125. L. H. Nicholson, <u>The Problem of the People</u>, *Beaver*, Spring 1959

The Beverley caribou herd moving North (Courtesy of Eaon McEwen)

Caribou herd passing a plane on a frozen NWT lake (Courtesy of Dr.J. Kelsall)

Caribou (Courtesy of Dr.J. Kelsall)

Dr. J. Kelsall with caribou (Courtesy of Dr.J. Kelsall)

Dr. J. Kelsall with white fox pelt(Courtesy of Dr.J. Kelsall)

De Havilland 'Beaver' carrying a canoe. Museum of Aviation, Ottawa (Frank Wade)

Housing construction, Inuvik. 1959
(National Archives of Canada PA 1112151)

Inuvik, 1958. note the utilidor running between the buildings above ground.
(National Archives of Canada)

The Roman Catholic Igloo Church. Inuvik, 1958   (Courtesy of Eaon McEwen)

The Alexander Mackenzie School, Inuvik, 1958   (Courtesy of Eaon McEwen)

Utilidor

Frank Wade (the author) with NWT Commissioner, Ben Sivertz (Frank Wade)

Chapter 9
More Court Work

In May 1957, Parker defended a famous Inuit of the day, one George Angulalik, on a murder charge. He it was who had given evidence in the Kaotok murder case in which John Parker had earlier been involved. In his capacity as witness, he had travelled "outside" to Yellowknife, had seen white society, and had learned something about non-native ways and non-native law.

Newsweek magazine described him as "the dandy of the tundra." A handsome energetic man with a broad Inuit smile, he was known in the north as the only Inuit to have his own trading post. He had been able to make the transition from traditional Inuit ways to modern Canadian entrepreneurship in the harshest of environments, an amazing achievement. His treatment of his Inuit trappers was very considerate, and he gave them more credit than the HBC. If they had a couple of bad years he would tide them over.

For a few years, the Bay had run a trading post on Wagstaff Island at the Perry River on the Arctic coast. However, there were only about fifty Inuit families in the Queen Maude Gulf area where it was located and the post did not pay, largely because of the cost of freight transport. In 1937, instead of closing the post, the company transferred it to Angulalik.[126] He would pay off the company over a period of years, and obtain his trade goods from the HBC post at Cambridge Bay, about 100 miles across the gulf. The local trappers were to bring in their high quality furs to him, in return for goods. The furs would then be transported to Cambridge Bay for payment.

He was successful not only because of his business acumen and energy but because he could live cheaply off the land, on caribou, seals, and fish. His operating costs were therefore much lower. Eventually, he made enough money to pay off the mortgage and to purchase two 35 foot diesel-powered schooners, the Sea Otter and the Tudlik, which he operated in the short summer season.

In 1949 he opened his own satellite post at Sherman Inlet on the Adelaide Peninsula, about 200 miles to the east. His son Oakoak and Oakoak's handsome wife, Suzie, who was half-Inuit and half-white, were a great help to him. A brother also worked for him. He would use his boats to transport goods and furs to and from this post, and would also charter them to the HBC to transport goods from Cambridge Bay to their trading post on Gjoa Haven on King William Island.

Richard Harrington, the intrepid Canadian photographer and author, writes that the post at Wagstaff Island under Angulalik was well kept but hardly snug. There was a windcharger to supply electricity and power for a radio but it didn't work. There was also a wood/coal-burning stove but it was kept at low heat. Coal in the far north was very expensive, at $240 a ton and wood was not locally available. Harrington, who was there in mid-winter, noted that the base boards and the inside windows were frosted over. He wrote in his book "I never remember being colder than I ever have been during those first hours in the trading post, waiting for my supper of caribou stew." Angulalik and his wife were quite happy with the temperature. The trick to survive such conditions, as Parker well knew from his own experiences, was to avoid moving too fast so as to reduce the rate of breathing and prevent the lungs from freezing — breathing through the nose was a good idea.[127]

Angulalik had not been educated in a mission school, so didn't speak English. The same applied to his son. After he had been taken into custody and was awaiting trial, he immediately started learning the language. He was able to understand a surprising amount by the time of his hearing and later trial. Inuit syllabics he didn't know either although he had a syllabic typewriter at the post. A local Inuit at Wagstaff Island would take long-hand dictation from Angulalik in syllabic characters, and then Angulalik would type the text out. The RCMP constable from Cambridge Bay would help him update his paperwork when he visited the island. When ordering trade goods, he simply copied the labels of the desired items. Usually the HBC employee was able to decipher his wishes, despite the oddity of some of the orders; $1/_2$ dozen cheap prices, 10 lbs women's underwear, 6 ointment, capsicum compound, beware of the eyes.[128] He once ordered some umbrellas, to the amazement of Hyslop, the HBC factor. These he painted white and traded to hunters who could hide behind them when stalking seals on the ice.

The charge against him was killing a man during a New Year's Eve party when some heavy drinking had been going on. He had written a letter to the RCMP in Cambridge Bay explaining the circumstances. The letter was typed in syllabics, which, after being translated, read as follows:

"I say a few words to the police. I got scared of man and ran away from him. Since long he been go after me. How I get mad with him Otoetak. I don't want to kill him. I couldn't help it. With a knife. In a party and drinking. And I poked him. He got after me and I couldn't help it.   People. Happy amongs them. Lots of people. Lots of them. They are fighting amongs them. He caught me and I poked him. In Norman's house. I was drunk. After that for myself when he died, when I got sober I like to kill myself. I was think about my family. Got nobody to watch for them and nobody to keep them. I don't know that when he go after me. I got scared of him. I don't want to do anything bad for people. He been bothering me. He been go after me. Since a long time.
He go after me and I get scared of him. I did it.[128A]

The Cambridge Bay policeman went to Wagstaff Island with an Inuit interpreter and interviewed Angulalik. He wrote down the accused's statement in English from the words given to him by the interpreter and charged Angulalik with murder. No-one else was present.

Apparently, Otoetak had been jealous of Angulalik's success for some time. He had been especially angry when Angulalik had made his son return some goods he had taken from the post without payment. Otoetak thought Angulalik should have let him have these because the Inuit share with one another. As a result, he had been harassing Angulalik over a long period prior to the fight at the party.

The Inuit don't usually fight with fists, but they generally carry small flat knives for cutting raw seal meat or fish. In the scuffle, Angulalik had made a good-sized cut in the lower body of the deceased and part of the bowel was protruding. Otoetak had died four days after the incident. In that time, he had been fed several meals in the belief that this would be good for him; in fact, nothing could have been worse. Simple first aid would have saved him. The bowel could easily have been pushed back inside the body and a strong bandage placed over it to keep it in place. It must have become strangulated and complications and infection had set in, causing Otoetak to die. If the radio at the post had been working, medical advice could have been obtained from Cambridge Bay.

Angulalik was taken back to Cambridge Bay and kept in the lock-up. The coroner's inquest and the preliminary hearing were held at Yellowknife to ensure that they were properly and fairly conducted. In keeping with Judge Sissons's strongly held views, the actual trial was to be held at Cambridge Bay, as near the scene of the crime as possible so that the accused could be tried by a jury of peers from his neighbourhood.

The preliminary hearing was conducted by Robert Bouchard, who usually acted as Crown prosecutor. John Parker appeared for the defendant and Frank Dunne from Edmonton appeared for the Crown. The evidence of the policeman and the Inuit witnesses at the party was led. Among the latter was Molly Etegoyak, the dead man's elderly sister with a tattooed face. She didn't know her age but admitted that her children had children. Lena Otoetak, the wife of the deceased, who had been at the party, said she didn't know how many guests there had been but she was sure there were more than she had fingers on both hands. At the end of the hearing, the accused was arraigned for trial.

This was held at Cambridge Bay in May 1957. On arrival, Judge Sissons was informed that some of the prosecution witnesses had not yet arrived. The pilot of the Wardair Otter aircraft, Don Braun, offered to fly out immediately to try and pick them up off the ice. An RCMP constable accompanied him and a few of the missing witnesses were found. The prosecution requested a delay until the rest were located but Sissons insisted that the trial proceed.

The courtroom was in the RCAF Arctic Survival School. Parkas were worn over suits and gowns because of the lack of heating in the building. The room was packed, the result of Sissons's instruction to the RCMP to visit the hunting areas on the island by sled and inform everyone that the trial was about to begin. He wanted make the Inuit aware of the work of the NWT court, understand how it worked, and see that their compatriots were being fairly treated. Most of the evidence would be in the Inuit language so they could understand a lot of what was happening.

This experiment seems to have succeeded. Sissons writes that he had a chance to watch the faces of the attending Inuit when the evidence was being led in their own language. They were fascinated with the novel proceedings, swivelling their heads towards each speaker as they had their say. When English was being used, they would start talking among themselves quietly. Sissons did not order them to stop because he felt they were trying to help each other to understand what was taking place.[129]

Sissons also wanted an all-Inuit jury. At first, both prosecution and defence agreed. However, at the last minute, prosecutor Dunne objected on the grounds that the Inuit did not take a serious view of a man using a knife. He rejected all the Inuit members of the panel and in the end the jury was all white, being made up of men who worked at the Cambridge Bay DEW line station.

The statement which Angulalik had first made to Corporal Jones, as translated by an interpreter, was disallowed as evidence by the judge. The reason for this decision was that there was no certainty that the statement reported by the corporal was what Angulalik had actually said. Corroboration was required. The policeman had not arranged for another Inuit to be present to confirm the translation. Mistakes were always possible even by the best Inuit translators, and Sissons agreed with Parker's contention that key words prejudicial to the accused might have been mistranslated. Sissons considered that this was an instance where he should be flexible and felt that his decision was within the law. Be that as it may, this testimony was vital to the prosecution because Parker was not going to put his client on the witness stand and expose him to cross-examination.

The judge also rejected the letters that Angulalik had written to Corporal Jones and Mr. Hyslop, the HBC factor, because what had been typed was copied from what his friend had written in Inuit syllabics. Guesswork about Angulalik's typed orders for goods was acceptable but guessing what he meant in his typed letters admitting guilt to murder was not permissible in a court of law.

These rulings having been made, the first of the witnesses was called. One Inuit confirmed that two letters had been sent by Angulalik, presumably to Jones and Hyslop. He stated that home brew had been drunk at the party and that he himself had passed out. Jimmy Taipanik testified that he had seen Angulalik and Otoetak hitting each other, but didn't actually see Angulalik stab the deceased. He had met both men the following morning and Otoetak had shown him his wound. Angulalik's knife was presented to him, and he had no problem in identifying it. Then the doctor who had conducted the autopsy confirmed that the deceased had died of a strangulated bowel which could easily have been cured by simple first aid.

The evidence left no doubt that there had been a fight between the two men at the party, that Otoetak had been wounded during the fight with Angulalik, and that he had died five days later as a result of an abdominal knife wound. But Parker noted that Otoetak had started the scuffle and argued that Angulalik's response was justifiable self-defence. Moreover, Angulalik had shown remorse for his part in the fight. The jury should consider the matter an unfortunate accident at a rather boisterous party.

Dunne went over the evidence carefully, saying that there was no doubt that Angulalik had committed the act that had lead to Otoetak's death, and that he should be found guilty. He admitted that there were mitigating circumstances but these could be taken into consideration when the judge passed sentence.

In his summing up, Judge Sissons reminded the jury they must base their decision on what they had heard from the witnesses about events during the fracas between the two men. These had taken place during a wild party. They must consider whether they had heard any direct evidence that Angulalik had caused the condition which led to the death of Otoetak. On the afternoon of the second day of the trial, the jury retired and within thirty-five minutes returned with a verdict of not guilty.

At about this time, John Parker handled another rather more bizarre case, the outcome of which illustrated how careful a lawyer must be in questioning witnesses. This proved to be an instance of asking one question too many. There must always be definite reason for a question and, even then, the demeanour, intelligence, and credibility of the witness must be considered. General fishing for information can be dangerous and it is better for the questioner to keep quiet if he or she has any doubt about the wisdom of the query.

Parker's client in this case was an ebullient East European miner who stood accused of attempted murder. His innocence he protested vehemently to Parker and, although he was rather emotional, he appeared to be sincere and truthful.

He had been a boarder in a house with another miner and his wife with whom he had previously lived in a mining town in Quebec. Consequently, he knew them quite well and got along with them, especially the wife. They had come to Yellowknife and he had followed them. One thing led to another, and in the summer of 1957, he and the wife had flown to Edmonton to spend a passionate month together there. The accused had even sent some photographs of the two of them to the husband, for a joke. He told Parker that the wife had been the original instigator of the trip, although he had willingly agreed. The wife he believed to be madly in love with him.

The accusation of attempted murder arose from a series of events which had occurred during their stay in Edmonton. The husband, of course, was furious and had a good idea of what was happening. Before their departure, the husband had borrowed an oil heater from a friend, the jeweller Pollock, and set it up and used it. During their absence, he decided he didn't need it any more and returned it to its owner. One cool evening the jeweller decided to use it. Normally he would have opened the small side-door and thrown in a lighted match. However, for some reason, he opened up the top, which, to his utter surprise and dismay, he found was packed with dynamite sticks. He immediately rushed over to the husband for an explanation and the husband's thoughts instantly turned to the man who had absconded with his wife. Was this an attempt to kill him? Without further ado, he reported the facts to the police.

Finally the two lovers returned to Yellowknife; maybe the shine had gone off the romance. The wife maintained that she had been forced to leave with the lodger at gun point. He had hidden the weapon under his coat and had kept nudging her with it on the aircraft.

Parker's client was immediately arrested and charged with attempted murder. Knowing of Parker's reputation from the Angulalik case, the client asked for his legal services. Parker questioned him about whether he could produce witnesses to back up his story. Yes, there were two close friends of his in Quebec from his "old country" who would do anything for him. He had already written to them to come and support him.

These men actually drove across Canada as far as Hay River and then flew on to Yellowknife. Parker interviewed them, but they had very little useful information to offer. Besides, John soon realised that they would not make trustworthy witnesses. Independently of each other, they had both affirmed their readiness to give any evidence that was required. It seemed a shame, however, that no use could be made of them, after they had come such a long way to help their friend. Parker told them to attend the trial as observers; they were to give him their assessment of the evidence. He would first listen to the Crown's case before deciding to call defence witnesses.

The case against the accused was not completely airtight. There was no direct evidence as to who had put the dynamite in the stove. This might have been done by the wife or someone else. It was not even clear that the intention was to kill the stove owner. Nevertheless, the circumstantial evidence against the accused was strong. He had access to dynamite, lived in the house, and could easily tamper with the stove. Moreover, his romantic attachment to the wife provided a motive to get rid of the husband.

The trial was presided over by Judge Sissons. The Department of Justice sent a handsome young and inexperienced lawyer — who made quite an impression on the Yellowknife women — to prosecute. John Winter, who was active in Yellowknife civic politics and was the accountant at Con Mine, was the chairman of the jury.

The facts of the case and the background circumstances were duly revealed by the witnesses for the prosecution. Parker was able to score a minor triumph in rebutting the wife's allegation that she had been forced to leave at gunpoint. This he did by reference to the photographs of her with the accused, several of which showed her smiling.

However, the Crown's evidence was very damning and Parker felt that his client stood condemned. The only ploy he could think of in the circumstances was to call the accused to give evidence on his own behalf. This was something he avoided, particularly in murder cases, but in this instance he felt he must make an exception. It was just possible that his client might impress the jury with his strong affirmations of innocence and sow doubts in their minds. Also, the client was eager to testify, and Parker felt that he would make a good witness.

In the witness box, the client dwelled upon his passionate month-long fling in some detail, with both the jury and the public hanging on his lips. It was the wife who had begged him to go. The wife was in the courtroom for all to see, and was a good-looking woman. He had been shocked to hear about the dynamite on his return and could not account for it. Under cross-examination, he freely admitted that he had easy access to dynamite underground and could have brought it to the house without difficulty.

Crown counsel then asked the question which Parker was convinced clinched the matter for the jury. Had there been any "familiarity" between him and the landlord's wife when they had all lived together in Quebec? The response was dramatic, spontaneous, and apparently quite honest. The accused, a huge jolly fellow, roared with laughter. When he had recovered himself sufficiently, he replied that there had been no relations between him and the wife. At the time she had several other boyfriends and he was low on the list. By now even some of the jury members were smiling and the public in the gallery was laughing openly. Sissons had to bang his gavel repeatedly to restore order.

No-one contradicted this evidence and the accused was duly acquitted.

Parker was involved in another rather odd Yellowknife case which could be called the "Stolen Gold Bars Case." His involvement, however, was not as central as he might have wished. The case concerned a young Australian miner called Tony Gregson. He was a happy-go-lucky character who seemed well-educated, and was certainly athletic, handsome, gregarious, and popular. A well-paid single miner, he was never short of cash or charm, and cut quite a swath through the ladies of the town.

He worked in Yellowknife before moving to Consolidated Discovery Mine, some sixty miles to the north and only accessible by bush plane or winter Cat train. After a year or so there, he informed the mine manager that he was moving on. This was normal for single men at remote mines. They could save a lot of money in a short time, since there was nowhere to go and nothing to spend it on — provided they didn't lose it all in gambling. Also, they would become bored and want to seek greener pastures. The manager expressed his regrets and assured Gregson that a job would be waiting for him if he decided to come back. When he was collecting his last cheque, the accountant told him about a small group insurance refund and asked where he wanted it sent. Tony had no intention of giving a forwarding address and replied, "Oh, send the cheque to the Vancouver Symphony Orchestra as a contribution from me."

Everyone in camp knew that the smelted gold was moulded into bars and prepared for shipment before the plane arrived every Friday to take them to Yellowknife for onward shipment. Two bricks amounted to a week's production. All gold produced in Canada then had to be sold to the Canadian Mint in Ottawa. The bars were carefully prepared for shipment, being tightly sewn in canvas and marked with a serial number and weight. When the plane arrived, they were put in a mail sack and turned over to the aircraft captain.

The plane used on this particular trip was a Wardair Otter, piloted by Max Ward himself. On these short trips he dispensed with a flight engineer. Ward was given the mailbag containing the bars, checked them and their serial numbers, and signed for them. He then took the bag into the plane and placed it in the baggage area at the back of the aircraft. This area was situated behind the passenger seats and was quite open.

There were two passengers on the flight, Tony Gregson and the mine foreman. The *News of the North* of 9 July 1954 reported that Gregson was acting as if he were slightly intoxicated. Two stops were made on the return trip. One was a few miles south, where the mine had a woodcutters' camp, to drop off groceries, equipment, stores, and mail.[130] At the second stop, further south at a power-line work camp north of Yellowknife, Max and the foreman got out of the aircraft for a short break. Gregson decided to stay onboard.

In their absence, he went aft to the luggage area and removed two more canvas-covered bars from his bag. These were bars of lead shaped identically to the company bars. The lead had been purchased from Jock McNiven, the manager of Negus Mine. Gregson kept a small boat with an outboard motor near the mine and McNiven was told that this odd purchase was needed for the boat. Moving back to the luggage area, Gregson quickly opened the unsealed mailbag and exchanged his lead bars for the real ones which he quickly hid in his own bag. Perhaps Gregson was disturbed in the act by the return of the pilot and the other passenger, because Ward did notice that someone had moved the luggage around when he came back aboard. Be that as it may, Gregson had stolen two bars worth $55,000 — a great deal of money in those days — for $20 worth of lead in a very carefully planned and slick exchange. Simply melting the lead ingot bars without anyone else's knowledge demanded considerable organisation.

On arrival in Yellowknife, Gregson alighted from the aircraft onto a floating pontoon without his luggage. This was the usual procedure, for the pilot would unload the luggage and give it to the passengers. Gregson must have had a few anxious moments at this stage, but managed to remain calm and avoid arousing suspicion. He kept his composure even when Ward, surprised at the weight of the baggage, joked, "What have you got in here, gold bars?" Tony merely laughed and took the bag as nonchalantly as he could.

He immediately took a cab to the Negus Mine jetty where he had his boat. His plan was to boat across to Hay River, a distance of 125 miles. This was a long way but the weather on the lake was usually good in July. On arrival at Hay River he would take a bus, plane, or hitchhike south. He hadn't got very far when the engine started to misbehave, so he decided to return. It was evening by the time he got back. Either improvising or acting on a back-up plan, he telephoned Wardair and chartered a plane to Hay River. He asked that it be made ready to leave as soon as he arrived.

In the meantime, Ward had delivered the mailbag to Frenchy's Transport where it was to be kept for safe keeping over the weekend. It was too late to turn it in to the Post Office which wouldn't open until Monday. As he was doing this, he met John H. Parker, the other John Parker in Yellowknife — they were always getting each other's mail. John H. was then a consulting mining engineer, and later became the mayor of Yellowknife before crowning his distinguished career as NWT commissioner.

This Parker had never held a gold bar in his hand before and asked Ward to open the mailbag and let him lift one out. As he did so, he asked Ward how much it weighed. On being told it was forty-eight pounds, he replied that he didn't think the bar was nearly heavy enough. Ward still did not think anything was amiss, and dismissed Parker's remark with a shrug, saying "Don't be ridiculous."[131]

It was later that evening that Ward received Gregson's call for a charter aircraft to leave right away for Hay River. Ward wondered why he didn't wait for the much cheaper regular CPA flight and, thinking the request rather odd, decided to report it to the RCMP. Just as he was picking up the telephone, Gregson arrived by cab, so Ward hung up. Gregson immediately paid cash for the flight and hurried out to the waiting plane with his bag. Little did Ward realise just how eager he was to depart. As soon as he was aboard, the pilot closed the door and took off. Ward decided not to bother with the police.

On Monday morning the gold bars were taken to the Post Office by Emil Lamoureux. The postmaster soon became suspicious. Firstly, the serial numbers didn't follow sequentially from those on the previous batch of bars. Secondly, the bars were found to be substantially lighter than those he was accustomed to handling. There was also a small mistake in the spelling on the address card, "Canadian Mint" being misspelled as "Canadien Mint." He decided to radio the mine. The mine office agreed that something was dreadfully wrong and told him to cut the canvas covers and inspect the actual bars. This was done, and the truth was out. Max Ward was contacted and it became obvious what had happened. The RCMP were notified and all detachments between Hay River and Edmonton were alerted. The bus from Hay River to Peace River, which it was known Gregson had taken, was searched but he had got off before arrival in Peace River. Despite a search of the area, he had disappeared with his gold. A later country-wide search also failed to find him.

It was well known that gold bars were insured for full current value right after being smelted, and Parker wrote that the incident was regarded as something of a joke in

Yellowknife. Max Ward didn't think so. He was very bitter with Gregson, whom he had trusted, and was very distressed about the affair.

Shortly after this, an insurance company contacted Parker and asked him if he would act on its behalf. It wanted him to find out about the circumstances of the theft and advise whether there had been negligence on the part of the carriers, and, if so, whether a suit could be launched against them. He refused because both Max Ward and Emil Lamoureux were old friends and clients.

From time to time reports were received that Gregson had been seen by people from the Territories while they were away on holiday or on business, but no-one turned him in. One friend encountered him in Detroit and Tony expressed pleasure at seeing him. He suggested a drink at the Book-Cadillac Hotel in half an hour, but never turned up.

On 27 June 1957, three years later, the *News of the North* included an item that Gregson had been caught in Sydney, Australia. He had been reported as a stowaway by the captain of the SS Cornwall. Later it was revealed that he had given the police a false name. However, after routine finger-printing, the police, still on the alert for him, discovered his real name. With some smart detective work, his print was matched to his name on an Interpol listing, which stated that he was wanted in Canada for the theft of gold bars. He was locked up and the RCMP were notified.

He was extradited within a month and returned to Halifax by ship in the charge of a Canadian immigration officer. He said he could have escaped from the ship at Fiji, but had given his word and decided to return to Canada to face the music. He was met by Corporal Bill Campbell of the Yellowknife RCMP and said with his usual aplomb, "Hello Bill, nice of you to come."

On his return to Yellowknife, the Department of Justice asked Parker to prosecute the case, but he refused, since he expected to be asked to act for the defendant. The thought of carving a defence out of what he knew of the case intrigued him. However, Gregson retained Don Hagel. Maybe he thought that Parker would refuse because he was such a good friend of Max Ward.

Much to Parker's surprise, Gregson pleaded guilty and Judge Sissons sentenced him to twenty-eight months and he was paroled after eighteen months. No mention was made of the disposition of the gold and it was never recovered.

Parker was hired by the mine's insurance company to conduct a watching brief. He was to sit in court, listen to the proceedings, and inform his clients of anything that might interest them.

Parker later discovered what had happened to Gregson during his three-year absence. His first problem was to sell the gold bars without arousing suspicion. Certainly it was too dangerous to attempt this in Canada and the States. He eventually learned that Cuba would be the best place. After he arrived on the island, he cut a big chunk off one bar and had little trouble in finding a willing purchaser after a casual conversation in a bar. After a fling on the island, he returned to Nova Scotia, presumably using a false passport. Here he purchased a small boat and went into the fishing business in a small Nova Scotia fishing port. He hired a young man to help him.

One day, his landlady came to his room saying that two RCMP officers wanted to see him. Fearing the worst, he adopted his usual jovial manner and came down to talk to them. He still had one gold brick and part of another in a locked suitcase in his room upstairs. They apologised for bothering him but wanted to know something about the man who was working for him.

After this close brush with the law, he decided to sell the boat and return to Cuba. Here he went through his ill-gotten gains at a fast rate because within two years or so, he got into difficulty with the Cuban authorities and was ordered to leave. He was forced to stowaway on a ship, in Cuba and elsewhere, to get back home to Australia. There was talk that he spent, lost, or was forced to give up what was left of his gold bars and so became a penniless destitute. So much then for the colourful tale of Tony Gregson.

BUILDING AN

Chapter 9 Notes

126. R. Harrington, <u>The Face of the Arctic</u>, p174
127. R. Harrington, <u>The Face of the Arctic</u>, p183.
128. R. Harrington, <u>The Face of the Arctic</u>, p102.
128A. Jack Sissons, <u>Judge of the Far North</u>, p89.
129. Jack Sissons, <u>Judge of the Far North</u>, p89.
130. Max Ward, <u>The Max Ward Story</u>, p129.
131. Max Ward, <u>The Max Ward Story</u>, p130.

Lake filled
Mackenzie Delta
Courtesy of
Eaon McEwen

HBC buildings,
Aklavik, 1951
Courtesy of Eaon McEwen

All Saints Anglican
Cathedral Church,
Aklavik, 1951
Courtesy of Eaon McEwen

Angulalik and his wife Cook/NWT Arhives N79-032-0013

Knut Lang from Aklavik who succeeded
Frank Carmichael on the NWT Council   Courtesy of Eaon McEwen

Chapter 10
More NWT Council Work

The next meeting of the NWT council was held in Ottawa from 14 to 23 January 1957. The commissioner, in his opening speech, covered many of the problems previously discussed, including education, the declining caribou herds, the poor fur market and, of course, the perennial liquor problem — a subject that always sparked heated discussion.

For the first time, budget items were itemised in detail. Native education was the major item — $894,000 out of $2,361,000. Revenue came mainly from federal funds, plus territorial liquor sales and other receipts.

On top of this, the Department of Health and Welfare as well as the Department of Public Works were to spend $34 million in the Territories from their own budgets, for a total of $36 million to be spent by all departments. This amounted to $1,775 per person which was lower than the prevailing Canadian national average.[132]

Commissioner Robertson, in his further comments on education, noted that the Ottawa staff were working hard to phase out all religious schools and to have all NWT schools publicly operating as soon as possible. Of the forty-eight schools then existing in the Territories, sixteen were operated by the churches — ten Roman Catholic and six Anglican. Thirty-two teachers taught 759 students, composed of 172 white students, 208 Native Indians, and 379 Inuit. Eleven of these schools were in small isolated Arctic communities and were only open part-time during the spring and summer. They were housed in tents, providing instruction to 300 Inuit students.[133] Many native children, particularly Inuit children, received little or no education at all.

Native students were to receive a general education to prepare them for simple jobs in the cash economy as well as receiving some instruction in traditional crafts and lore. The Native instruction was very rudimentary as far as hunting and fishing went. Some of the brighter pupils would receive additional vocational training to help them become artisans. Even those who preferred to follow the life of their parents in the bush would benefit from this education. Instruction would be in English but Native languages would be permitted outside the classroom.

Mr. Robertson hoped that this plan would help allay the distress of many northern Natives stemming from the downturn in the trapping trade and the reduction of the caribou herds. It was felt that once Natives had completed their training, and this would take time, there would be sufficient jobs for them in communities around the

Territories. No education would be arranged for adult Natives, nor would Inuit children in very remote areas in the Arctic Islands benefit immediately from this scheme. They would be left until last because a formal education for them would be difficult to arrange, and was considered less pressing. They were far from white communities and would have great difficulty in adjusting to a totally new culture.

During the ensuing debate on the commissioner's speech, council members seemed pleased with the plans to establish a new common education system, but had some reservations. There were many doubts going through their minds. Would there be any jobs for the Natives? Would companies hire them? Would the Natives be able to handle the curriculum? What if they couldn't get a job and, lacking wilderness skills, could not live off the land? What kind of psychological effect would there be on them; their being thrust into a completely different environment? Would they be neither fish nor fowl, in limbo between two cultures? What did the Natives themselves think about this? Had they been consulted?

Louis Audette, in a speech at this meeting, put into words what was bothering many of his council colleagues. He was particularly concerned about the future of the Inuit who lacked the Native Indian social organisation: "They have always lived individual lives without social organization, without government, without armies and without concerted effort beyond the level of the head of the family."

Drawing on historical analogy, he went on..."the Indians, a fine proud race, had been humbled by the white man's greed and desire for territory, when he used alcohol to undermine them. The same thing could happen to the Inuit. The sudden alteration of life for them was because of the white man's desire to invade his territory, to extract from it the riches he may find there, and to gain military strategic ends [a reference to the Cold War]. This was because the white man held the wealth, the power, and the overwhelming numerical majority. He was doing this, no matter what the cost to an unfortunate people and without their agreement.[135]

This line of thinking was behind the deliberations of most of the council members, particularly as regards education and alcohol abuse. They were worried that what they were approving would not be in the best interests of the Natives. There was also the gnawing sense of guilt that it was all being done without their consent.

Parker was not so hesitant in voicing his opinions. The basis of his thinking on most political problems came from a firm set of principles based on Greek philosophy, Christian belief, and British constitutional history. He reiterated his argument that the Native population were Canadians and, as such, were entitled to the same rights and freedoms as other Canadians. He was the one on the council who had led the fight to get government-run education for the Natives, along with better health services and housing. The Native Indians had their rights under their treaties, but they would never be able to look after their interests and fully participate in Canadian life until they had become educated and learned about western culture. The same applied to the Inuit. They had never signed any treaties and so education was even more important for them.

In this context, he welcomed the great economic opportunities in the north, with major mining, petroleum, and gas prospects, and greatly increased tourism. He could see a great many NWT Natives becoming part of this development once they were educated.[136]

But in council more immediate problems also attracted his attention. He, like several other members, believed that all Inuit children, no matter where they lived, should be given education right away and that this should not be left until later. Parker was critical of the tent schools, advocating permanent structures and year-round education.

There was a consensus among council members that Native social and economic conditions had improved in recent years. Progress was being made but much more needed to be done. Conditions in the Mackenzie District were very distinctive. Several members referred to the problems of Natives in the Mackenzie area, who had more contact with whites than other native groups, in adjusting to white culture. They had formerly led a slower way of life dictated by the flow of the seasons and the cycles of animal life. As they settled in white communities, they faced a busier, more regulated way of living with wage employment and modern suburban living.

Also they had to face the hardships of terrible winter conditions and awful housing exacerbated by the diminishment of caribou herds, the lifeblood of many Natives, and the decline in the fur trade. The situation was deplorable for many Inuit families, particularly the caribou Inuit in the barren lands.

More emphasis and resources would have to be devoted to areas outside the Mackenzie District. Parker pointed out that the DEW line was employing many Inuit and helping to relieve distress, but, unfortunately this was not nearly enough. Much more needed to be done. Solutions were costly and difficult to implement because of the great distances, the terrain, and the weather. It took time to institute programmes.

Despite the feeling of optimism for the future, and the belief that Native conditions were beginning to improve, council still felt a great deal of frustration about Native affairs. More money and resources were needed in order to overcome these critical problems as quickly as possible. A battle plan was needed to wage war against the acute distress of the barren lands Inuit in particular.

That apart, the Department of Public Works with its centralised bureaucratic practices, was being unjustifiably tardy in the construction of new schools. Parker and others were extremely critical of the department on this score. Public Works seemed to have no idea about northern building problems and ignored experienced northern building businesses. Parker, in his usual colourful language, dubbed the department "incompetent," and its workers "a hopeless group," saying that construction must be hastened before "pupils become eligible for the old age pension or at least reached maturity." It was suggested that contracts for smaller projects be handled at the local level to speed up matters.

One bright spot was the sharp decline in the incidence of Native TB because of the excellent work being done by the health departments in finding and treating cases. Adequate funds and resources were now finally available to tackle a problem that had afflicted the Native population since the twenties. The delay in providing such services had been a national disgrace. However, at last, the government had done something about it.

Once again, council gave attention to the Native liquor prohibition and all the old arguments for and against were aired. The outcome was an agreement that all Natives be allowed to drink beer in those few communities that had taverns.[137]

While Native affairs featured prominently in the council's deliberations, other subjects were also addressed, especially the state of the economy. In his opening address, Commissioner Robertson had noted that economic activity was down slightly from the previous year but future prospects looked favourable. There was the DEW line, major government work at Inuvik and Frobisher Bay, the hoped-for Pine Point railway, and expected expansion in the mining, oil, and fishing industries.

Other evidence bore his comments out. Cominco was satisfied that there was an estimated 60 million tons of lead-zinc ore in its thirty-six square mile Pine Point Mine. It was a very viable mining project that would run for years and years. Financing was ready and it was only a matter of the Northern Alberta Railway being extended north. Once that happened, construction and production at the mine site could be immediately started. Council passed a resolution urging the minister to convince his cabinet colleagues to provide the $55 million needed to extend the line. Once it was completed, freight costs to Yellowknife would fall by 20 to 30 per cent and the Territories would start to boom.

Moreover, it had definitely been established that the barren lands contained large copper deposits which were ripe for exploration. Oil searches were being carried out in the Yukon and geologists were predicting that prospects in the Mackenzie basin were just as good, if not better. Also, there were large stands of timber below Great Slave Lake suitable for pulp production. Lumbering had just started around Fort Smith, and several million board feet had been shipped out by water in 1956. In addition, results at the federal experimental farm at Fort Simpson had been promising. It was reported that there might be 1.5 million acres of arable land in the southern part of the Territories between the Mackenzie and Liard rivers. And finally, the Social Credit government of British Columbia was planning to build a railway into the Peace River country and Fort Nelson. Eventually it could be extended 200 miles up the Liard River to Fort Simpson.

So the January 1957 meeting ended on a positive note. Business expectations for the Territories were excellent and it was hoped that more jobs would be opening up. It was agreed that every effort must be made through training and government support to ensure that northerners, both white and Native, filled these jobs.

In a sense, this mood reflected the wider situation in Canada. At this time, there was great optimism in the economic future of the country and this applied particularly to the north. Universities, boards of trade, and even political parties were sensing this and conferences on the subject were being routinely held. Parker spoke at one such conference on northern development organised by the Edmonton Chamber of Commerce. He was then president of the Yellowknife Board of Trade and his message was that what was needed above all else was more government funds for transportation and more initiative from the private sector. His speech was entitled "Northwest Territories 1945-65." In talking about mining, transportation, and education in the Territories to date, he conceded that "progress had not been as rapid as hoped, but that more had been done in the past ten years than in the previous one hundred." He stressed the unrivalled mineral richness of the Precambrian Shield which covered most of the Territories and the conclusion of the Gordon Commission that, with increasing world demand, minerals would account for more than a third of all Canadian commodity exports. With improved road and rail transportation in the north, mineral production in the Territories could reach a scale unknown in any Canadian province.

The next council meeting, starting on 2 June 1957, was held for the first time at Frobisher Bay on Baffin Island in the high Arctic. Commissioner Robertson, in his opening address, referred to the long history of the island going to back to the 1500's and Martin Frobisher. He alluded to its use as a wartime air-staging post by the Americans, and its subsequent role in that capacity for civilian aircraft flying between Canada and Europe. Frobisher Bay was also an expanding government administrative centre providing services to the eastern Arctic Inuit. New buildings were being constructed, and council members were invited to inspect these during the course of the session.

The agenda for the session covered subjects previously discussed with no new or controversial items. Among the more salient issues was a new financial agreement between the Territories and the federal government which required that capital costs for education be repaid by the Territories over a twenty year period from local taxes. As the northern economy increased the local population would be required to take on more financial responsibility. It was agreed that the Department of Northern Affairs must ensure that NWT inhabitants were covered by the new Hospital Insurance and Diagnostic Services Act then being discussed in the House of Commons.[138] Also, once the new act came into force, the Native population should not be deprived of any healthcare services that they were entitled to under current legislation. The usual complaints and suggestions were made by members, often the outcome of consultations with all their constituents, both white and Native. Elected members continued to be a good conduit of communication between all parts of the Territories and the Ottawa bureaucrats.

Several of the suggestions affected Native Indians specifically. It was proposed that a hunting area be set aside north of Great Slave Lake for the exclusive use of the Dogribs. The tribe felt that white hunters and trappers were interfering with their hunting rights. Also, in connection with this area, a proposal was made that a royalty be levied on commercial fishing on Great Slave Lake. This money could be used for enforcing conservation practices. The question of over-fishing by commercial operators was again discussed. The Native Indians felt that fish stocks were being depleted to their detriment.

It was also pointed out that Indian reserves in the south had full mineral and oil rights. As there were no reserves in the Territories, it was suggested that a percentage of the territorial revenues obtained from natural resources should be set aside for the benefit of the Natives.

As to that old bone of contention, the scale of rations for destitute families, an increase was proposed in cases where the male breadwinner was in hospital. Rations in these circumstances should be higher than normal because, in many instances, the wife could not hunt, fish, or trap to provide additional income or food.

However, the highlight of the session was the passage of a formal resolution, after considerable discussion, recommending that the residents of the eastern part of the Territories, the districts of Franklin and Keewatin, although few in number, be given the franchise to elect two new members to council. This area formed almost half the Northwest Territories but its many problems were not being given sufficient attention. Among the most pressing of these was the desperate condition of the barren lands Caribou Inuit. The area had been administered from Ottawa with little or no involvement by its residents. Existing council members were not elected to represent them, although they tried to keep informed of their problems and see that they were not entirely overlooked. Given poor communications and the huge geographical area of Franklin and Keewatin, which included the high Arctic islands, the Arctic coast, and the barren lands, it was hard for currently elected members to keep abreast of issues in this area.

This session of the council occurred against the backdrop of the 1957 federal election in which northern affairs featured so prominently. Erik Neilsen writes in his book "The House is Not a Home" that, when he was preparing for the 1957 federal election, he felt the Yukon Territories were not getting a fair shake as far as roads, telephone services, bridges, radio service, education, and housing were concerned.[139] He brought this to the attention of Alvin Hamilton, a Conservative leader, at the 1957 party convention. Hamilton came to the Yukon during the ensuing campaign to help Neilsen, and was much taken with the territory and its future. He got Diefenbaker interested and the leader referred to the north in many of his speeches.[140] This emphasis was still novel in the country and lent itself nicely to populist rhetorical flourishes, even if Diefenbaker's criticisms of the Liberals for neglecting the north were rather overdone. Parker, the good Conservative, did not have so direct an influence on electoral strategy, if only because he could never afford to fly out to the party conventions.

The Liberal party was finally beaten in the 21 June 1957 election, with 112 Conservative members being elected, 105 Liberal, 25 for the CCF, 19 for the Socreds, and 4 for other parties. Diefenbaker formed a minority government and Doug Harkness was appointed the Minister of Northern Affairs and National Resources. Very soon afterwards, on 22 August 1957, he was succeeded by Alvin Hamilton.

In January 1958, the NWT council met in Yellowknife with Gordon Robertson, the commissioner, still in the chair. His main item for discussion was the alleged crisis in the caribou population. In 1955 Kelsall had reported the herds being reduced to below 300,000. Now, it was thought they were down to almost 200,000. This was clearly unacceptable.

The basic trouble seems to have been low calf drops in the previous seven years. This reduction in the regeneration of the herds meant that they were not keeping pace with natural mortality rates and excessive hunting. Drastic measures were therefore needed if herds were not to become extinct.

Severe changes to the hunting regulations were introduced. The killing of female caribou was prohibited between January and July inclusive. No caribou calves were to be killed at any time until they were fourteen months old. The tremendously wasteful practice of feeding caribou meat to sled dogs — Dr. Kelsall regarded this as a major problem — was to be prohibited. They would have to make do with frozen fish instead. The use of .22 calibre rifles was to be stopped, because these weapons were not accurate at longer ranges and often only maimed the caribou, which would then die a lingering death in the bush. Those whites who had special "grandfather" privileges to hunt caribou were told to stop such hunting. More severe punishments were introduced for wasteful caribou hunting, for example, leaving portions of the carcase to rot or the senseless slaughter of herds. Dr. Kelsall thought that poor hunting practices almost equalled the legitimate kills in a season. Beyond these concrete measures, a future quota system for the regions was discussed which envisaged limiting the kill to 7,500 per year.[141]

These regulations were approved by council and also the provinces of Alberta, Saskatchewan, and Manitoba. However, for obvious reasons, they were very difficult to enforce. They probably did help as did other measures such as visiting camps to monitor caribou hunts, providing nets to promote fishing, restricting amounts of ammunition to hunters, and maintaining some predator control. However, Kelsall believed that the problem slowly corrected itself. For some strange reason — possibly the discovery of new pastures — the herds avoided the areas where the Native hunters were. Thus herd decline, even in the barren lands, may have been more apparent than real and not as serious as was supposed. Kelsall admitted that despite all their hard work studying the herds, the real answer was incredibly elusive. Whatever the explanation, the herds began to recover gradually.

The chairman reported on a more positive subject. More Inuit were being employed in mining; seventy were working in the Rankin Inlet nickel mine.[142] Some were also employed in survey teams on the west coast of Hudson Bay, on South Baffin Island, in the Coppermine area, and on the Belcher Islands. They were also working as stevedores, boat crews, ore packers, camp cleaners, diamond drill helpers, and some were being trained as prospectors. This was very encouraging, particularly for Parker who was so keen on Natives becoming involved in private enterprise.

With his usual gusto, he entered the debates of that session. Once again, he railed against the excessive controls on Native liquor consumption, which, he claimed, forced Natives to drink in secrecy. He also pushed for the immediate construction of the Pine Point railway. But his strongest criticisms were reserved for government plans on Native education — his favourite hobby horse.

He served notice that he was going to conduct a campaign against the construction of new government boarding schools for juvenile pupils. His feelings on this subject arose from his observations during his travels through the Territories of the effects of mission education on Native children and family life. It was, he strongly held, wrong to make six- to eleven-year-olds go to schools so far from their own communities and it would be much better for these youngsters to be educated at or much nearer to their homes. Hostels for junior pupils, he said, meant that "the continuity of the home would not be maintained and the Native culture and language [would be] destroyed." He continued, "I am horrified to think of sending a six-year-old child hundreds of miles away to an unknown settlement and a school he had never seen." It wasn't a matter of a white child going to a boarding school (he himself had been to one as a very young child); it was a matter of a child going to a completely different environment and culture. "Such a child cannot grow up as part of his family, and has little if anything in common with them when he returns home. We are, in fact, adopting a system we criticize in other countries.[143]

However, he agreed that after the age of eleven the Native children could go to the large regional-school hostels then being constructed. Moreover, he asserted, this approach would actually be cheaper on a per capita basis. The regional schools would not have to be so big because the school population would be spread over the local schools and the regional schools.

These comments received the favourable attention of the Edmonton Journal, which embodied them in an editorial entitled "A Question of Humanity." [144] It was Erik Watt, the well-known Yellowknife journalist and author, who covered the 1958 council meetings for the Edmonton Journal. He recalled Parker for his dynamism, his admirably colourful speaking style, and his concern for the Native people. The white men on council at that time, he feels, had a genuine interest in their Native constituents and did their best to stand up for them and protect their interests.

White Canadians, historically, have gone through a number of phases in their attitudes towards Natives. At first they considered them as enemies and dangerous. Then they regarded them as backward and lazy and in need of instruction in white religious and moral values. Others considered them to be special people with special rights deserving of protection, and arising from their status as the original occupants of the country. A view quite prevalent in the Territories during the thirties and forties was that the Natives were a dying race. Many subscribed to Rousseau's "Noble Savage" ideal which portrayed the Native as unsullied by the worst of western ways, and living in idyllic circumstances in the forest and on the prairie plains. There was also the Canadian love affair with Native dress and art, which continues to this day. These works of art are considered to be the finest representation of Canadian society and are exhibited around the world.

There was also the middle path, which is the path that John Parker took . He felt Natives must be brought into the twentieth century through modern technical education, not just simple job training to be crop farmers or housewives, an approach that had failed on the prairies in late 1800s. Parker once said that the Natives, particularly the Inuit, were smart enough to be brain surgeons or top lawyers provided they were given the proper education. He also said that, as in any group of people, they were not all angels and he had come across some poor specimens in the course of his career.

However, it was also felt in the council that, in addition to being given this modern education, Natives must also be allowed to keep their languages and their culture. In fact this should be promoted as it was an important unique part of Canadian history and should thus be kept alive. At most meetings there were proposals or motions passed concerning some aspect of council's "responsibility to ensure retention of the Native culture."

One supposes that all these ideas were in the minds of the white councillors to some degree as they battled with the problems of their Native constituents. Certainly there was tremendous admiration and respect for the ability of the Inuit and the northern Indians to survive in the harsh northern conditions. There was also the presumption that the NWT Natives, as they became more educated, and this has become a fact, would be able to run for office and be elected to council and finally have a direct say in the management of their own affairs.[145]

Mistakes were made, but usually by the arbitrary Ottawa establishment, far removed from the scene, and not by the local representatives. This is not to say that

Commissioner Robertson and his staff were totally at fault. It was due to his leadership and their energy that so much was achieved for the Natives during the fifties.

By this time, John Parker's sojourn in the NWT was, unbeknown to him, drawing to a close, but not before Diefenbaker called a quick election in March 1958 to end his minority government. It was a landslide victory with the Conservatives winning 208 seats, against 48 for the Liberals, 8 for the CCF, and 1 other. But the Liberal incumbent in the Mackenzie riding, Merv Hardie, just held onto his seat in the face of a determined challenge from John Winter, the Conservative candidate. Indeed, Hardie was the only Liberal MP left west of Ontario. The count for the riding was Hardie 2670 and Winter 2047. Erik Neilsen, a Conservative, won a close race in the Yukon and went on to be a cabinet minister and bring northern problems into the Canadian limelight.

Perhaps Parker was right not to have accepted Dief's earlier invitation to run. Yet, with his success on council and his prominence in the Territories, he might have taken Yellowknife for the Conservatives. He certainly would have been a very successful federal politician with his energy, his outgoing personality, his colourful speeches, and his knowledge of the north.

FOX MOTH

Chapter 10 Notes

132. NWT 1957 & 1983 Budgets

	1957*	1983**
	$	$
Health	245,000	50,939,000
Health (DH&W)		19,600,000
Welfare	123,000	29,061,000
Welfare (DH&W)		4,100,000
Municipal	68,000	88,202,000
Administration	127,000	12,016,000
Education	894,000	67,367,000
Liqour Sales	1,014,000	
Housing		28,367,000
Justice		21,238,000
Tourism		17,016,000
Interest		11,976,000
Highways		13,773,000
Other	10,300,000 DPW	30,388,000
	36,461,000	374,487,000
Population	20,500	47,000
Per Person	$1,775	$7,967

* Financial Post, 23 February 1957

** NWT data Book, Outcrop Press, 1986

1992/93 Federal Budget per person - $5,372

133. Department of Health and Welfare Report 1957/58 - Report of NWT Commissioner Gordon Robertson.

134. Ivan Mouat, Superintendent of Native Schools in the Keewatin District in the 50's says Inuit leaders at Baker Lake gave lectures to students in their own language about Inuit lore and folk tales and gave them demontrations of Inuit arts and crafts.

135. Audette's speech to January 1957 Council. Audette's papers.

136. 1989 federal government report on Inuit Arctic lands called "Building Our Economic Future." It covered 59 communities. Iqaluit (old Frobisher Bay), Inuvik, Tuktoyaktuk had good "in and out" transportation, communications, government administrative centres and a range of viable private enterprises. Six communities were "swing" centres with unemployment, but with a market potential. 46 were underdeveloped, with high unemployment with consequent social ills. It was estimated that 2,789 jobs were needed. Donald Purich, The Inuit and their Land , the story of Nunguit, (James Lorimer, Toronto, 1992), p50.

"Despite the best intentions of Council in the 1950's and its optimistic hopes for the future, the employment problems of the Inuit have not improved much even today. A sad outcome of all their efforts"

137. It is interesting that when Gordon Robertson was interviewed on the CBC TV <u>Newsmagazine</u> programme on 20 January 1957, he spent most of his time discussing the native liquor problem and not the other important matters that had been covered in the NWT Council meeting. National film archives. National Archives 76-11-352.

138. The Hospital and Diagnostic Services Act was passed in July 1958.

139. Erik Neilson, <u>A House is not a Home</u>, , Diefenbaker was the first Canadian prime minister to visit the north when he went to Whitehorse in 1958.

140. Erik Neilson, <u>A House is not a Home</u>, p 82.

141. Interview with Dr. Kelsall, September 1994.

142. Unfortunately the Rankin Inlet mine stopped operations in 1962.

143. *Edmonton Journal*, 5 June 1957.

144. *Edmonton Journal*, June *1957*, Editorial

> *A Question of Humanity*
> *In our desire to assist our northern native children to grow into full citizens with opportunities for improvement and advancement equal to those of the rest of Canada we should not forget that they are human beings. For this reason the federal government should give sympathetic attention to the complaint of John Parker, Yellowknife member of the Northwest Territories Council, at its current session. Mr Parker criticised as "inhuman" the government program involving the construction of large school hostels which would take many young pupils hundreds of miles from their homes for extended periods.*
> *There is merit in Parker's suggestion for small hostels attached to existing day schools in settlements along the Mackenzie River, for the accomodation of children of tender years. He would limit the use of larger hostels to pupils at the high school level.*
> *Keeping pupils of, say, six to twelve years in their own communities would not only avoid the heartbreak and loneliness of sending them great distances to a strange environment but would expose their families to the benefits of civilised education.*
> *Apparently no change will be made in the current program of construction but in any future planning Mr. Parker's suggestion will be taken into consideration. Native children are not little machines any more than white children.*

145. A.W.R. Carrothers, a law professor, was asked by the Pearson Liberal government in 1965 to chair a commission to look into NWT future constitutional changes. He reported that he found the Inuit and the Native Indians were not interested in such matters. The Indian chiefs were only interested in the proper enforcement of the NWT treaties and the Indian Act, which they understood. But representation on the NWT Council was not a priority. John Hamilton, <u>Arctic Revolution</u> ps 91 and

115. This changed as Native younger men and women became educated and became leaders. In 1992, the Mulroney Conservative government reached an accord with the Inuit leadership to split the Territories into two parts and this later took place when the new territory of Nunavik was formed.

Chapter 11
Tragedy and the Kikkik Case

The Northwest Territories council met in Ottawa on 14 July 1958 for its summer meeting. This was to be last session that Parker attended, since he had been appointed by the Conservative government as the judge of the Yukon Territorial Court, a position he was to assume in September.

Most of Commissioner Robertson's opening speech dealt with the terrible tragedy that had occurred in the barren lands in the early part of the year when a number of caribou Inuit had starved to death. This episode, of course, stemmed from the decline in caribou herds which had preoccupied the council during its three previous sessions. However, this was the first time during Parker's incumbency on council that a detailed report of conditions in the barren lands had been tabled.

In general terms, the peculiar hardships faced by the caribou Inuit had been exposed years before in Farley Mowat's book, *People of the Deer*, published in 1952. It described his visits to the area in 1947 and 1948 and was very critical of the HBC, the missions, the RCMP, and particularly the Department of Northern Affairs for not providing more help to the caribou Inuit. His narrative had first been serialised in the American magazine Atlantic Monthly before being published as a book, in which form it became a bestseller and caused a sensation. Even Mowat admitted that the book had its faults, in John Parker's view, an understatement.

But Mowat was not the only author to take an interest in the barren lands. At about this time, Richard Harrington, the Canadian photographer and writer and a good friend of Parker, wrote a book called *The Face of the Artic,* published in 1952, which included a description and photographs of the area in 1950. Harrington actually saw Natives on the verge of death, with their sled dogs dying all about them. All this had been brought on by the virtual disappearance of the large herds of caribou. Only scattered groups of animals were sighted that year. By Harrington's reckoning, a family of four, two adults and two children, with eight to ten sled dogs, would require five caribou a week, or 260 a year, to live comfortably.[145A]

It is not difficult to envisage the disastrous impact of the disappearance of the great caribou herds on the Ahearmiuts and Padleimiuts (caribou Inuit). With no caribou meat, the sled dogs would be the first to die. The Inuit would be forced to travel by foot, making life much more arduous. It would be difficult to visit traplines or make the usual caribou hunting expeditions of up to 100 miles (in Inuit terms, "two sleeps away"). Tired and weakened by lack of food, hunting groups would struggle to stalk the wily caribou. Alternative foodstuffs, such as fish from under the ice-cap, were neither that easily caught nor that nutritious.

Harrington was much less critical of the HBC than Mowat. He had found Henry Voisey, the half-Inuit HBC trader at the Padlei post 100 miles inland from Hudson Bay, extremely sensitive to the needs of the destitute. Of the local missionary he was less enamoured, and he felt that the Department of Northern Affairs was unaware of the seriousness of the situation.

This last point is perhaps explicable. Reports of deaths in winter had become so routine that they were accepted by government as a fact of life in this godforsaken region. Relief supplies had been flown in from time to time, and, during the fifties, some family groups had been transferred by air to other lakes where it was thought they would fare better. Perhaps in response to Mowat's and Harrington's reports, Minister Lesage announced in 1954 that six northern service officers would be appointed to live and work with the barren lands Inuit.[146]

Nonetheless, the problems of these pepole were highly complex and almost intractable. At root, however, they stemmed from the near disappearance of the caribou herds, and if these didn't return, there were no obvious alternative solutions. Moreover, simply establishing what was happening was a major task in itself, given the vastness and inhospitableness of the region and the dispersal of the populace. It was easy to criticise government policy, but there were no simple remedies.

This, then, was the context of Commissioner Robertson's report to council. He went on to detail the several tragedies that had occurred over the last winter, tragedies that had taken the northern service officers so much by surprise. In one instance, seven members of the group living at Henik Lake had died. This was particularly disturbing, since the band had recently been resettled there because it was thought that the caribou would be more plentiful. Moreover, Henik Lake is only fifty miles from Padlei, yet the people were too weak to cover even this distance for help. Once reports came in, however, immediate action was taken by the RCMP and government field officers, Robertson said, probably preventing further deaths

Even worse were the sixteen deaths in the Garry Lake area in the far north, near Thelon Game Sanctuary about 150 miles northwest of Baker Lake. Robertson noted that full information on these deaths was still not available. Two deaths from starvation had also occurred on Chantrey Inlet, on the Arctic coast east of the Adelaide Peninsula.

Robertson continued that this was the worst known instance of mass starvation in the north, reiterating his belief that the present situation was not due to a change in caribou routes but to a "vast collapse in numbers." He pointed to the difficulty in devising alternatives for the inland Inuit. They could not be moved to where they could get jobs because they lacked the necessary skills and the change of culture would be too drastic for them. Nor could they be moved to relief camps without destroying their self-reliance and initiative. They could not even be provided with radio transmitters, because of the weight of the batteries. Furthermore, the government could not station personnel near to every tiny group. Indeed, including RCMP, there were ten government officers plus approximately 100 whites in an area about half the size of Manitoba.

Despite these grave difficulties, Robertson announced that certain actions were being immediately taken. Firstly, patrols by the RCMP and the northern service officers were being better coordinated. Secondly, emergency caches of food were being established, and thirdly, more air patrols were being instituted.

Even with these actions, he could not guarantee that the problem would not recur. Ultimately, the only solution was to get the caribou herds back up to strength. More people were working on a new caribou study with more testing stations but it was not expected that the caribou would come back in large numbers in the near future.

The long-term solution might be reducing dependence of the Natives on the caribou and providing an alternative means of livelihood. One plan, which had been started, was to move 120 inland Inuit, over time, to Tavani, seventy miles north of the Manitoba border. The new community would live a different life that would not be too different. White whale and caribou hunting would persist, as would traplines, but a handicraft cooperative would be started to open new avenues of work, and health services and vocational training would be provided. A key objective in this plan was to ensure that "the basic fabric of the Keewatin Inuit culture be maintained." However, Robertson had to concede that the plan might be wrong one and one could only do what seemed correct at the time.

As usual, many suggestions and ideas were introduced by council members during this session. The subjects of debate tended to conform to a pattern that was by now familiar to Parker. Overall, "Trapping" was debated more times during his time on council than any other subject, followed by "Education" and then "Relief" and then the "Caribou Decrease." True to form, these topics were aired in one guise or another during this session.

Also during this session, all the members strongly urged that responsibility for natural resource management be transferred to the council from the federal government. If this were done, the territorial government would more closely resemble the provincial governments and more rapid and suitable economic development would result. Parker took comfort in this proposal since he had reached the same conclusions years before.

He had long been an advocate of northern development, and always remained one. Not surprisingly, several years later, in 1976, he came out strongly against the recommendations of the Berger Commission which suggested that proposed northern gas and oil pipeline construction be delayed pending further study and the settlement of native land claims. Parker responded with a long article in the Globe and Mail. He believed that the pipeline should be built immediately. Its construction would ease the native unemployment problem to some degree, and its postponement would probably not have much effect on the settlement of land claims. Moreover, delay would inflate the cost of construction, an important argument which Parker used to considerable effect.

So Parker's participation on the NWT council came to a close and it would not be long before he took up his judgeship in the Yukon. But in that last year in the Northwest Territories, Parker also added further lustre to his legal career by serving as Crown prosecutor in the most famous murder trial in the Territories, the Kikkik case. This incident arose from the recent tragic winter events among the barren land Inuit of Henik Lake when seven of their number had died, two of them by murder.

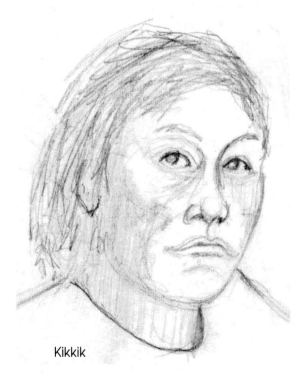

Kikkik

Kikkik was a woman born into the Ahearmiut Inuit who lived in the remote Ennadai Lake area of the barren lands, 250 miles west of Hudson Bay. They lived in one of the harshest environments in the world with little contact with the outside. Farley Mowat has written that their first encounter with government officialdom was in 1948 when they were visited by an RCMP officer who noted their names and gave them their number tags, so that they could claim their family allowances and emergency rations. [147] It seems extraordinary that this situation could exist in mid-twentieth century Canada.

Kikkik and her husband, Halo, and children, along with other family members, were moved by the government by air to Henik Lake, about 100 miles from the coast. As Harrington had discovered, these families were having a terrible time. By 1957, they had lost all their dogs, could no longer hunt caribou, and were slowly starving to death. In February 1958, they were on their last legs, living on fish and caribou hides only.

Among this group was Halo's brother, Yahah, and his family, and the leader of the group, Ootek, who was a half-brother of Kikkik and a supposed shaman, and his wife, Howmik, and children, were also there. They were the last of a number of families to leave for Padlei, some fifty miles away, to get their destitute rations from the HBC trading post. At this point, Kikkik had five children to look after: a twelve-year-old girl called Ailoyoak, her eldest; Karlak, a son; two young girls, Nesha and AnnaKatha; and baby Noahak, eighteen months old.

Halo's family and Ootek's families had been amicable in the past, but bad blood had recently arisen between them. Halo was the hard worker, whereas Ootek was somewhat of a dreamer, rather lazy, with pretensions to being a shaman and a leader. Certainly, Ootek was a poor provider and Halo had given him food from time to time. Even so, his wife and children were in terrible condition. They had little food, ragged clothing, and dreadful shelter. In fact, there had been a dead baby in the tent for several weeks at the time of the events under consideration. It was Parker who unearthed these facts about the family.

The two men had apparently got into a violent argument when Ootek heard that Halo, Kikkik, and family had decided to go to Padlei, leaving Ootek and family to fend for themselves, since Yahah and his party had already left. Ootek knew he was too weak to reach Padlei and implored Halo to stay. He knew that Halo's departure would sound the death knell for his family.

Halo, on the other hand, must have concluded that the survival of his own family was of more importance than staying to help Ootek. He may have even suggested to Ootek that he and his family accompany him and he would do his best to help them. Also there was a distinct possibility that, once at Padlei, help would be sent for Ootek.

Maybe the weather and living conditions and lack of food were so bad and relations between the two families so strained that there was no rational discussion between the two men. The last thing in the world that an Inuit would do was to refuse to help another Inuit, since assisting another person was a sacred part of their tradition. In this instance, Halo must have reasoned that his family came first.

On 7 February 1958, against this background of growing tension, with the temperature at 45 degrees below and high winds and driving snow, Ootek borrowed Halo's gun to try and shoot some ptarmigan. Ootek, who was not a good hunter, was weak and probably semi-delirious from hunger. Later, in a freezing blizzard, while Halo was huddled over his fishing lines on the frigid lake, Ootek surprised him and shot him dead with the rifle.

Meanwhile, Kikkik became alarmed when Ootek did not return the rifle. Because he had been behaving strangely of late, she determined to retrieve it before he did some harm. In Ootek's shelter, she found him waving the rifle about frantically. Without hesitation, she began to wrestle with him in an attempt to get it back, and, being the stronger, pinned him down on the snow. She called out for one of her children to find their father and to bring him to her assistance as quickly as possible.

Her eldest child soon came hurtling back in terror, shouting in the howling wind that her father was dead. Kikkik immediately realised that Ootek must have been the culprit and ordered Ailoyoak to bring her knives right away. All the while, she held the struggling man beneath her, yelling at him, but she could get no satisfactory answer from him. She knew Ootek's character well and must have felt that he was capable of yet worse misdeeds. Once she had the knives, she used them on Ootek and killed him. She left two knives, upright, on either side of Ootek's head, an odd thing to do, but possibly an Inuit tradition. With the strong resolution which she displayed throughout this tragic story, she then got her children to help bring her husband's body back to the shack. There, Halo was laid out ceremoniously under the sleeping ledge.[148]

The next morning was still very cold but the storm had abated. After feeding her children, she dressed them in all the clothing they possessed and prepared them for the hazardous trek to Padlei. She tore the canvas roof from her shelter, cut it in half, and laid a part of it over Halo's body. Then she put Nesha and AnnaKatha under some deer skins on the sled. Some of their skin clothing was to be used for food, so they would not be properly dressed to walk in the drifting snow. Baby Noahak she strapped to her back beneath the hood of her parka. Karlak and Ailoyoak were to walk beside her.

Just then, Howmik came over and asked Kikkik what was going on and where Ootek was. Her reply was that he must have gone on ahead to Padlei to get help. She made no mention of the stabbing or of Halo's murder. Howmik didn't argue and staggered back to her tent.

Kikkik left immediately, leaning into the wind as she pulled the sled. What a dramatic sight she and her little family must have made as they struggled across the lake and up the windswept trail in the terrible cold. Slowly they disappeared behind a small hillock towards their destination, which she hoped to reach in under a week. She walked as quickly as she could, hoping to cover up to ten miles a day. The little party made good progress the first day.

Towards the end of the afternoon, feeling very tired and depressed, they were delighted to come upon Yahah and his family ahead of them. Yahah had been making slow progress, as his wife Alesha was not well — her condition was later diagnosed as tuberculosis — and his child had frost-bitten feet. After awhile they stopped and decided to camp for the night. Yahah made a small temporary igloo for shelter and they chewed on some frozen caribou before trying to sleep.

The next day, 9 February, the wind increased, the temperature plunged, and the howling storm returned. Conditions were terrible yet they had to press on. With the traditional stoicism of the Inuit in the face of adversity, they struggled on into the wind. Kikkik, who had to pull the sled, had a particularly difficult time. By late afternoon, the Yahah family with Kikkik's two eldest children were a mile ahead of her. That night Yahah built an igloo for his group and came to Kikkik to erect a very makeshift shelter of skins and the sled for her. At this latitude in the barren lands, the treeline is far to the south, so that there were no branches to be had for protection. There they spent a particularly bad night.

Next morning Yahah suggested that he and Alesha go on ahead pulling the sled with their child in it. He estimated they were only about three days away from Padlei. Kikkik should stay in the temporary igloo with her children and he would arrange for help to be sent to them at once. Before leaving he fed some caribou guts to Kikkik and the children.

Kikkik then spent five fearful days there huddled together with her children with nothing to eat, waiting for help. They managed to make a fire and were able to drink some hot water, and the baby was breast-fed. However, by the morning of 15 February, she had given up hope of help and decided that they must move again. She wrapped AnnaKatha and Nesha in skins and pulled them along on a piece of canvas. The baby was put on her back again and off they staggered.

They made only a few miles that day and it was through sheer will-power and Kikkik's determination to save her children that they did so. Unbeknown to them, they were only twenty-six miles away from their goal. Luckily the trail was well marked and they were going in the right direction. Kikkik was too tired to make a proper camp. She just dug a large hole in the snow with a frying pan and she and her children got into it and covered themselves with the skins and canvas. They spent a very cold night indeed there.

In the meantime, 13 February, Yahah's party had safely arrived at Padlei. Trader Voisey immediately radioed the RCMP at Eskimo Point. The next day, a plane rescued Howmik and her family from Henik Lake. It also retrieved the bodies of Ootek and Halo. These were taken directly to Eskimo Point and not via Padlei, so Kikkik and her children were not sighted.

On 15 February — the day Kikkik resumed her march — the plane wasted the whole day flying to Rankin Inlet to get the coroner, instead of searching for Kikkik. Voisey had thought it would fly to the search area and had not despatched his assistant by dog team to rescue Kikkik, which could have been done within a day. The air search thus far had been badly bungled.

On 16 February, she decided to leave the Nesha and AnnaKatha and press on with the two oldest children and the baby. The need to drag the two young ones was slowing the progress of the party and endangering the lives of all of them. Kikkik knew that the the two of them would probably die, but with all the fatalism of her people, she accepted the harsh reality of the situation. There was always the slim hope that she could help them from Padlei. She ordered them to stay under the covers, out of the extreme cold, until someone came. The remaining members of the party battled on until, by chance, they reached a deserted trapper's hut that was fairly snug. Here she decided to stay until rescued.

On this day, 16 February, the RCMP Beaver aircraft flew to Padlei from Eskimo Point, took on Voisey, and set off to find the igloo that Yahah had built and where it was presumed Kikkik still waited. It was quickly discovered and the plane was able to land nearby. Finding no-one there, Voisey directed the pilot to follow the trail. As they flew over the cabin, Kikkik and her children rushed out to wave at them. The plane landed and the rescue was finally effected. Kikkik, strangely, told a constable that the two other children had died and she had buried them.

By this time, she was seriously crippled from pulling the children through the snow and could hardly straighten her back. Parker recollected that at the preliminary hearing in Eskimo Point she still couldn't walk and was actually crawling around on all fours.

The RCMP began to suspect that perhaps Kikkik was not being completely truthful. Next morning it was decided to send out Constable Laliberti with an Inuit interpreter, Jimmy Gibson, from Padlei by dog team to find the bodies of the children. They proceeded down the route towards the spot where Kikkik had left them.

Parker remembered that a dramatic moment in the Kikkik trial, among many dramatic moments, was when the constable described how they came upon the children's den. The ears of the sled dogs suddenly pricked up indicating that something was amiss. As they swept along, he and his aide began to hear the low cries of a human in distress. These were the cries of AnnaKatha from under the canvas. She was still alive when they found her but Nesha, who had crawled out from under the skins, had frozen to death. The party spent the night at a trapper's shack and the constable was amazed at the politeness and restraint of the child, despite her recent traumatic experiences and her acute hunger.

After this, it was decided to keep Kikkik in custody at Eskimo Point and her surviving children were taken from her and cared for by a white family. An igloo, twelve feet in diameter, was built outside the RCMP post, and she lived there with another Inuit woman who was her guardian. Doug Wilkinson, a northern expert and author, was brought in to act as interpreter when she was interrogated.

Judge Sissons, who presided over her trial, wrote that she was an unusually small woman who knew exactly what was happening and why she was being charged. She always conducted herself with grace and poise and calmness, and exemplified the toughness of the Inuit. Farley Mowat claimed that she was not told of AnnaKatha's survival until it suited her captors, which is hard to believe.

After two preliminary hearings, at one of which Parker, as Crown prosecutor, was present, her trials started on 14 April 1958. They were held at Rankin Inlet which had reasonable facilities and which lay near the location of the crime, thus ensuring that she had a jury of local peers. There were two trials because there were two distinct charges against her. Firstly there was the murder of Ootek, and secondly there was the abandonment of the two children.

The court was held in the recreation hall of the local nickel mine. Justice Sissons sat at a small desk on a platform raised about a foot above the floor. The platform also contained a chair for the witnesses. This was done so that the audience could see the proceedings. The remainder of the throng were at floor level. In front of the judge, slightly to his left, sat the court clerk. On the judge's left, the court recorder occupied a small table. John Parker, the Crown prosecutor, faced the judge with his back to the audience, mostly Inuit women. Next to him sat the defence lawyer, Sterling Lyon, a Winnipeg attorney who later became the attorney general and then the premier of Manitoba. To the right of the judge, the accused sat with her Inuit guardian, an RCMP officer, and the court interpreter. On the other side of room the six members of the jury sat. Two of these were Inuit men.

The Kikkik case received wide attention in the world press. Time-Life sent a reporter and a photographer. Farley Mowat wrote an article about it for Macleans and included a chapter on it in his book *The Desparate People*. Unfortunately, Mowat did not write in great detail about the trial proceedings, and neither did Sissons nor John Parker, who died in 1992. The trial transcripts are not now available. It is therefore difficult to establish exactly what happened during the trial.[149]

Sissons notes that he opened the trial by giving a brief talk on the history of the jury system and how it began in England. This was carefully translated into Inuit. The charge of murder was then read by the clerk of the court.

Henry Voisey, the Padlei HBC trader, testified that he knew both Ootek and Halo. He had never heard of trouble between the two men and was surprised to learn of the murder, since extreme violence was rare among the Inuit. Ootek was a shaman and he knew that these men often had power over other Inuit and might be feared. He explained that a shaman enforced societal norms such as special eating and other habits, and conducted ceremonies to exorcise evil spirits which the Inuit believed caused illness and bad luck. They could go into trances. However, he had never heard any bad reports about Ootek. Under cross-examination, he could not say whether Ootek sometimes behaved strangely, either because he was a shaman or through lack of food.

Corporal Gallagher testified about the RCMP plane movements and the separate rescue of Howmik and Kikkik and their respective children. He also recounted the retrieval of the bodies of Halo and Ootek.

The defence requested that a translated signed statement, made by Kikkik when she was interrogated by the RCMP, be read to the court. Judge Sissons removed the jury and conducted a hearing to satisfy himself that the statement was voluntarily made. Duly content that it was, he recalled the jury and the statement was read out.

"I asked Ootek why he was cleaning the rifle and
he answered, "I am taking the snow off it." I was afraid
and told Ootek to leave the rifle alone. Ootek did not

answer and continued to clean the rifle.

I took hold of the rifle and Ootek held it also. Ootek said, "I won't bother you and you let it go." I let go of the rifle and Ootek started pointing the rifle at me. He had the rifle at his shoulder in firing position. I jumped and grabbed the barrel near the muzzle. The rifle went off and the bullet just missed my head as I had pushed the rifle sideways ... After the bullet we started to fight for the rifle ... I knocked Ootek over. Ootek was pretty weak and chilly ...

I was right on top of him and I called for my Ailoyoak ... I thought that Halo was still alive. I asked Ailoyoak to take away the rifle and said, "As soon as you get the rifle away you bring your father to help me." Ailoyoak got the rifle and started running towards the jigging hole to get her father.

Ailoyoak returned, was crying and saying, "My father is shot and is dead." I asked my daughter if this is true. My daughter said, "It's real true, my father dead."

I asked Ootek why he had shot Halo and Ootek answered, "It's not my fault, my wife told me to kill Halo."

... I asked Ootek how I could look after my family now that he had killed my husband. Ootek answered, "You will get lots of family allowances and will be all right after." I answered, "I could never look after them." ... We did not talk again and I still held Ootek down.

I then ... asked my daughter to bring me a knife. Both Ailoyoak and Karlak bring me knives which they got at the igloo.

I then tried to stab Ootek with the large knife my daughter had brought but it would not work, as it was dull. I stabbed once near the right breast with the large knife but it would not go in. Ootek grabbed the knife with his right hand and took it from me. When he grabbed it away he struck his forehead some place and I got the knife back and dropped it and picked up the little knife which my son Karlak handed me. Karlak was standing beside Ootek and I. As soon as I got the small knife I stabbed in the same place. The knife went in and I stayed on Ootek until he died. When Ootek stopped moving I removed the knife and stood it up in the snow behind Ootek's back."

In Canadian criminal law the prosecution need not proceed on the basis of the charges made against the accused, but can use a lesser but similar charge, an "included" charge. In this instance, Parker, in his address to the jury, asked for a verdict of manslaughter. He felt the verdict of murder was not appropriate. The charge of murder can be dismissed if the accused exercised her right of self-defence for her person or for anyone under her protection. It can also be dismissed if a person has been provoked to a very serious degree.

The charge of manslaughter is often used if murder cannot be proven and misadventure does not apply. In other words, manslaughter means that the accused can be held responsible for the death where self-defence was not applicable and provocation was not severe. Parker argued that this pertained in the present instance. The evidence showed that Kikkik was not likely to be killed by Ootek. During the fight between Kikkik and Ootek she had complete control. Even the possibility of a future attack was out of the question. Ootek was in a weak condition and once the rifle had been taken from him, he would not be able to cause Kikkik or her family bodily harm.

There was no doubt that she had been provoked. Halo, her husband, had been killed by Ootek and she considered Ootek deserving of death. However, he argued that Kikkik should not have resorted to stabbing the deceased. She could have dealt with Ootek, if he had attacked her or her children, before she left the next day. Therefore, she was guilty of manslaughter. He added that, if she was found guilty, every consideration should be given to awarding her a suspended sentence bearing in mind the strong mitigating circumstances of the case, and the very difficult situation she had found herself in.

Lyon, the defence council, maintained that there was no case for either murder or manslaughter. He said there were mitigating circumstances for both self-defence and provocation. It was not only her life that was threatened but her children. She was living in an isolated spot without police or other agencies to aid her. If she herself had been incapacitated in any way, her children would have been left in a perilous state. The evidence pointed to the fact that Ootek had been acting in an odd way and could have caused serious bodily harm to her or her family . There was thus sufficient provocation for the charge of manslaughter to be dismissed. He concluded that Kikkik herself felt that she had done no wrong.

Sissons, in his charge to the jury, referred to cases brought before the Privy Council of Great Britain with reference to Native peoples. He mentioned Lord Chief Justice Goddard's dictum in connection with evidence of self-defence and provocation in murder cases: the test must be what the ordinary Native person would do in the accused person's circumstances. This implied that English common law should be more leniently applied in such cases.

Judge Sissons continued, "In this present case we have a very primitive Eskimo society which has not changed very much and is still very insecure and unsettled, with no policemen within one hundred and fifty miles." Kikkik could be found guilty of murder if the jury found beyond reasonable doubt that she killed Ootek without justifiable cause. Otherwise, she must be found not guilty. She could be found guilty of manslaughter if they were satisfied beyond reasonable doubt that her act was intentional or unprovoked or that she had used unnecessary force in defending herself and her children. Otherwise, she must be found not guilty. If they found that Kikkik acted in self-defence or in defence of her children in a justifiable way, then she could be found not guilty.[150]

It was late afternoon, and the jury returned in ten minutes with a verdict of not guilty.

Later, at 7.30 pm, the second trial began. This time Kikkik was charged on two counts, one for causing the death of her daughter Nesha through criminal negligence, and the second for unlawfully abandoning her daughter AnnaKatha so that her life was endangered.

Yahah gave evidence explaining what had transpired during his journey with Kikkik and her family. In a dramatic development, the twelve-year-old daughter Ailoyoak also gave evidence. A photograph taken at the trial shows her looking so small on the witness chair, with her legs dangling well off the floor. She was very composed, and her story came out slowly, sentence by sentence, as Voisey interpreted.

Corporal Gallagher rehearsed the story of the rescue of Kikkik, Ailoyoak, Karlak, and the baby from the abandoned cabin. He said the temperature was between 30 and 40 degrees below zero when they arrived. All the survivors had with them was one Indian blanket, one deer skin, a frying pan, and two mugs. Kikkik had said to him that the others had died during the night, Nesha from bellyache and AnnaKatha from convulsions.

This statement puzzled everyone. Why, after all her brave exertions, did she resort to such a lie? However, the judge allowed an interpreted statement she had made to Gallagher to be admitted as evidence. He felt that it explained her actions and statements at this stage to some extent. She admitted that both children were alive when she put them in the covered hole on the trail. When asked why she had left them there, she replied that they could not walk any more and were too heavy to drag. If she had continued with them, the lives of all the family would have been endangered. Why had she not said where AnnaKatha and Nesha were, when she knew there was a chance to save them? She replied, "I was afraid to say." Possibly Farley Mowat was right in suggesting that at this point "coherence left her," presumably because of her ordeal. Judge Sissons agreed.

Constable Laliberti rounded off the testimony with his heart-rending account of the discovery of AnnaKatha and Nesha.

Parker conceded in his final address that Kikkik had not committed a wanton act of cruelty but had done what she felt was best for her family, although she had lied to Corporal Gallagher. Lyon said very little. The jury was out for a very short time and found her not guilty. Kikkik accepted her freedom quietly and with dignity and managed a smile. Sissons wrote that she never seemed to doubt the outcome of the trial.[150]

An excellent one hour documentary on the Kikkik case was made by the Montreal film-maker Ole Gjerstad and written by Elisapee Karetak for the Canadians Women's TV channel. It showed that Kikkik received a very fair trial and was well treated by the white court. Gjerstad read the original transcript of this book.

Some new evidence came out of the programme. Apparently the Inuit families were harshly removed by air to Henek Lake, being forced to leave behind some of their belongings and, what was more valuable, their food. The place they were sent to was far worse than the old lake they were forced to leave. Annakatha, Kikkik's young daughter who was found alone on the trail with her dead younger sister, was interviewed and was extremely well- spoken and educated as were her brother and sisters.

Kikkik never spoke a word to her children of the murder and the trial. It was only much later that they read Mowat's "The Desperate People" and found out what actually happened. Kikkik has 150 descendents, although she herself is now dead. Many of them have forgiven the white people who brought these unhappy times upon them.

What was so interesting was how well her her children turned out. It would have been so heartening for the men who worked with Parker on the NWT Council and who worried so much about whether they were doing the right thing, to see the documentary.

And so Parker's career at the Northwest Territories bar reached its dramatic climax. New challenges and triumphs awaited him as a judge in the Yukon. He was to enjoy himself thoroughly there and loved the people there just as much as he did his NWT friends. However, he always regarded his days in the Northwest Territories as the most exciting and productive of his life, and this was the point where he wanted any book about him to end. I would not want to flout his wishes.

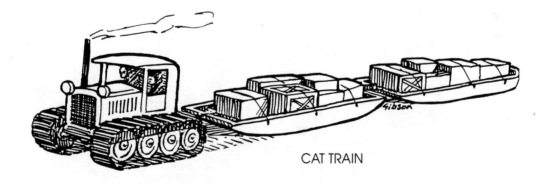

CAT TRAIN

Chapter 11 Notes

145A It seems strange that these people were dying of starvation as far back as 1952, yet it wasn't brought to the attention of the NWT Council until 1957. This was the fault of Ottawa.

146. 1957 NWT population found in Audette's papers indicates 1038 Inuit in Chesterfield Inlet (including Coal Harbour on Southampton Island, Repulse Bay and Melville Peninsular), 267 in Baker Lake but no figures for Padlei or Eskimo Point.

147. Farley Mowat, <u>The Desperate People</u>. p 88.

148. Farley Mowat, <u>The Desperate People</u>, chapter 13. Mowat gives details of the Kikkik case taken from court records and interviews with some participants. Also the thoughts and writings of John Parker regarding the case. Also Judge Sissons, <u>Judge of the Far North</u>, p 99.

149. J Sissons, <u>Judge of the Far North</u>, p 99

150. No trace of the court transcripts of the case could be found in either the National Archives, departmental records or the Yellowknife court records or the Yellowknife archives. It is believed that they are in cardboard boxes in the Yellowknife archives storage room, awaiting the attention of some summer student in the future. It is amazing there is no official record of one of Canada's famous criminal cases.

Bibliography

Balikci, Asen, <u>The Netsilik Eskimo</u> (Garden City, NY: Natural History Press 1970)

Berger, Thomas R., <u>Northern Frontier, Northern Homeland</u> (Vancouver: Douglas and McIntyre 1988)

Blackman, Margaret, <u>Sadie Brower, Neakok, an Inupiag Woma</u> (Vancouver: Douglas and MacIntyre 1989)

Calef, George, <u>Caribou and the Barren Lands</u> (Toronto: Firefly Books 1981)

Camsell, Charles, <u>Son of the North</u> (Toronto: Ryerson 1954)

Dickerson, Mark, <u>Whose North?</u> (Vancouver: UBC Press 1992)

Finnie, Richard, <u>Canada Moves North</u> (Toronto: MacMillan 1948)

McCurdy Gould, Gladys, <u>Jock McMeekan's Yellowknife Blade</u> (Duncan: Lambrecht Publications 1984)

Naomi, Jackson Grover, <u>AY's Canada</u> (Toronto: Clarke Irwin 1968)

Harrington, Richard, <u>The Face of the Arctic</u> (Toronto: Nelson 1952)

Hoffman, Arnold, <u>Free Gold, The Story of Canadian Mining</u> (Toronto: Rinehart 1947)

Hume, Stephen, <u>Ghost Camps, Memory and Myth in Canada's Frontier</u> (Edmonton: Newwest Publishers 1989)

Hunt, Barbara, <u>Rebels, Rascals and Royalty</u> — The Colourful North of Laco Hunt (Yellowknife: Outcrop Press 1983)

Kelsall, J.P., <u>The Caribou</u> (Ottawa: Department of Indian Affairs and Northern Development and Canadian Widlife Service 1968)

Lebourdais, D.M., <u>Men and Metals</u>, The Story of Canadian Mining (Toronto: McClelland and Stewart 1957)

Lower, J. Arthur, <u>Canada, An Outline History</u> (Toronto: McGraw-Hill Ryerson 1991)

McMahon, Kevin, <u>Arctic Twilight</u> (Toronto: Lorimer 1988)

Morton, Arthur S., <u>Hudson's Bay Company</u> (London: HBC 1934)

Mowat, Farley, <u>The Desperate People</u> (Toronto: Little Brown 1959)

Nagle, Ted & Jordan Zinovich, <u>The Prospector, North of Sixty</u> (Edmonton: Lone Pine 1989)

Newman, Peter C, <u>Renegade in Power, The Diefenbaker Years</u> (Toronto: McClelland and Stewart 1963)

Neilsen, Erik, The House is not a Home (Toronto: Macmillan 1989)

Peet, Fred J., Mines and Moonshiners (Victoria: Sono Nis 1983)

Government of the Northwest Territories, People and Caribou in the Northwest Territories (Yellowknife 1989)

O'Malley, Martin, The Past and Future Land, The Berger Commission Story (Toronto: Peter Martin 1976)

Phillips, R.A.J., Canada's North: My Life with Louis St. Laurent (Toronto: University of Toronto Press 1975)

Price, Ray, Yellowknife (Toronto: Peter Martin 1967)

Price, Graham, "Remote Justice, The Stipendiary Magistrates Court in the Northwest Territories (1905 to 1955)," unpublished MA thesis, National Library of Canada, Ottawa 1986

Rea, K.J., The Political Economy of the Canadian North (Toronto: University of Toronto Press 1968)

Robertson, Gordon, Northern Provinces, A Mistaken Goal (Montreal: Institute for Research and Public Policy 1985)

Robertson, Joe, From Prairie to Tundra: Judge of the Far North (Toronto: McClelland and Stewart 1968)

Sutherland, Alice, Canada's Aviation Pioneers (Toronto: McGraw-Hill Ryerson 1978)

Jackson, Susan, (ed.), Yellowknife, NWT, An Illustrated History (Sechelt: Norwest Publishing 1990)

Thompson, Dale C., Louis St. Laurent, Canadian (Toronto: Macmillan 1967)

Ward, Max, The Max Ward Story (Toronto: McClelland and Stewart 1991)

Watt, Erik, Yellowknife, How a City Grew (Yellowknife: Outcrop Publishers 1989)

Whyard, Florence, Ernie Boffa, Canadian Bush Pilot (Anchorage, Alaska: Northwest Press 1984)

Wilkinson, Doug, Arctic Fever: The Search for the Northwest Passage (Toronto: Clarke Irwin 1971)

Zaslow, Morris, The Northern Expansion of Canada 1914-1967 (Toronto: McClelland and Stewart 1988)

Canada's Northwest Territories

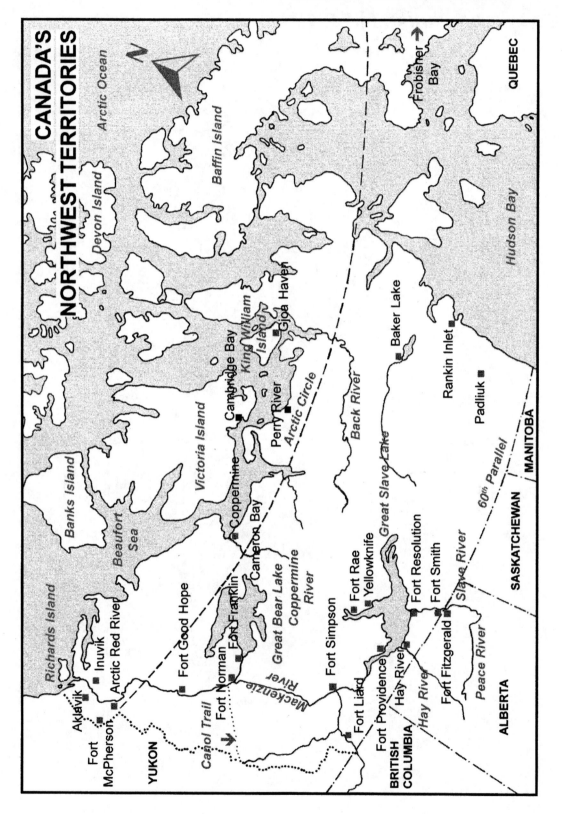

Yellowknife, NWT. 1947

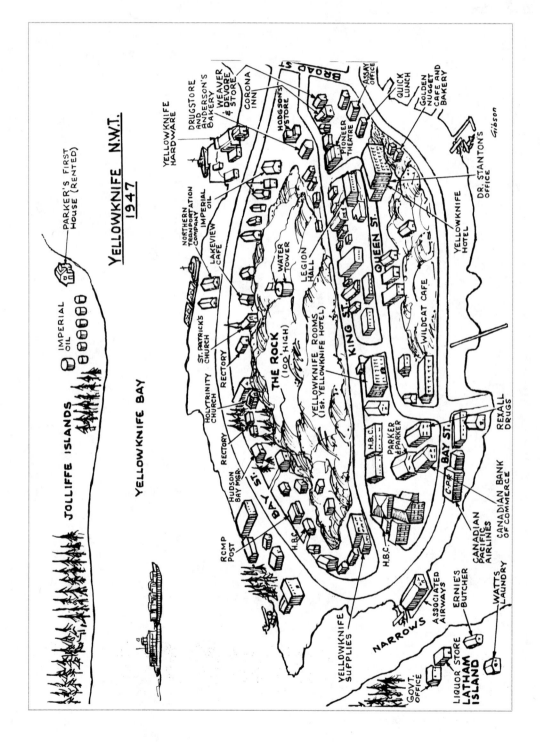

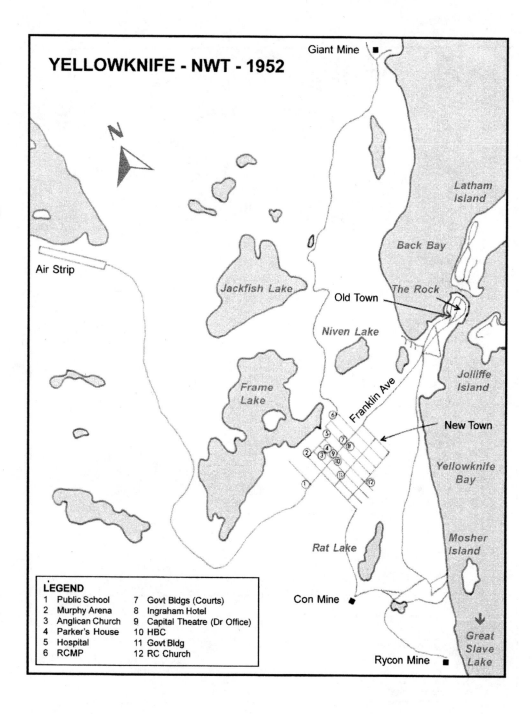

YELLOWKNIFE - NWT - 1952

Air Strip

Giant Mine

Latham Island

Back Bay

The Rock

Jackfish Lake

Old Town

Niven Lake

Jolliffe Island

Frame Lake

New Town

Franklin Ave

Yellowknife Bay

Rat Lake

Mosher Island

Con Mine

Great Slave Lake

Rycon Mine

LEGEND
1 Public School   7 Govt Bldgs (Courts)
2 Murphy Arena   8 Ingraham Hotel
3 Anglican Church   9 Capital Theatre (Dr Office)
4 Parker's House   10 HBC
5 Hospital   11 Govt Bldg
6 RCMP   12 RC Church

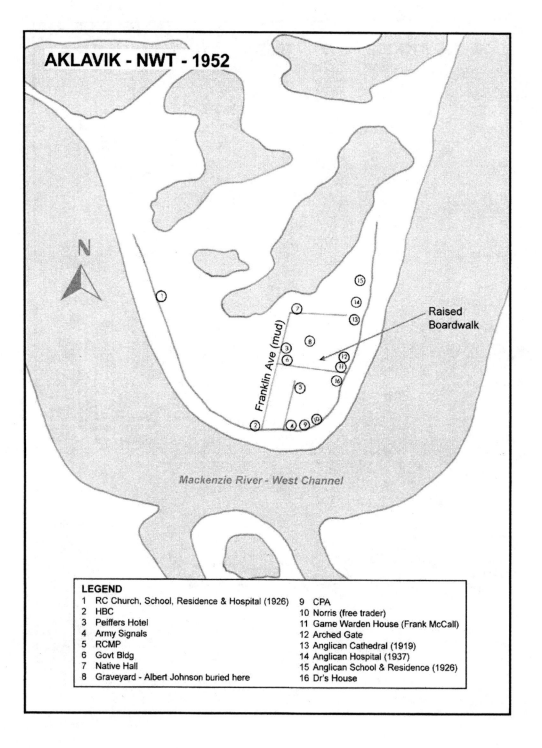

AKLAVIK - NWT - 1952

N

Franklin Ave (mud)

Raised
Boardwalk

Mackenzie River - West Channel

LEGEND

1	RC Church, School, Residence & Hospital (1926)	9	CPA
2	HBC	10	Norris (free trader)
3	Peiffers Hotel	11	Game Warden House (Frank McCall)
4	Army Signals	12	Arched Gate
5	RCMP	13	Anglican Cathedral (1919)
6	Govt Bldg	14	Anglican Hospital (1937)
7	Native Hall	15	Anglican School & Residence (1926)
8	Graveyard - Albert Johnson buried here	16	Dr's House

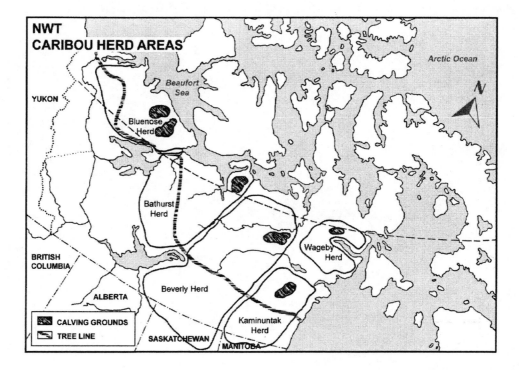

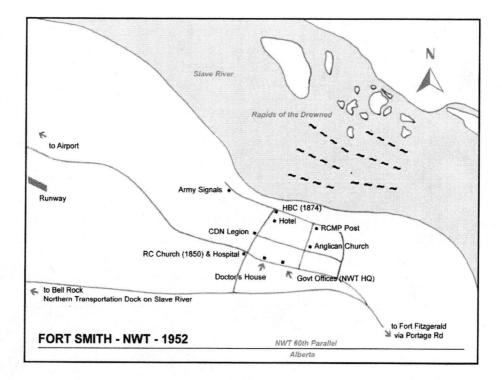

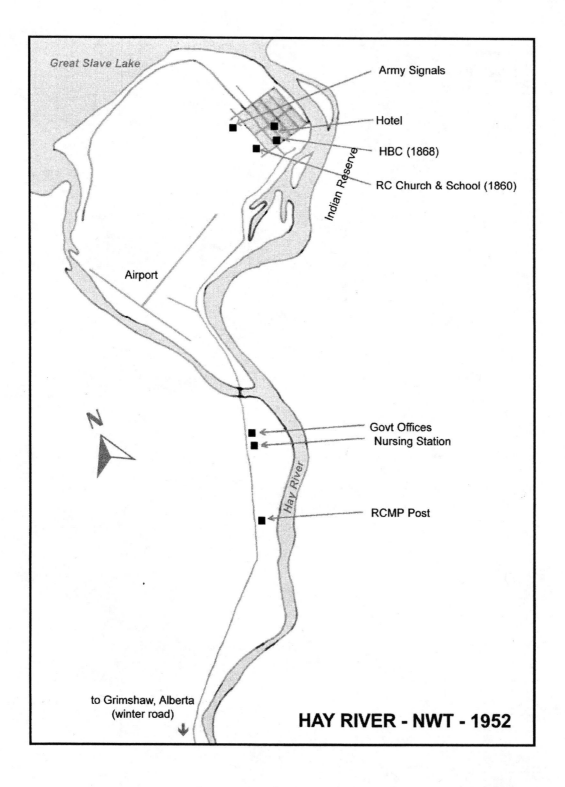

Great Slave Lake

Army Signals

Hotel

HBC (1868)

RC Church & School (1860)

Indian Reserve

Airport

N

Govt Offices
Nursing Station

RCMP Post

Hay River

to Grimshaw, Alberta
(winter road)

HAY RIVER - NWT - 1952

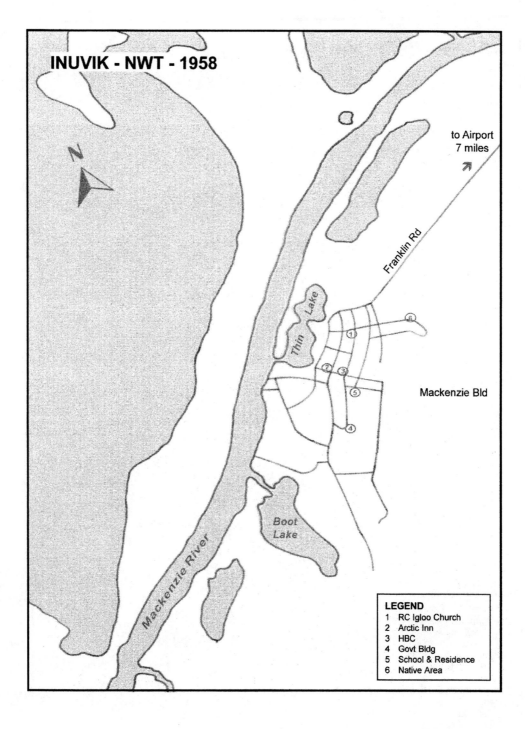

INUVIK - NWT - 1958

to Airport
7 miles

Franklin Rd

Thin Lake

Mackenzie Bld

Boot Lake

Mackenzie River

LEGEND
1 RC Igloo Church
2 Arctic Inn
3 HBC
4 Govt Bldg
5 School & Residence
6 Native Area

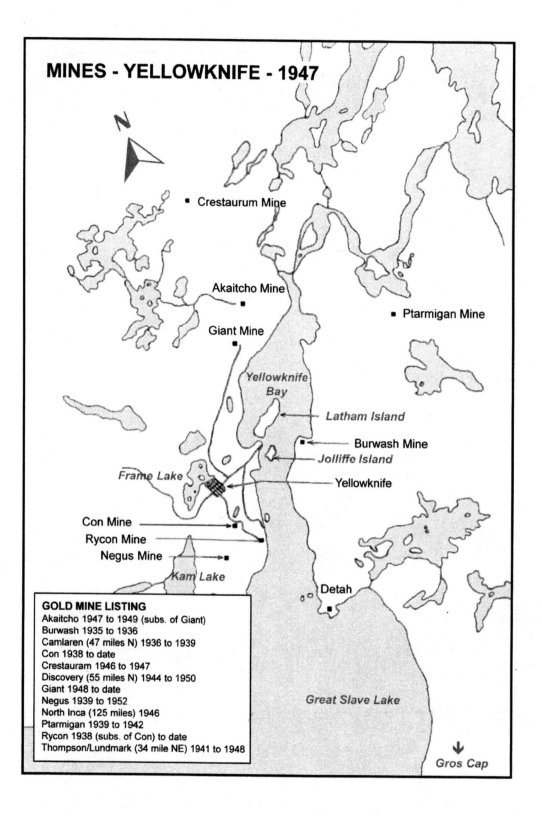

MINES - YELLOWKNIFE - 1947

N

Crestaurum Mine

Akaitcho Mine

Ptarmigan Mine

Giant Mine

Yellowknife Bay

Latham Island

Burwash Mine

Jolliffe Island

Frame Lake

Yellowknife

Con Mine

Rycon Mine

Negus Mine

Kam Lake

Detah

GOLD MINE LISTING
Akaitcho 1947 to 1949 (subs. of Giant)
Burwash 1935 to 1936
Camlaren (47 miles N) 1936 to 1939
Con 1938 to date
Crestauram 1946 to 1947
Discovery (55 miles N) 1944 to 1950
Giant 1948 to date
Negus 1939 to 1952
North Inca (125 miles) 1946
Ptarmigan 1939 to 1942
Rycon 1938 (subs. of Con) to date
Thompson/Lundmark (34 mile NE) 1941 to 1948

Great Slave Lake

Gros Cap

Index

ISBN 1-41204243-7

9 781412 042437